SPEAKING and RELATING
in the Information Age

ELIZABETH GRAHAM

FOUNTAINHEAD PRESS

As a textbook publisher, we are faced with enormous environmental issues due to the large amount of paper contained in our print products. Since our inception in 2002, we have worked diligently to be as eco-friendly as possible.

Our green initiatives include:

 Electronic Products
We deliver products in non-paper form whenever possible. This includes pdf downloadables, flash drives, and CDs.

 Electronic Samples
We use Xample, a new electronic sampling system. Instructor samples are sent via a personalized web page that links to pdf downloads.

 FSC Certified Printers
All of our printers are certified by the Forest Service Council, which promotes environmentally and socially responsible management of the world's forests. This program allows consumer groups, individual consumers, and businesses to work together hand-in-hand to promote responsible use of the world's forests as a renewable and sustainable resource.

Recycled Paper
Most of our products are printed on a minimum of 30% post-consumer waste recycled paper.

Support of Green Causes
When we do print, we donate a portion of our revenue to green causes. Listed below are a few of the organizations that have received donations from Fountainhead Press. We welcome your feedback and suggestions for contributions, as we are always searching for worthy initiatives.

Rainforest 2 Reef

Environmental Working Group

Cover design by Linda Beaupré and Ellie Moore

Text design by Deborah M. Lindberg

Copyright 2015 by Elizabeth Graham

Books may be purchased for educational purposes.

For information, please call or write:

1-800-586-0330
Fountainhead Press
2140 E. Southlake Blvd., Suite L #816
Southlake, TX 76092
www.fountainheadpress.com
customerservice@fountainheadpress.com

ISBN 978-1-59871-963-5

Printed in the United States of America

Table of Contents

Table of Contents

Preface

The ability to communicate effectively in public settings, relationships, groups, and in society is at the core of civic engagement and a central component of a civil society. Learning to accomplish goals, share ideas through dialogue, assume leadership roles, and affect social change through public engagement requires a deep understanding of communication theory, principles, and practices, topics featured in this course and textbook.

Hiring agents, business professionals, and health care specialists consistently identify communication skills as a singular determinant of students' personal and professional success. You will find that cultivating the skills necessary to engage in meaningful and consequential dialogue in face-to-face and mediated environments is a valuable and worthwhile endeavor.

This textbook begins with a survey of the field of communication in the information age. Several models are presented that feature the process of communication beginning with the linear and interactive, and concluding with the transactional model. The chapter concludes with a discussion of how speaking and relating with others has been influenced by the information age. Next up is a discussion of the interface among perception, self, identity, and communication. Identity is managed through our manner, appearance, and verbal and nonverbal communication so that others perceive us, as we desire to be perceived. The subsequent chapters address the components of public speaking including organizing and delivering a speech, selecting and researching a topic, supporting ideas, listening, and common types of speeches, specifically informative and persuasive speaking. A subsequent chapter on the value and importance of verbal and nonverbal communication is featured and the influence of culture, context, age, and gender are explored. Finally, the last two chapters are devoted to communication in context including personal relationships and small group settings.

This textbook is infused with real-world examples and exercises are created to illustrate course concepts. Key terms are boldfaced throughout the text, and brief chapter summaries are provided at the end of each chapter. Please note that this textbook contains several chapters (1, 3–10) reprinted with permission from *Public Speaking in the Communication Age* (2014). Southlake, TX: Fountainhead.

If you dedicate the appropriate time and effort to the study and practice of this material, you will improve your communication skills and reap the rewards associated with being an effective communicator.

I wish you a wonderful semester as you embark on this exciting endeavor.

ABOUT THE AUTHOR

The year was 1976 and I was sitting in my first college class at John Carroll University, a small Jesuit college outside of Cleveland Ohio. The course was Public Speaking and I was apprehensive about the subject matter and fearful of speaking in public. Lucky for me, the instructor of the course was exceptionally talented and I learned to control my anxiety and I even came to like public speaking. My second course was Interpersonal Communication and it was then that I knew that I had found my academic home and I was going to be a Communication major. My interest and enthusiasm for Communication, cultivated in those early college courses, continued and after graduating with my Ph.D. from Kent State University I started my career as a college professor at Ohio University and later moved to The University of Akron.

Over the years I have taught undergraduate and graduate courses in Interpersonal Communication, Small Group Communication, Organizational Communication, Public Speaking, Statistics, and Advanced Communication Presentations and other related subjects. In addition to teaching, I am also interested in conducting research. I am interested in studying textbook delivery systems such as p-books and e-books. I hope to determine which platform students prefer and if textbook format enhances learning and enjoyment of the reading material. I like to travel, garden, swim, cheer for Cleveland sports teams, and engage in good conversation.

In my thirty years of teaching I have learned that success in this course is assured if you attend class, read the textbook, and ask for assistance from your professor when necessary. I think you will find the subject matter personally and professionally relevant and useful today and in the future.

Introduction

Welcome to the Introduction to Communication course, COM 101, offered by the Department of Communication and Dramatic Arts at Central Michigan University. I am delighted you have chosen to learn about the art and science of communication. The concepts and skills that you will master in this course will provide you with the foundational knowledge necessary for you to thrive in your future career and life choices.

More specifically, this course is designed to enhance your ability to:

1. Understand the rich tradition of the field of communication from an historical, theoretical, and applied perspective.

2. Acquire the skills necessary to craft and deliver effective public speeches.

3. Develop the skills necessary for improved communication in a variety of settings, including your personal relationships, group environments, the workplace, and your community.

4. Appreciate how theories and concepts can be applied to communication problems in various contexts.

5. Grow as professionals equipped with the skills and practical experience required to meet the social, professional, and personal challenges of the twenty-first century marketplace.

I hope you find this course and textbook both personally engaging and professionally enriching. Let's now get started on this exciting journey.

CHAPTER 1

An Introduction to Speaking and Relating in the Information Age

Marcus was sitting in his communication class as a college sophomore. He was not anxious about giving presentations to his classmates. He just questioned why he had to take this class. "I'm a mechanical engineering major, when am I going to have to give speeches," he said to a friend the day before. "I'll take it because I have to, but I just don't see the point," he lamented. Marcus was also thinking about why he had to take a class focusing on communication in interpersonal relationships and group settings. I've been communicating my whole life and it's natural, what can I possibly learn? Marcus looked at his teacher, absorbed some of what she had to say, and then his mind drifted off as he looked ahead to joining friends for lunch after class.

Marcus's rumblings are typical of many students sitting in a communication competency class. Let's consider his concerns. Why should a mechanical engineering major have to take such a class? Well, when any person advances in a career, he or she acquires information and accumulates experiences that would be valuable to share with other less experienced coworkers. These experiences are often shared in a public presentation of one form or another. If part of your career advancement leads to an administrative or managerial position, presentations are frequently given to subordinates for purposes of training, or presenting updates on organizational initiatives. You may also wish to give a presentation persuading superiors to accept a new idea you have developed. These are just professional opportunities for public speaking, however. If you ever wish to present your ideas or arguments at a town hall meeting, or a political rally for a local candidate, you will need public speaking skills. Less formal events also call for public speaking such as giving a toast at a family member's wedding or anniversary celebration, or at the beginning of a holiday meal. You may also find yourself in front of your son or daughter's soccer team, giving a motivational pep talk as they head into a playoff game. In short, over the course of our lives many opportunities emerge for us to speak publicly in order to inform, persuade, entertain, motivate, and celebrate. These opportunities will arise in professional, political, community, and educational settings as well as in gatherings of family and friends. The more you know about the components of public speaking, and the more comfortable and enthusiastic you feel about speaking, the more effective you will be in the various settings in which you are called upon to speak.

Now, let's consider Marcus's concerns about the need to learn more about communicating in interpersonal relationships and group settings. Some people *are* naturally at ease and successful in their interpersonal relationships and in being an effective group member; however, communication is always at the core of all problems occurring in these relationship settings. A close friend appears to be going through a difficult time, but they are hesitant to open up. What can you do? You are involved in a romantic relationship and your partner says, "I'm feeling smothered?" How do you respond? You contribute your ideas in a group meeting expecting support from everyone and someone says angrily, "You always think you know the right answer. Can you please give the rest of us a chance?"

We can all benefit from learning additional skills that will allow us to improve our communication in interpersonal relationships and group settings. To learn these skills, you first need to know what the skills are and when they should be used, and second, you need the opportunity to actually practice the skills. The best way to learn about the skills and to master them is through structured experiences. The plan in this book is for you to learn skills helpful to interpersonal relationships and group settings and to master them through structured experiences as well as through reading about them.

INTRODUCTION

In this chapter, you will be provided with a brief foundation of some important concepts related to understanding how the communication process works from the perspective of different models of communication. Then, the types of human communication will be addressed as well as the importance of communication competence. Finally, some common myths about human communication will be dispelled.

WHY STUDY COMMUNICATION?

Communication is classified as the seventh most popular field of undergraduate study, often because of its relevance in conveying knowledge and skills into a variety of career settings. Studying communication also helps you learn how to maintain healthy and enduring relationships through enhancing skills to show support, manage conflict, and understand varying communication styles that are unique to your own. Through the study of communication, you can also learn how to become a more engaged citizen. When you develop stronger critical thinking skills, you are better able to express your own opinions and values. In short, enhancing communication aptitude allows you to improve your personal and professional well-being while also enhancing your ability to become a contributing member of society.

It is easy to assume that because you have been communicating your entire life, it is not necessary to study communication in a formal setting. It is important to remember that formal study allows you to improve upon your current skills. Just like musicians continue to take voice lessons and athletes seek personal trainers to improve their performance, studying communication allows you to learn how to make your communication behaviors even more effective.

COMMUNICATION MODELS

Linear Model of Communication

The **linear model of communication** was the first model created to describe the communication process. This model portrays communication as something that one person presents to another individual. In this model, communication runs in one direction, and involves seven elements.

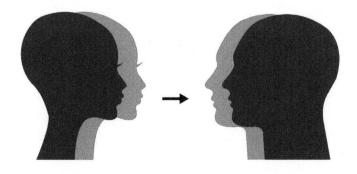

The first element is the **source,** or the speaker. The speaker formulates the idea he or she desires to communicate and constructs a message that successfully expresses that idea to another person or persons. A speaker must translate his or her ideas into words, which is referred to as the **encoding** process. Encoding involves moving from an abstract idea to one having meaning through using symbols understood by another person. The final outcome of encoding is a **message,** which refers to the idea the source originally sought to communicate to another person. This message is then presented over a **channel.** In a face-to-face communication setting, this is the air that carries sound waves from the speaker's mouth to another person's ears. "The channel is both the route traveled by the message, and the means of transportation" (Verderber, Verderber & Sellnow, 2014, p. 352).

To this point, these concepts seem reasonably straightforward, and you may be thinking how could it become puzzling or how could a person's message be misunderstood? Well, even in the initial stage of encoding a message, and presenting it over a channel, speakers can choose words not clearly representing their intentions. Secondly, the speaker may also choose words that the receiver does not comprehend or recognize. These are two small ways this straightforward process can produce a breakdown in creating shared meaning. Potential communication problems, however, are not linked only to the source in the linear model. Let's consider how the linear model clarifies what unfolds after the message travels over the channel to a receiver.

When a source sends a message using symbols, it is delivered to a **receiver** who gives meaning to it in a process labeled as **decoding.** Importantly, in order to give meaning to the message, a receiver must understand how he or she encoded it. When applying this concept to a communication situation receivers must comprehend the symbols or language the speaker uses.

As stated previously, this may appear simple, but we can all recall situations when we received messages while not completely understanding them. This can occur when reading an email from your boss, receiving directions from a stranger, and even conversing casually with your roommate at the end of a long day. We can share a common language, but give different meanings to specific words and phrases. In other words, we may process words differently than the speaker intends. This could result in confusion between speaking partners. Decoding problems also take place when we do not listen carefully.

An additional factor that can hinder accurate decoding is **noise,** the last component of the linear model. Noise involves anything that alters the message after it is sent. Noise may be of a physical or psychological nature, and it always impedes the communication process.

What are the different types of noise senders and receivers may encounter in a communication situation? Physical noise may include sounds other than the voices of each speaker, visual distractions or barriers, poor vocal projection, hunger, fatigue, illness, or physical pain. Psychological noise may include a preoccupation with thoughts other than the message being presented, an emotional reaction to the topic of discussion, prejudice toward the message sender, an unwillingness to listen, or resistance to the message.

The linear model illustrates several fundamental components of the communication process; however, it has some problems that limit its ability to capture the creation of shared meaning when people communicate with one another. Do listeners simply absorb information exactly as it was intended by a source in all situations? Most of us would question such a simple characterization of the communication process. In response to this over simplification, communication researchers modified the linear model to include more dynamic responsibility for receivers. This led to the interactive model of communication.

Interactive Model of Communication

The interactive model of communication develops our understanding of the communication process through taking into consideration the fact that messages flow simultaneously between sources and receivers. As we clarified previously, the linear model considers the communication process complete once the receiver decodes the sender's message. The interactive model is not as limited. Instead, the interactive model shows us how both the sender *and* receiver are involved in encoding and decoding messages.

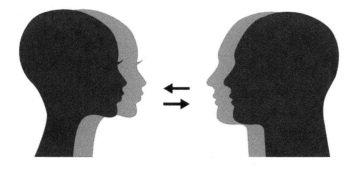

The interactive model varies from the linear model by including the process of **feedback.** Feedback takes place once the receiver has decoded the sender's message. This process is in essence the receiver's reaction to the message. This new message then flows one way, back to the sender, who then becomes the receiver of the feedback to the initial message.

When a sender says something, the receiver processes that message and reacts to it using verbal or nonverbal messages. The original sender then receives that reaction, providing closure to the communication process. Including feedback in the communication process provides us with a more accurate representation of what occurs when two or more people converse.

A second additional element in the interactive model of communication is including the **environment.** By including the environment we reach a deeper appreciation for the communication context than the reference made to noise in the linear model. Even though noise is a component of the environment, it does not represent the entire context. The environment represents the total communication context in which messages are sent and received, involving numerous distinctive components that both aid and impede the communication process (e.g., physical and psychological noise, beliefs, message content, historical moment, participants, relationships, physical setting, values, emotions, etc. . . .). Both senders and receivers should contemplate these features of the environment when encoding and decoding messages.

The interactive model offers us more insight into the communication process than the linear model does; however, it does not adequately represent the complexity of feedback in that process. Senders and receivers do not wait when offering feedback to one another. To develop more precise knowledge of the communication process, it is necessary to consider the transactional model.

The Transactional Model of Communication

The interactive model falls short once we realize that in any communication situation we both send (encode) and receive (decode) messages concurrently. The **transactional model of communication** offers us a more accurate understanding of communication behavior through recognizing that communication is continuous. This means that we play the roles of sender (source) and receiver concurrently in almost every interaction.

We both send and receive messages concurrently.

The transactional model is exceptionally helpful in describing the dynamic nature of face-to-face communication, whether we are involved in social conversations or in a formal public speaking event. In every communication situation, the sender or speaker is responding in real time to how the receiver is responding to the message. If the sender notices heads nodding off when giving a presentation, perhaps he or she adds passion to his or her voice to gain attention back from the audience. This impromptu alteration in the planned presentation is a consequence of feedback received from audience members.

The transactional model of communication allows us to realize that no communication situation ever develops precisely as planned because we must continuously adjust to the feedback we receive. For our intentions in this course, this dynamic model helps us to recognize that all communication situations initiate a transactional process between sender and receiver, where all individuals are involved in concurrently sending and receiving messages. Now that we have a model that allows us to understand the complexity of the communication process, let's consider speaking and relating in the information age.

SPEAKING IN THE INFORMATION AGE

We are living in the **information age,** an age in which communication, technology, and media converge and deeply permeate daily life (Edwards, Edwards, Wahl & Myers, 2013, p. 3). **Convergence** speaks to the ways in which face-to-face communication and different forms of technologically mediated communication overlap and intersect. As applied to public speaking, it means you can connect through the Internet to people all over the world who have written blogs about your topic or have uploaded images and videos that help you to develop your ideas. As you work on your speech you can also post comments or questions on Facebook, asking your friends to help you find information or develop an argument. When you post on Facebook, sometimes you will have to wait for responses, other times responses will be received instantly.

The information age also provides opportunities for speakers to connect with others not only in face-to-face contexts but digitally connect with others in distant locations around the world. For example, a sales representative can give a multimedia sales presentation on Skype and connect with clients all over the U.S. as well as internationally. And, in such a situation, it is important to recognize that when we connect with others through technologically mediated communication, there are different issues we must attend to than in a face-to-face speaking environment. For example, have you insured that the lighting in your location allows you to be seen clearly by others viewing you on screens in remote locations? Have you loaded your graphics, web sites, or videos so they are at your fingertips for a seamless presentation? Have you removed distracting applications from your computer such as email notifications or social media alerts?

In the information age we also need to recognize that any time we give a presentation we may be recorded, sometimes surreptitiously by a person holding up a phone or planting a recording device in an area that is out of our sight. This has caused some embarrassing situations for people in recent years. For example, when Michael Richards (who played Kramer on *Seinfeld*) was performing a stand-up comedy routine at Laugh Factory in Los Angeles he became angry with a group of hecklers who were African American. Several people took video recordings of his tirade, which included the use of racial epithets and the intimation that such behavior fifty years ago would have resulted in a lynching. Within minutes his racist rant was posted on social media and eventually the mass media. Although he apologized publicly, his career was hurt for years afterward. If you wish to see Michael Richards's angry response to the audience members at Laugh Factory, you may find it on YouTube at http://www.youtube.com/watch?v=BoLPLsQbdt0. Then, if interested, you may see his public apology on *Late Show with David Letterman* on YouTube at http://www.youtube.com/watch?v=EC26RI-Ria8.

Michael Richards's racist rant was broadcast on social and mass media

In the political arena, there was also an interesting and widely publicized recording that may have influenced a national election. Specifically, a hidden camera was used at a Republican fundraiser in 2012, capturing candidate Mitt Romney talking about people likely to vote for President Barack Obama. He stated:

> There are 47 percent of the people who will vote for the president no matter what. All right, there are 47 percent who are with him, who are dependent upon government, who believe that they are victims, who believe the government has a responsibility to care for them, who believe that they are entitled to health care, to food, to housing, to you-name-it—that's an entitlement. And the government should give it to them. And they will vote for this president no matter what.... These are people who pay no income tax.... My job is not to worry about those people. I'll never convince them they should take personal responsibility and care for their lives.

The videotape was widely disseminated to all major media outlets with Democrats spinning the story that Mitt Romney does not care about 47 percent of the U.S. population. Many political analysts agree that the comments damaged Romney's campaign significantly. If you wish to read more about this event you may read an article written by David Corn of *Mother Jones* magazine (Corn, 2012). The video of Romney making the 47 percent comment may be found on YouTube at http://www.youtube.com/watch?v=M2gvY2wqI7M.

Romney's comments damaged his campaign.

Although you may never see yourself doing stand-up at a comedy club or giving a speech as a candidate for political office, we may give presentations in class, as part of our jobs, in our local communities, or in volunteer organizations. In the information age we need to be aware that anything we say can be easily recorded and broadcast on social media or in other public venues. If we say something that is hurtful to others or we present ourselves in a way that is easily subject to criticism, our personal and professional lives may be hurt significantly.

When we give presentations that are both face-to-face and involve audience members who are connected through technologically mediated communication, we may interact afterwards in ways that connect people across the world. If the people who are connected represent many diverse groups, a very spirited and culturally enriching dialogue may surface. And, because we may upload our presentations to social media or to blogs, conversations about our ideas can continue well beyond the ending of that presentation.

Listening in the information age offers opportunities and presents challenges. When listening to a presentation we may use a mobile device to find the sources a speaker cites while he or she is speaking to check for accuracy or potential bias. Listeners can

Technology can distract us from the message.

also connect with others by holding up a mobile device that allows friends or loved ones to see and watch the same presentation you are listening to. The downside of the information age from a listening perspective, is allowing our connection to technology to distract us from the message the speaker is presenting. Listening is an issue we discuss more extensively in Chapter 9.

Because technology permeates our daily lives, that influences our public presentations as well. When we give speeches we know our audience will expect us to use technology such as our computers or digital cameras, or integrate media clips found on the Internet to draw listeners into our presentations.

Speakers are also creating **digital narratives,** media presentations in which a speaker tells a story using full motion video with sound, animation, or other non-physical media (e.g., electronic files). In this speaking format, the speaker is not face-to-face in real time with an audience; rather he or she connects to others digitally in a virtual world. So, when we think about public speaking in the information age, we need to recognize that regardless of who we are, or who our audience members are, no one is far from the presence of technology, media, and communication (Edwards, Edwards, Wahl & Myers, 2013). Public speaking is addressed more completely in other chapters of this book.

RELATING IN THE INFORMATION AGE

In the information age we also need to recognize that technology permeates our daily lives. Prensky (2001) coined the terms *digital natives* and *digital immigrants*. A digital native is a person who was born in an era in which digital technologies such as computers, cell phones, video games, and digital cameras were in wide use. They have no memory of not using these technologies. Communication through technology and media is how communication occurs, sometimes more so than face-to-face communication. Digital immigrants remember living lives in which technology and media were not so wrapped up with our day-to-day communication, but they have learned to adopt these forms of communication, recognizing, sometimes regretfully, that we will never return to a non-technologically mediated, media saturated world.

Because communication is a central part of our lives, we need to recognize that it can occur in a range of contexts. In just the course of a single day, a person can watch television, surf the Internet, converse with other people for a short time or at length, solve problems in a group setting, and even deliver a formal presentation. It is necessary to identify each of these wide ranging contexts in order to understand why and how we communicate. Developing this understanding will be helpful in studying communication more effectively.

When a person engages in **intrapersonal communication,** he or she is *communicating internally with his or her own self.* Intrapersonal communication is the internal communication that occurs within our own minds, the mental processing of decisions we must make, the choices we have made, and even the conversations we desire or need to have. It can sometimes be referred to as "self-talk." It can be both positive and negative or even civil or uncivil.

Interpersonal communication is *communication with other people that can range from considerably personal to considerably impersonal.* This type of communication usually occurs between two people as a *dyad* or in a small group, which involves fewer than six people. The essential component of this type of communication is that it involves relationships. When communicating on an interpersonal level, we are establishing, maintaining, and disengaging from relationships with others. There are many forms for these types of communication. For example, we may connect with others face-to-face, by cell phone, via text message, through social media, or by email.

It is common during interpersonal communication to be civil towards those we like and uncivil towards those who we do not like. Most of us have probably also recognized that it is easier to listen to and communicate with people we identify as similar to us. Even so, we sometimes find ourselves communicating civilly with those whose company we do not enjoy and communicating uncivilly towards loved ones.

Group communication, sometimes referred to as *small-group communication,* arises *when we interact with a small, but organized assembly of people.* Group communication usually involves a focus or goal. It takes place when we communicate as a team, study or work group, collective or committee, or even hobby, club, or political group. When we communicate in groups, we often are guided by rules or specific intentions. We may discuss strategies or plans that steer the interactions. Group communication can be formal or informal, and group members often assume specific roles. These roles can range from team leader or chairperson, to recorder or behind-the-scenes organizer. In order for a group to become effective and successful, civil and ethical communication must be used. When group members turn against one another, uncivil and unethical communication can consume the group. Just as in interpersonal communication, in the information age groups can interact face-to-face or through a variety of computer mediated forms of communication such as Skype or other means of videoconferencing. Group communication is explored more completely in Chapter 13.

COMMUNICATION COMPETENCE

A **competent communicator** is one who engages in appropriate and effective communication (Canary & Spitzberg, 1987, 1989). *Appropriate communication* is communication that does not violate relationally or situationally sanctioned rules. For example, a married couple may establish a relational rule of, "When we argue, we will not yell at each other." *Effective communication* achieves the valued goal of the communicator. For example, a person is an effective communicator if he or she successfully explains to a coworker how to perform a new task. Let's examine in further detail some additional aspects of communication competence in order to clearly explain how it affects the communication process.

Because communication competence is evaluated over time in relationships, competent communicators must consistently use appropriate and effective communication rather than use these forms of communication only sporadically. As a consequence, the label of competent communicator is one that can neither be acquired nor lost quickly. One embarrassing comment in a business meeting does not make you an incompetent communicator. On the other hand, one successful persuasive presentation does not mean you will always be considered a competent communicator.

To observe that a competent communicator succeeds *in specific contexts* means that communicators may be perceived as more competent in some circumstances than in others. For example, Aiden loves making his friends laugh in the cafeteria, but is terrified of speaking publically in his classes. Aiden is perceived as more competent in small group contexts, but not in public speaking situations. On the other hand, Ava can eloquently present in class during a speech, but has a difficult time making friends in her residence hall. Ava is considered more competent in public speaking situations than in interpersonal ones.

When it is said that a communicator is *perceived* to be competent, this means that communication competence is in the eye of the beholder. There is no fixed standard by which someone can evaluate communication competence. In order to attain communication competence, one must alter communication behaviors to match the expectations of individual receivers, relationships, and contexts rather than following general prescriptions for communication.

To *deliberately use appropriate and effective communication behavior* is to be capable of picking and choosing among a range of communication behaviors, and selecting those most likely to be perceived as both appropriate and effective in a particular situation. When you evaluate the behaviors you have used in the past in order to accomplish your goals, you can build upon and improve your communication competence. Similarly, when you know what others deem to be appropriate and effective communication behavior, you have access to the information you need in order to meet their expectations.

Suggesting that competence includes *reaching mutually desirable effects* means that both you and your communication partners feel content with the results of your communication efforts, at least a majority of the time. For example, two roommates, Noah and Dan, decide to get a job together at the library. One day, Noah texts Dan at the last minute to cover his shift. Dan complies, and Noah feels he was a competent communicator because he was successful at solving *his* problem. However, if Dan is frustrated because Noah forgot about a basketball game he wanted to attend during that shift, he may not feel the same way about Noah's request. Dan, in this instance, may question the appropriateness of Noah's communication.

So, communication competence is multifaceted. It is concerned with accomplishing personal goals while also expressing concern for others, identifying their needs and opinions, including their ideas, and being willing to adjust your goals in order to mesh with theirs. These communication behaviors are likely to lead to perceptions of communication competence.

MYTHS ABOUT HUMAN COMMUNICATION

Communication involves the continuous process of sending and receiving verbal and nonverbal messages between two or more people. Though this seemingly straightforward process is the subject of this text, it is in reality rather complex. To effectively study human communication we need to examine some of the common myths about the process so we may become better communicators in different settings.

MYTH 1—THE MORE ONE COMMUNICATES, THE BETTER ONE'S COMMUNICATION WILL BE.

Though this statement seems logical, the same idea is weaved into the popular belief that practice makes perfect. Practice is only capable of making communication effective if you are practicing the correct behaviors and skills. So, if you are practicing incorrect habits, you are likely to become a less effective communicator. Consequently, it is important to learn and practice the principles of appropriateness and effectiveness in communication with others.

MYTH 2—WHEN TWO PEOPLE ARE IN AN INTERPERSONAL RELATIONSHIP, NEITHER PERSON SHOULD HAVE TO COMMUNICATE NEEDS AND DESIRES EXPLICITLY.

It is easy to assume that your relationship partner should intuitively know what your needs and desires are, but this assumption is at the center of many interpersonal problems. People are incapable of mind reading, and to expect this of them creates barriers to open and honest communication.

MYTH 3—INTERPERSONAL OR GROUP CONFLICT IS AN INDICATION THAT THE RELATIONSHIP OR GROUP IS IN DANGER.

Conflict is an inevitable part of interpersonal and group communication. If managed effectively, conflict could even benefit the individuals and the relationship. For example, when a married couple manages a difficult conflict, producing a solution each person finds desirable, the relationship is strengthened. Or, when a group is able to overcome unproductive arguing when tackling a complex task, they may feel more motivated to work with each other in the future.

MYTH 4—STRONG COMMUNICATORS ARE BORN, NOT MADE.

Though some learn the principles of appropriate and effective communication earlier than others, communication is a developed proficiency. Anyone can build their communication skills when learning the principles of human communication and given the opportunities to practice them.

MYTH 5—THE FEAR OF PUBLIC SPEAKING IS NEGATIVE AND MUST BE ELIMINATED.

Most people who speak publicly are nervous. What is important is to learn how to *manage* that fear, making it work for you rather than against you. Anyone is capable of becoming a more effective speaker regardless of their current level of communication apprehension.

SUMMARY

This chapter began by describing different models of communication. The three models that were covered were the linear, interactive, and transactional. The transactional model is the one communication researchers recognize as providing the most accurate depiction of the communication process.

The second section of the chapter described how speaking and relating have been impacted by the information age, an age in which communication, technology, and media converge and deeply penetrate daily life. As applied to speaking and relating, living in the information age allows speakers, friends, and coworkers to connect to people all over the world. This can offer incredible opportunities for dialogue among people representing diverse ideas and cultures. Speakers also need to be aware of potential risks such as being recorded and having our speeches or conversations uploaded to social media and other outlets. For listeners, the information age allows us to connect friends in remote locations to a speaker, or to critically evaluate speeches by checking the Internet for sources that relate to the speaker's topic. However, the very technology we use for such purposes may also distract us from the message we are in the audience to hear. The permeation of technology in our daily lives connects us to people, but it also raises the expectation that we use that technology effectively and expertly in communicating our messages whether face-to-face or digitally.

In the final section of the chapter we described five common myths that discourage effective communication. The five myths were: (a) the more one communicates, the better one's communication will be, (b) when two people are in an interpersonal relationship, neither person should have to communicate needs and desires explicitly, (c) interpersonal or group conflict is an indication that the relationship or group is in danger, (d) strong communicators are born, not made, (e) the fear of public speaking is negative and must be eliminated.

REFERENCES

Canary, D.J., & Spitzberg, B.H. (1987). Appropriateness and effectiveness perceptions of conflict strategies. *Human Communication Research, 14,* 93–118.

Canary, D.J., & Spitzberg, B.H. (1989). A model of perceived competence of conflict strategies. *Human Communication Research, 15,* 630–649.

Corn, D. (2012, December 31). The story behind the 47 percent video. *Mother Jones.* Retrieved April 23, 2014, from http://www.motherjones.com/politics/2012/12/story-behind-47-video?page=2

Edwards, A., Edwards, C., Wahl, S.T., & Myers, S.A. (2013). *The Communication Age: Connecting and Engaging.* Thousand Oaks, CA: Sage.

Prensky, M. (2001). Digital natives, digital immigrants. *On the Horizon, 9*(5), 1–6. Retrieved April 23, 2014, from http://www.marcprensky.com/writing/prensky%20-%20digital%20natives,%20digital%20immigrants%20-%20part1.pdf

Verderber, R.F., Sellnow, D.S., & Verderber, K.S. (2014). *The Challenge of Effective Public Speaking in a Digital Age* (16th ed.). Stamford, CT: Cengage Learning.

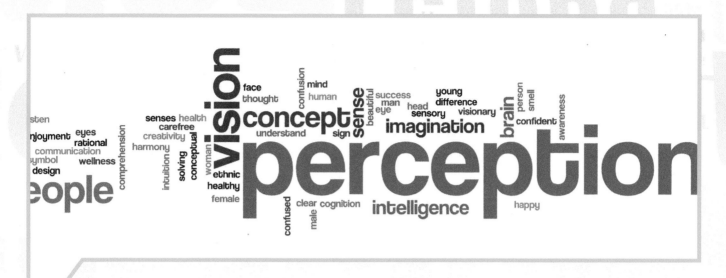

CHAPTER 2

Perception, Self, and Communication

"I was announced Homecoming Queen my senior year. To most girls, this is a dream come true. To me, this was my worst nightmare. I guess people could say I have self-esteem problems, and maybe I do. The students in my school always tell me how pretty I am, how I have the coolest clothes, and even the best hair. I receive multiple comments on my media pages complimenting my physical appearance, but nothing complimenting me on the true beauty that I know I have under all that. Before I leave the house everyday, I look into the mirror and try to see the physical attractiveness that everyone sees, but I never do. All I see is me, just me. Normal hair, normal eyes, normal face.

Little does anyone know, all I want in life is to be seen as something other than just a pretty face. I make good grades and I am always trying to improve myself intellectually. The thing is, no one notices. They only care about my newest look and my physical appearance. I want to make a difference in the world. I don't want other girls to feel like I do, invisible. I want others to see the real me. I am more than the pretty girl. People are always talking at me or about me; no one is ever talking to me."

– Beautiful and Empty

INTRODUCTION

As Beautiful and Empty's story illustrates, being deprived of the opportunity to be seen as you wish to be seen is the ultimate denial. When perception of one's self image is not supported by significant others, self-esteem suffers. As much as we are free to define ourselves, we are dependent on others to affirm and support that definition. Beautiful and Empty is struggling with the limited and incomplete picture others have of her. After reading this chapter, you will be able to offer Beautiful and Empty suggestions for how she can cultivate the social confirmation that she desperately desires.

In this chapter you will learn about the perception process. How you select, organize, and interpret and assign meaning to behaviors and messages is influenced by several contributing factors, including your background, past experiences, and communication skills. We will focus on increasing perceptual accuracy and factors that influence perception, including individual differences. In the second part of this chapter we will explore the development of self through communication. Then, we will examine the self-concept, self-esteem, and self-awareness. Additionally, several theories and concepts will be introduced that will offer insights that explain why we compare ourselves to others, succumb to self-fulfilling prophesies, and engage in identity management activities. Reflecting on your communication behavior and exploring one of life's fundamental questions, your identity, is an initial step in the development of your interpersonal communication competence. Let's first begin by talking about perception.

THE PERCEPTION PROCESS

Perception is the process by which we become aware of people, objects, events, and activities in the external world and make sense of that stimulus. How we interpret and assign meaning to behaviors and messages is influenced by our background and past experiences. The perception process can be organized into three steps: **selection, organization,** and **interpretation.** Commonly employed, these three steps are continuous, interdependent, and involve all five senses. In the next section we will discuss each of the four selection activities.

Step 1: Selection

Selection is not a unitary activity but rather encompasses an elaborate series of processes that include: selective attention, selective exposure, perceptual accentuation, and selective retention.

SELECTIVE ATTENTION

Selective attention occurs when we direct our attention to certain stimuli and ignore others. We do not attend to everything in our environment, nor could we. We are selective in our attention and discerning in our choices. Why do certain stimuli get our attention? Why do other stimuli fail to garner notice? Two factors influence the selection process and include stimuli that are in our immediate proxemic space and stimuli that are unusual or novel in some fashion. Think about the last time something or someone made you stop what you were doing and redirect your attention. Most would agree that it is near impossible to ignore a loud siren, perhaps because we know that it signals trouble and peril for someone. If you are like me, when I am in the car and I know that there is an incident up the road, as I approach the scene, I tell myself that I am not going to look at the carnage; I am going to face forward and proceed past the wreckage. Unfortunately, I find myself succumbing to the all too common practice of "rubbernecking," and I realize that I am not in control of my choices and often the stimuli is simply too difficult to ignore. We do not always consciously choose to attend to particular stimuli, sometimes we are in the right (or wrong) place at the right (or wrong) time) and the selection process is largely influenced by what appears in our midst.

Selective attention is also influenced by novelty including odd and unusual stimuli. What was it about the situation that was so unusual? Why did it capture your attention? Chances are you observed something or someone you have not seen before. Expectations and previous experience define much of what we would term novel or unusual stimuli. For example, a man wearing a skirt is considered odd in western society, unless we happen to be in Scotland and the skirt happens to be a kilt, a traditional garment worn by Scottish highlanders. How about an incident in which a dog bites a woman? This is unfortunate but not a terribly unusual occurrence. However, a woman biting a dog would likely get lots of attention for its sheer novelty.

In March 2012, actor Alicia Silverstone shared a video online in which she engaged in "kiss-feeding" her son. There is nothing unusual about a mother feeding her child however, prechewing food and then transmitting it to a child via a kiss garnered much fan fair. Premastication, a centuries-old feeding practice, carries many health benefits for babies and is considered a bonding activity as well as a feeding method (Konner, 2010). In California and other parts of the world, this practice is considered akin to breastfeeding and would not attract much attention. In the majority of the United States however, premastication is frowned upon and considered unsanitary and unnecessary, signaling that **cultural** and individual differences are at play.

SELECTIVE EXPOSURE

Selective exposure refers to conscious efforts to seek out stimuli that are consistent with our beliefs, values, and attitudes. Jeremy Sherman, writing for *Psychology Today*, laments that it is all too common to run across people who will not consider alternative views or even facts that run contrary to their opinion. He claims, "We all engage in selective exposure and for the same reasons. Truly hearing challenges to our assumptions is freaking exhausting! One's whole metabolism recoils and bridles at the hassle and cost

Expose yourself to contrary and opposing views—cognitive stretching.

of having to remodel our beliefs to fit new information" (Sherman, 2014). To only expose yourself to what you already believe is to short-circuit the very purpose of education, experience, and personal growth. As F. Scott Fitzgerald reminds us, "The test of a first-rate intelligence is the ability to hold two opposed ideas in mind at the same time and still retain the ability to function." Release yourself from your familiar moorings and expose yourself to contrary and opposing views, think of it as cognitive stretching.

PERCEPTUAL ACCENTUATION

Perceptual accentuation occurs when needs influence perceptions and lead us to see what we expect and want to see. In effect, we magnify or accentuate that which will satisfy our needs and wants. Have you ever gone grocery shopping when you were hungry? Chances are you bought far more food than necessary. When needs are foremost in our mind, perceptual distortions are likely and we have a tendency to act impulsively and make poor decisions. For example, after a particularly painful breakup, you find yourself in need of personal affirmation. On an evening out with friends you notice that a man at the end of the bar appears interested in you. You surmise this because he has been staring at you all night. After you engage in some nonverbal displays of interest with one another, he ventures over to your table. He sits down with you and your friends and soon after, the two of you are deep in conversation with one another. By last call you find that you are very interested in this man and hope the night does not end soon. Your friends signal that it is getting late and it is time to go home. Your facial expression indicates to them that you are not interested in going home and would rather spend time with this new person. Your friends escort you to the bathroom and emphatically insist that you do not go home with this man. They say that this is classic rebound behavior and your judgment is not to be trusted. They leave you little choice in the matter. When you return to the table you see that your new friend has left the bar. Although you feel worse than you did before, you are thankful that your friends saved you from making a bad decision, fueled by a weak moment and skewed perceptions.

SELECTIVE RETENTION

We have creative and subjective memories that are largely self-serving. **Selective retention** refers to the decision to minimize messages that are painful, unpleasant, or inconsistent with our self-image. In short, we remember the good and forget the bad. We retain thoughts that are consistent with who we think we are and discard those that do not support this perception. Perhaps your parents fondly refer to their high school and college days as the best time of their lives and counsel you to also appreciate your college days. Was it really the best time of their lives? Perhaps they are selectively (mis)remembering.

Selective retention is in evidence when family and friends share memories of a loved one who has passed away. As time goes by, the deceased person ceases to have any questionable qualities and is now awash in positive memories that reference only complimentary personal traits. Perhaps the most telling example of selective retention can be seen in former inmates of Auschwitz who hold reunions in which they grow sentimental over remembered jokes and experiences.

Step 2: Organization

Organizing perceptions is a complex activity that is characterized by several cognitive decisions, arrived at with varying degrees of awareness. We use organizational structures to make sense of the stimuli selected in Step 1. Stimuli are organized into **schemata,** which are cognitive templates. Think of schemata as metaphoric file drawers in our mind that serve as an organizing mechanism for incoming information. Organizational schemata explain how the same symbol can be interpreted as both a letter and a number. For example, in the first series below, the second symbol 13 signifies the letter *B* but in the second series *13* is recognized as number *13*. Context and proximity are consequential and influence the organization and interpretation of stimuli.

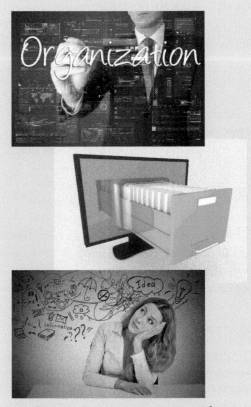

Organizing perceptions is complex.

A 13 C   12 13 14

Perceptions are organized by applying four types of cognitive schemata, which include: prototypes, personal constructs, stereotypes, and scripts.

1. **Prototypes:** A prototype is a sample or model and represents the most typical or ideal example of a person, group, place, object, activity, or relationship. Incoming stimuli is organized according to an existing prototype. For example, many people have an existing prototype of an ideal relationship partner. A potential romantic suitor is evaluated and measured against the qualities and characteristics identified in the prototype. Chances are some potential partners will be more consistent with the prototype than others.

2. **Personal Constructs:** Constructs are individually created mental representations of how we interpret and organize people, events, and objects. Each person's construct system reveals what is important to them and is based on personal experience. People differ in the number of constructs they employ in the organization process, as some have elaborate systems and others, particularly children, have very few.

   A construct can have two bipolar opposites such as "good/bad," "attractive/unattractive," "generous/cheap," and "useful/useless," and we assess where someone or something fits along the continuum between the two extremes. Constructs are applied to incoming stimuli and help organize our perceptions (Kelly, 1955).

3. **Stereotypes:** Generalizations and judgments about people and situations without regard for differences is the essence of stereotyping. When we ignore differences to simplify perceptions we are being cognitively lazy. Stereotypes are shortcuts in processing stimuli because we draw inferences about people, events, and objects without regard for the facts.

4. **Scripts:** Scripts are developed to organize routine and predictable communication. We know what is expected in familiar situations and we organize our perceptions and communication accordingly. There are expectations about how various scenarios unfold such as how greetings are enacted and we invoke a tried and true script without much conscious awareness. A typical script depicting two friends unexpectedly running into one another follows:

Tanya: "Hey Rochelle, how ya doin'? It's been awhile."

Rochelle: "Everything is all good, you know, just hangin' in there. How about you?"

Tanya: "Oh you know, same old thing, nothing much to tell."

Both parties understand that they are employing the script used for a friend you haven't seen in some time. Rochelle and Tanya know that the other is not expecting an elaborate response to the question "How ya doin'?" If either party did offer more than a cursory response, it would be unusual and unexpected. We rely on scripts for much of our initial and routine communication with others. If and when a novel circumstance arises, a different script is crafted and one's communication repertoire is enhanced.

Scripts organize routine communication.

Step 3: Interpretation

In the third step of the perception process, we make sense of our perceptions through interpretations, explanations, and attributions of another's behavior. Consistent with the selection and organization perception steps, interpretation is subjective and influenced by personal and contextual factors resulting in a very complex activity.

ATTRIBUTION THEORY

The initial step in sense making is to understand why people do the things they do. Fritz Heider developed the **attribution theory** in 1958 to describe the process by which we cultivate explanations for peoples' behavior, their motives, and intentions. Heider believed that attribution was necessary to determine if behavior is the result of dispositional causes or the result of situational factors. Is a person's disposition responsible for this outcome or is the behavior due to some external environmental cause? These questions and others are at the heart of the attribution theory.

As we make sense of what we perceive, we can be inaccurate.

In the process of making sense of what we perceive, we sometimes make snap judgments, ignore critical pieces of information, and draw quick conclusions that can lead to inaccurate judgments. Two types of systematic attribution errors are detailed below.

ERRORS IN ATTRIBUTION

Self-Serving Bias.   The tendency to attribute one's successes to internal dispositional causes and one's failures to external uncontrollable factors is the essence of the self-serving bias. We do this primarily to protect our own self-image (Spitzberg & Manusov, 2015) and give ourselves the benefit of the doubt. For example, if you get a new job, it is due to your work ethic and talent. On the other hand, if you do not get the job, it is because the person interviewing you was a self-involved old fart. Kelsey's story illustrates the self-serving bias in action.

> I wasn't feeling well so I missed a class and received a zero on an in class quiz. The professor wouldn't let me retake the quiz because I did not email him about my illness. I blamed the entire situation on the professor being unsympathetic and inflexible. I realize now that I was not taking responsibility for my problem and my shortcomings, it was much easier to attribute fault to the professor rather than myself.

Fundamental Attribution Error.   The tendency to attribute others' behaviors to internal (i.e., personality, dispositional) rather than external (i.e., environment, chance) causes. For example: the cashier gave you the wrong change because he doesn't know how to count, not because he was distracted by an announcement being made over the loudspeaker. The driver cut you off because he is a jerk, not because of noisy children in the car.

INCREASING PERCEPTUAL ACCURACY

PERCEPTION CHECKING

While it is all too easy to make perception errors, there are several strategies you can use to minimize misperceptions. **Perception checking** involves offering descriptive statements to your conversational partner that explains your perception of a situation. After you describe your *perceptions,* request clarification to determine if you interpreted the situation correctly. Stress that it is important for you to know if your understanding is consistent with his or her intentions. Statements such as, "what I hear you saying is.... Am I correct in my perception of this situation?" Perception checking takes the guesswork out of the perception process.

CONFUSING FACT WITH INFERENCE

Confusing fact with inference is a common perceptual error. A fact is an observable and undeniable truth. An inference is a conclusion based on probability. When reaching conclusions, it is imperative to recognize which aspects are rooted in assumptions (i.e., inferences) and which are based in truth (i.e., fact). Both facts and inferences are integral to decision-making; the key is to be mindful of the tendency to overstate an inference and underplay a fact.

FROZEN PERCEPTIONS

If you have cringed at the comment from a relative that sounds something like, "Oh my, you have grown up so much, how did that happen?" then you already know what frozen perceptions are. We have a tendency to think that everything stays the same, especially in our absence. Change is constant, children grow up, get taller, develop independence, and become young adults. Your Aunt Marge has not seen you since you were twelve years old and as illogical as it sounds, she is genuinely surprised to see that you are no longer that same young child, even though six years have passed. Denying the inevitability of change by relying on frozen perceptions contributes to misperceptions.

INFLUENCES ON PERCEPTION

The perception process, particularly the selection, organization, and interpretation of stimuli is influenced by several factors including impression formation principles such as the implicit personality theory, the halo and horned effect, and the primacy/recency principle. Individual differences influence perception and will be also explored.

Impression Formation Principles

IMPLICIT PERSONALITY THEORY

The **implicit personality theory** occurs when we form impressions of others and organize certain characteristics with other characteristics because we desire stability in our judgments and order in our evaluations. If we observe several qualities in a person, we make the assumption that other qualities are also likely to be present. In other words, we assume similarity even in the absence of adequate information that support or deny the view. For example, let's imagine that you notice that your neighbor volunteers as a "Big Brother" for disadvantaged local youths and helps people in the neighborhood care for their lawns if they are sick or unable to do so themselves. From these observations you readily surmise that your neighbor is not only kind and generous he is also probably intelligent too. You chose this quality, rather than unintelligent because intelligence is consistent with the other known characteristics (i.e., kind and generous).

HALO AND HORNED EFFECT

Closely aligned with the implicit personality theory is the **halo and horned effect.** Psychologist Edward Thorndike coined the terms halo and horned effect in 1920 to describe the tendency to form an impression based on your knowledge of one trait. Initial positive (i.e., halo) or negative (i.e., horned) perceptions lead to subsequent positive or negative attributions. For instance, physical attractiveness is a powerful positive attribute and can be parlayed into additional positive perceptions such as leadership potential

(Verhulst, Lodge, & Lavine, 2010), viability of employment (Samovar, Porter, & McDaniel, 2009), and sociability (Guerrero, Andersen, & Afifi, 2014). Once the perception is cognitively registered in our mind; subsequent actions and interactions tend to support the original perception. We are not accustomed to appreciating the contradictory characteristics of people or tolerating the ambiguity that comes with being human. The reality is, most of us are a mixed bag of contradictory, competing, and inconsistent attributes.

PRIMACY/RECENCY

Primacy/recency effect is the third impression formation principle. There is considerable evidence that suggests that what comes first is more influential than what comes last. Solomon Asch was one of the foremost thinkers to extensively explore the implicit personality theory and the primacy/recency effect. Asch's (1940) research tested whether what comes first or last has the most compelling effect on perceptions. He found that people described with the first set of qualities listed below were perceived differently than those described with the second set of qualities.

> Person A: **intelligent, industrious,** impulsive, critical, stubborn, and envious
>
> Person B: envious, stubborn, critical, impulsive, **industrious,** and **intelligent**

You probably noticed that both sets of words are the same, however the order of appearance is altered. Results of Asch's experiment revealed that people evaluated person A more favorably than person B. Asch's findings help explain how we arrive at first impressions and why they carry more perceptual weight than later impressions. Perhaps you recall drawing an inaccurate conclusion about someone after a brief first meeting. Can you identify factors that contributed to your erroneous conclusion? It is not unusual to change your impressions of someone after you have had the opportunity to get to know the person better. Your willingness to adjust your first impressions is a testament to your ability to change in light of additional information. Let's now move on to the discussion of individual differences in perceptions.

Individual Differences

There is considerable evidence that men and women differ in their perception behavior. For example, women favor more psychological characteristics than men do and seek more information before they form impressions. Men form faster impressions and compared with women, are more concerned with physical characteristics. Women are more perceptive in reading nonverbal behaviors and are especially sensitive to deciphering emotional and facial expressions (Wood, 2013). There are sensory differences between men and women too that can affect perceptual abilities. For example, women are better at perceiving smells than men and men are more likely to experience hearing loss and sight deficits before women. There are limited differences between men and women regarding sense of taste and touch (Chitale, 2009). Perceptions are affected by sensory abilities; which can influence selection, organization, and interpretation of communication behavior.

Perceptions are affected by senses.

As we mature from children to young adults we generally become more sophisticated communicators, skilled at selecting, organizing, and interpreting perceptual stimuli. Age is generally accompanied by education and experience, which contributes to the development of schemata, a key perceptual skill. From a developmental perspective, the ability to judge emotions expressed reveals that children improve in their accuracy with age. For example, a three-year-old can recognize laughter; five-year-olds can recognize pain, anger, fear, horror, and surprise, and fourteen-year-olds can recognize contempt (a mix of hate and anger).

Before we move on to the next section of this chapter, remember Beautiful and Empty? What advice do you have for her? What can she do to alter the limited and incomplete perception others have of her? What role has Beautiful and Empty played in the impression others have of her?

THE DEVELOPMENT OF SELF THROUGH COMMUNICATION

> "What we are and what we see ourselves as being seems to be constantly under construction and reconstruction, with the architects and remodeling contractors largely being those with whom we have close interactions."
>
> Arthur Aron, 2003, p. 443

The development of self is largely a communication enterprise. Through interactions with significant others, identities are constructed and managed, expectations are forged, and behaviors are influenced. Several theories and concepts will be introduced that offer insight into how and why we compose and compare ourselves to others, succumb to self-fulfilling prophesies, and engage in identity management activities. Reflecting on your communication behavior and exploring the components of self and identity is an initial step in understanding the multiple influencing agents that have contributed to who you are today. Let's get started by talking about the various components responsible for the development of self.

The Development of Self

As Arthur Aron suggests, the self develops through communication with others. When we communicate we develop our self-concept based on the appraisal and treatment we receive from others. This feedback gives us information for confirming or altering our behavior and in effect, our **self-concept.** George Herbert Mead, a sociologist, was among the first to emphasize the social origins of self, believing that communication with others is a significant contributor to self-concept. He conceptualized this process and termed it **symbolic interaction theory** (Mead, 1934). It is through other's judgments and evaluations of us that we develop a sense of ourselves. Starting at birth, we receive and process judgments from others that influence our perception and definition of ourselves. In turn, our self-concept influences how we communicate with others. This cyclical process occurs throughout our lifetime.

SELF-CONCEPT

How do you become you? There are several contributing sources that influence the development of your self-concept. We define ourselves in so many ways that it is more accurate to speak of a "collection of selves" as self-concept has many authors. Sources of self-concept include: significant others, family, friends, and teachers. If people think positively of you, you tend to think positively of yourself.

As we compare reflections, not surprisingly we tend to pay more attention to some people and less to others. One's self concept is relatively enduring and develops over the course of a lifetime; however, the most significant developments occur between the ages of fourteen and twenty-three, although significant events can change your self-concept at any time.

We show different sides of ourselves to different people and in effect, we play different roles in different relationships. We are simultaneously both friend and teammate; child and parent; superior and subordinate; and teacher and student. Fluidity between and within roles reflects behavioral flexibility, a core component of interpersonal competence.

Reflected Appraisals.   Not only are we influenced by the treatment we receive from others but we also form impressions of how we *think* others view us. This process is termed **reflected appraisals.** These appraisals help us form a mental image of ourselves. The process of gathering information about how others judge us is captured in the metaphor the **looking-glass self,** developed by Sociologist Charles Horton Cooley (1902). This mirror image of ourselves is reflective of how we think others see us. Like Mead, Cooley believed that we develop our sense of self through interactions with others. Consistent with the image reflected in the mirror, people imagine their own appearance, intelligence, and likeability from the treatment received from others. These perceptions contribute and shape our definition of self and ultimately our identity.

Self-concept has multiple influencing agents, including context and culture. We are all products of the time in which we are born and come of age. If you are reading this chapter, you are more than likely a member of the millennial generation, so named because you were the first generation to come of age in the new millennium. Although dates vary somewhat, most agree that millennials mark the generation born between the years 1982 and 2002. Millennials are described as discerning and selective, close to their parents, confident, team-oriented, wired multi-taskers, electronically literate, and not terribly inclined to read newspapers or books (Howe & Strauss, 2000). If you are a member of this generation, do these qualities describe you?

A yearly study titled "Freshman Survey, Fall 2014" conducted by the Higher Education Research Institute (see Eagan, Stolzenberg, Ramirez, Aragon, Suchard, & Hurtado) reported that the social habits of college freshman are changing. Based on survey responses from more than 150,000 first-year students, they found that time spent on social media increased to upwards of six hours per week. Simultaneously students report that they feel increasingly less confident in their interpersonal skills. It is likely that the two trends are related, however research shows that social networking compliments rather than replaces face-to-face

A mirror-like image of ourselves, the looking-glass self, is developed through interactions with others.

communication (Guerrero et al., 2014). Nonetheless, the high level of social media use has prompted some researchers to believe that this behavior is indicative of an addiction (Kuss & Griffiths, 2011). No other generation has had to navigate the perils and pitfalls presented by such a powerful and pervasive social medium.

In 2014 there was a news report that the American Psychological Association concluded that taking selfie pictures was an indicator of a mental disorder (Foster, 2014). Although the report was a prank, many accepted the story as true because they believed that the millennial generation is narcissistic and the selfie is a prime indicator of this generation's self-indulgence (Kluger, 2015). While this characterization is debatable, given the predilections of millennials to explore facets of self and participate in self-expression activities, it is not surprising that in 2013, the word "selfie" was voted Oxford Dictionaries Word of the Year. Your self-concept is influenced by many factors including when you were born, your peer group, and societal forces beyond your control.

Another key facet of self-concept and identity is your name. Naming trends are reflective of societal trends. Your name can be an indication and a celebration of your culture, race, ethnicity, and identity. Yet throughout history, and particularly during World War II, ethnic groups changed their surname (i.e., last name) to avoid notice and seamlessly integrate into society. For example, to escape imprisonment by the Nazis, Jewish people changed or altered their last names, and some Germans modified their surnames to prevent antagonism from Americans. The cost of freedom and peace was high for these people, as they abandoned the names that reflected their heritage and culture.

Other social movements have resulted in interesting naming trends. For example, Roland Fryer and Steven Levitt (2004) examined the birth records of children born in California between 1961 and 2003 and concluded that there are distinct differences between the given names (i.e., first names) of black and white children. Their research revealed that in the 1960s, parents chose relatively similar first names for their children, regardless of race. However, by the 1970s that pattern changed, and many black parents engaged in distinctive naming practices. The authors believe that this naming trend was the result of the Black Power movement, which affected African American identities and is reflected in their children's names. Today there are far fewer crossover names for white and black children.

Does a white first name contribute to economic success more than a black first name? Fryer and Levitt (2004) concluded that the name given to children does not impact children's future financial success but does reveal much about the parents doing the naming. Perhaps the financial outlook is not affected by a name, but recent research suggests that there are social implications associated with one's first name. Reactions to first names appearing on a dating site were gathered from 12,000 adult participants, and the authors concluded that a bad first name is consequential and can lead to loneliness and low self-esteem (Gebauer, Leary, & Neberich, 2011). Other studies refute the claim that a first name can unduly influence one's life trajectory (Levitt & Dubner, 2005). As is evident, many factors serve as influential and powerful determinants of your identity and self-concept. Are you pleased with your name? Have you considered changing your name now or in the future?

SELF-ESTEEM

In addition to being susceptible to others' view of us, we too invoke evaluations and judgments of ourselves. You may have heard the phrases "don't be too hard on yourself" or "you are your own worst enemy." Both comments signal that we engage in self-assessment. How you feel about yourself is referred to as **self-esteem** and signifies the value you place on yourself—your perceived self-worth.

Self-esteem is the value you place on yourself.

The Social Comparison Theory.   The social comparison theory was developed by Leon Festinger in 1954 and explains how self-esteem develops. He believed that humans evaluate their self-worth by comparing themselves to others, usually those in one's peer group. For example, you might recall feeling quite satisfied with your performance on a Communication Theory test until you discovered that your roommate scored ten points higher than you did. Before you knew your roommate's score, you were content with your performance on the test, but your self-esteem plummeted when you compared your score to your roommate's score.

Self-assessments can be unreasonably positive or negative, often as a result of choosing inappropriate reference groups. For example, the current pressure on young men and women to develop bodies that are simply unrealistic (i.e., stick-thin women and sculpted men) has resulted in eating disorders, drug use, low self-esteem, and unhealthy self-concepts. In response to this problem, a bill is under consideration in France that would criminalize featuring unusually thin women in advertisements, and other European countries are ready to follow (*Time,* 2015). Consider Deanna's story about comparison:

> "I have struggled with my self-esteem since I was eight years old. I felt like I was never good enough or pretty enough like the other girls my age. Sure I had friends, but I always felt like the "fat" friend. Today I would be called the "Duff" (designated ugly fat friend). When I was ten years old, I was 4'8" and weighed 233 lbs. I am now twenty-three years old, and it still hurts when people post comments on Facebook or in my YouTube comments calling me "ugly," "fat," and "lazy." I am now in a weight-management program, and my goal is to get down to a healthy weight. My advice to everyone is to think before you stereotype people because you don't know what they are going through and your words can impact them immensely."

As Deanna's story illustrates, self-esteem is influenced by social comparisons with others and the hurtful words expressed by others. To enhance self-esteem, you might find yourself behaving in ways that solicit approval from others. Unfortunately, the approval of others can come at the price of disapproval from yourself, especially if your behaviors are inconsistent with your self-concept. Researchers (Lee, 2014; Park & Lee, 2014) observed that Facebook provides users with ample opportunity to engage in social comparison between self and others, and it can affect self-esteem and life satisfaction adversely. Consequently, feelings of inadequacy have prompted some Facebook users to deactivate their accounts.

High self-esteem has many social and emotional benefits such as a higher degree of happiness, less depression, lower delinquency, and improved academic performance. There are also some drawbacks to high self-esteem, including the tendency to engage in high-risk behaviors. Perhaps misplaced confidence and an ill-founded belief in one's ability to escape consequences fuels this behavior.

The Self-Fulfilling Prophecy.   Self-concept and self-esteem affects expectations and subsequent communication behaviors. The **self-fulfilling prophecy** is characterized as a belief that comes true because we act as if it is true. In effect, we behave in ways that confirm and conform to our own or others expectations. Robert Merton, a sociologist, coined the term in 1948 and claimed that self-fulfilling prophecies may be self- or other-induced. Self-induced prophecies are the result of convincing yourself that something will occur, and your very actions ensure that the outcome does, indeed, happen. For example, let's imagine that you are very insecure about your social skills and do not think you are physically attractive. This view of yourself contributes to your tendency to stay home and shy away from any social events or interactions with others. Consequently, you do not know many people and do not receive many invitations to socialize. You readily conclude that you are a social misfit and too unattractive to be included in any social events.

Have you lived up to or down to your expectations of yourself? How about others' expectations? An other-induced prophesy is illustrated in a classic experiment conducted in 1968 by Robert Rosenthal and Lenore Jacobson. They demonstrated that teachers who believed certain students were intellectually gifted treated those students as though they were gifted, which actually increased their I.Q. scores. They also found that children who were deemed low achievers and treated as such, acquiesced to the teacher's perception of their limited abilities. Take a moment and think about how self- and other-perceptions have contributed to your success and failure? Tyler's story is compelling and illustrates the power of self-perceptions.

> When I first started college I had way too many negative views about myself, and I let these negative views control me. My negative thoughts led me to believe that it was impossible for me to excel in college. This view contributed to my below-average effort and this resulted in below-average grades. This is when I lost all hope. I was on the verge of giving up, dropping out, and finding a below-average job to fit my below-average life.

SELF-AWARENESS

Self-awareness, often considered the result of mindfulness, requires a commitment to conscious awareness of self and others. Psychologist Erika Carlson (2013) suggests that mindfulness can lead to self-knowledge. By being mindful, nonevaluative, and attentive, you will be more open to information about yourself and your effect on others. As with most communication skills, this can be learned. You can increase your self-awareness by engaging in the following behaviors:

- Practice mindfulness and self-monitoring
- Develop an awareness of effective communication
- Monitor your communication
- Be more sensitive to oneself
- Practice new communication behaviors
- Gather feedback from others

The Johari Window. Researchers Joseph Luft and Harry Ingham developed a visual model termed the **Johari Window** in 1955 to illustrate the many facets of self (see Luft, 1969). Information known and not known to self are cross-examined with information known and not known to others to produce four windows: open, blind, hidden, and unknown self. The **open self** represents information about you that you and others know and could include information about your age, ethnicity, political leanings, financial holdings, fears, hopes, and desires, as well as other pieces of information you choose to share about yourself. The **blind self** represents information unknown to you but known to others. The **hidden self** includes information known to you but hidden from others. The **unknown self** refers to information that neither you nor others are aware of.

The four quadrants, also called windows, are flexible and change shape depending on whom you are talking to. The more you share with others and the more you know about yourself, the larger your open self becomes. Likewise, the more secrets you keep, the larger your hidden self becomes which in turn result in a smaller open self. Sometimes friends will share with you information about yourself you were not aware of, such as a nervous habit or your tendency to interrupt others in conversation. When this occurs, your blind self shrinks and your open self enlarges. The same result can be accomplished when the unknown self is revealed to both you and others. Any reductions in your blind,

Mindfulness can lead to self-knowledge.

hidden, and unknown self will result in increases in your self-awareness and self-concept. Take a moment and reflect on a significant relationship in your life and draw your own Johari Window in reference to this specific relationship. What does the drawing of the windows reveal to you? Are there any changes you would like to make?

	Known to Self	Not Known to Self
Known to Others	**OPEN** Information about yourself that you and others know	**BLIND** Information about yourself that others know but you do not
Not Known to Others	**HIDDEN** Information about yourself that you know and others do not	**UNKNOWN** Information about yourself that you and others do not know

The Johari Window

PRESENTING THE SELF

Identity Management

Identity is comprised of how we perceive ourselves, how others perceive us, and how we feel about these perceptions. Identity provides a structure to organize the many facets of self and includes our relationships (e.g., daughter, son, mother), roles (student, athlete, care giver), goals (graduate from college, move to New Hampshire, get a job), personal qualities (smart, kind, sincere), accomplishments (honor roll, president of student senate, debt free), group or cultural membership (member of: Irish American Club, Habitat for Humanity, Golden Key Honor Society), and appearance (true redhead, pretty, conservative dresser). Not all of these qualities define us in equal measure, as some facets of identity are more important than others. You may enjoy your work with the student senate, but it is probably not as central to your identity as being a son or daughter. However we define ourselves, we tend to act in accordance with that definition as "identity incorporates expectations and guides behavior" (Guerrero, et al., 2014, p. 37).

Identity management occurs in face-to-face settings and on social networking sites. Both platforms serve as a means to present an idealized image we wish to project to others. For proof of this claim, visit a social networking site and you will see displays of smiling people, new cars, wedding and baby announcements, promotions, and other representations of good news. As is evident, there is a tendency to present a positive rather than negative identity of oneself online. Electronic self-presentations allow for total control of your image—at least what you choose to post. In addition to poor personal choices that result in ill-advised postings, uncomplimentary information shared by others can be problematic and have given rise to cottage industries dedicated to online reputation repair.

Regardless of the forum, as a society we have become increasingly concerned, and some would say consumed, with our identity since the 1960s (Guerrero, et al., 2014). Although baby Boomers and others are active in online self-expression and image management, it is the millennials who have taken center stage in this domain (Ledbetter, Mazer, DeGroot, Meyer, Mao, & Swafford, 2011). Further efforts to characterize millennials were offered by the Pew Research Center (2010):

> "Millennials…embrace multiple modes of self-expression. Three-quarters have created a profile on a social networking site. One-in-five have posted a video of themselves online. Nearly four-in-ten have a tattoo (and for most who do, one is not enough: about half of those with tattoos have two to five and 18% have six or more). Nearly one-in-four have a piercing in some place other than an earlobe" (p. 1).

Millennials' self-expression can be explained in part by Erving Goffman's (1959) belief that we are social actors, continually performing our identity. He likened the presentation of self to a theatrical performance in which we play multiple roles. He argued that we alter our performance to suit the context and the audience. The goal of the performance is to enact an image that is personally constructed and socially approved.

Identity Management Theory. Rooted in Goffman's identity work, William Cupach and Todd Imahori developed the **identity management theory** in 1993 to explain how interpersonal competence is the result of the negotiation of mutually acceptable relational and cultural identities (p. 118). We accomplish this by presenting to others our **face,** which is a socially approved image that we create. The management and maintenance of face is termed **facework** and refers to the verbal and nonverbal behaviors that reinforce our own and other's face.

We present to others a face—*a socially approved image that we create.*

Self-Monitoring. Self-monitoring is an important component of image management. One of the skills necessary to increase awareness is termed **self-monitoring.** Self-monitoring involves closely monitoring your own behavior and the reactions you receive from others. People differ in their degrees of impression management. Mark Snyder (1974) identified two classifications of self-monitors—high and low. As expected, high self-monitors are acutely aware of their surroundings, their own behaviors, and the impact they have on others. This awareness permits them to make adjustments in their communication to meet the demands of the situation and the participants. Image management is important, and high self-monitors recognize the value of controlling their self-presentation to create a desired impression. You have undoubtedly met a high self-monitor. You probably noticed that they are socially adept and good conversational partners. Although you might think of high self-monitors as socially attractive, it is natural to wonder if they are being authentic or simply resorting to chameleon-like behavior to achieve desired outcomes.

Low self-monitoring behavior can be a choice or a skill deficiency. Some low self-monitors simply do not consider the effect of their behavior on others. They do not actively adjust their communication behavior to meet the demands of the context, and this can result in awkward social situations. However, some low self-monitors do not have the necessary skills to adjust their communication in response to circumstances. In essence, low self-monitors are not behaviorally flexible and do not know how to behave in new ways when necessary. There are, however, several advantages to communicating with low self-monitors. Their motives are transparent, they are easy to read, and they tend to engage in a bald-faced honesty in most interactions. You probably know someone who qualifies as a low self-monitor and might describe that person as someone who communicates without a filter.

If you are tempted to think that identity management behaviors are manipulative, you are wise to be wary. However you should know that not all identity management efforts are unethical, and many are quite necessary. For example, it is expected that you put on your best self for a first date, an interview, or the first time you meet your future in-laws. Attire and grooming would be given special attention, as would your posture and facial expressions (i.e., stand up straight and smile). This behavior is not deceitful but rather demonstrates your knowledge of the appropriate skills necessary for the specific circumstance. Your new supervisor might have a tendency to tell long and irrelevant stories, but it behooves you to act interested and be respectful while you listen.

Have you heard the phrase "fake it till you make it?" You might find yourself in situations that prompt you to act more assured than you really feel, and to verbally and nonverbally display a persona that you feel you have not earned or is an inauthentic representation of who you are. Relax; you are not the first person to push the boundaries between what is real and what is possible. Knowing when and how to act in new ways when necessary is a navigational skill that is necessary for successful personal and professional development.

SUMMARY

In this chapter we explored the perception process and the selection, organization, and interpretation of stimuli. The three steps represent a continuous and interdependent process that involves all five senses. Our background, past experiences, and communication skills influence the interpretation and assignment of meaning to behaviors and messages. Practicing perceptual accuracy skills can minimize attribution errors. Perception checking, avoiding confusing fact with inference, and recognizing the fallibility of frozen perceptions is necessary for authentic communication to flourish.

The second half of the chapter was devoted to the examination of self-concept, self-esteem, and self-awareness. Several theories and concepts were introduced that offer insights that explain why we compare ourselves to others, succumb to self-fulfilling prophecies, and engage in identity management activities. We manage our identity through our manner, appearance, and verbal and nonverbal communication so that others see us as we desire to be seen. Our goal is present our best self to friends, teachers, romantic partners, and significant others. The link among perception, self, identity, and communication is powerful and has implications for how you view yourself. Be mindful of the influencing agents in your life and remember, who you are is largely the result of your communication with others.

REFERENCES

Aron, A. (2003). The self and relationships. In M. R. Leary & J. Tangney (Eds.), *Handbook of self and identity* (pp. 442–461). New York, NY: Guilford.

Asch, S. E. (1946). Forming impressions of personality. *The Journal of Abnormal and Social Psychology, 41,* 258–290.

Carlson, E. (2013) Overcoming the barriers to self-knowledge: Mindfulness as a path to seeing yourself as you really are. *Perspectives on Psychological Science, 8,* 173–186.

Chitale, R. (2009, July 20). Men can't hear: Sex-linked sensory differences. ABC News Medical Unit. Retrieved from http://abcnews.go.com/Health/MensHealthNews/story?id=8114257

Cooley, C. H. (1902). *Human nature and the social order.* New York, NY: Scribner's.

Cupach, W. R., & Imahori, T. T. (1993). Identity management theory: Communication competence in intercultural episodes and relationships. In R. L. Wiseman & J. Koester (Eds.), *Intercultural communication competence* (pp. 112–131). Newbury Park, CA: SAGE.

Eagan, K., Stolzenberg, E. B., Ramirez, J. J., Aragon, M. C., Suchard, R. S., & Hurtado, S. (2014). The American freshman: National norms. Fall 2014. Retrieved from http://heri.ucla.edu/pr-display.php?prQry=160

Festinger, L. (1954). A theory of social comparison processes. *Human Relations, 7,* 117–140.

Foster, B. L. (2014, November 19). The persistent myth of the narcissistic millennial. *The Atlantic.* Retrieved from http://www.theatlantic.com/health/archive/2014/11/the-persistent-myth-of-the-narcissistic-millennial/382565/

Fryer, R. G., & Levitt, S. D. (2004). The causes and consequences of distinctively black names. *The Quarterly Journal of Economics, 119,* 767–805.

Gebauer, J. E., Leary, M. R., & Neberich, W. (2012). Unfortunate first names: Effects of name-based relational devaluation and interpersonal neglect. *Social Psychological and Personality Science, 3,* 590–596. doi: 10.1177/1948550611431644

Goffman, E. (1959). *The presentation of self in everyday life.* New York, NY: Anchor Books.

Guerrero, L. K., Andersen, P. A., & Afifi, W. A. (2014). *Close encounters: Communication in relationships.* Los Angeles, CA: SAGE.

Heider, F. (1958). *The psychology of interpersonal relations.* New York, NY: Wiley.

Howe, N., & Strauss, W. (2002). *Millennials rising: The next generation.* New York, NY: Vintage.

Kelly, G.A. (1955). *The psychology of personal constructs.* New York, NY: Norton.

Kluger, J. (2014). *The narcissist next door: Understanding the monster in your family, in your office, in your bed—in your world.* New York, NY: Riverhead Books.

Konner, M. (2011). *The evolution of childhood: Relationships, emotion, mind.* Cambridge, MA: Harvard University Press.

Kuss, D. J., & Griffiths, M. D. (2011). Excessive online social networking: Can adolescents become addicted to Facebook? *Education and Health, 29,* 63–66.

Ledbetter, A. M., Mazer, J. P., DeGroot, J. M., Meyer, K. R., Mao, Y., & Swafford, B. (2011). Attitudes toward online social connection and self-disclosure as predictors of Facebook communication and relational closeness. *Communication Research 38,* 27–53. doi:10.1177/0093650210365537

Lee, S. (2014). How do people compare themselves with others on social network sites? The case of Facebook. *Computers in Human Behavior, 32,* 253–260. doi: 10.1016/j.chb.2013.12.009

Levitt, S., & Dubner, S. (2005). *Freakonomics: A rogue economist explores the hidden side of everything.* New York, NY: William Morrow.

Luft, J. (1969). *Of human interaction.* Palo Alto, CA: National Press.

Mead, G. H. (1934). *Mind, self, and society.* Chicago, IL: University of Chicago Press.

Merton, R. K. (1948). The self-fulfilling prophecy. *Antioch Review, 8,* 193–210. doi:10.2307/4609267

The Oxford Dictionaries Word of the Year 2013 is... | OxfordWords blog. Retrieved from http://blog.oxforddictionaries.com/2013/11/word-of-the-year-2013-winner/

Park, N., & Lee, S. (2014). College students' motivations for Facebook use and psychological outcomes. *Journal of Broadcasting & Electronic Media, 58,* 601–620. doi: 10.1080/08838151.2014.966355

Pew Research Center. (2010, February). Millennials: A portrait of generation next. Retrieved from http://www.pewsocialtrends.org/files/2010/10/millennials-confident-connected-open-to-change.pdf

Rosenthal, R., & Jacobson, L. (1968). *Pygmalion in the classroom.* New York, NY: Holt, Rinehart & Winston.

Samovar, L., Porter, R., & McDaniel, E. R. (2009). *Communication between cultures* (12th ed.). Belmont, CA: Thomson.

Sherman, J. E. (2014, February 25). Selective exposure: Calling inconvenient news irrelevant. Toward an intergalactic natural history of blindered thinking. Retrieved from https://www.psychologytoday.com/blog/ambigamy/201402/selective-exposure-calling-inconvenient-news-irrelevant

Snyder, M. (1974). Self-monitoring of expressive behavior. *Journal of Personality and Social Psychology, 30,* 526–537.

Spitzberg, B. H., & Manusov, V. (2008). Attribution theory: Finding good cause in the search for theory. In D. O. Braithwaite & P. Schrodt (Eds.), *Engaging theories in interpersonal communication: Multiple perspectives* (pp. 37–49). Thousand Oaks, CA: SAGE.

Thorndike, E. (1920). A constant error in psychological ratings. *Journal of Applied Psychology, 4,* 25–29. doi:10.1037/h0071663

Time Magazine (2015, March 30). World. p. 17.

Verhulst, B., Lodge, M., & Lavine, H. (2010). The attractiveness halo: Why some candidates are perceived more favorably than others. *Journal of Nonverbal Behavior, 34,* 1–2. doi:10.1007/s10919-009-0084-z

Wood, J. T. (2013). *Gendered Lives.* Boston, MA: Wadsworth.

Note: Special thanks is extended to The University of Akron students Sara Holderbaum, Deanna Moore, and Kelsey Yaich for generously sharing their personal stories and granting permission to print them in this chapter.

CHAPTER 3

Organizing Your Speech

Evan decided to give his first speech on a topic very familiar to him. For the past several years he had worked for a landscaping company. Due to his strong work ethic and love for landscaping, Evan had recently been promoted to a supervisory position and given responsibility for helping homeowners design their gardens.

Given his extensive experience with landscaping, Evan felt a good topic for his demonstration speech would be planning a garden for a new home. He spent hours preparing visual aids showing how gardens could be structured. Evan also spent a great amount of time explaining carefully some of the technical aspects of caring for a garden. The night before the speech Evan believed his knowledge of the subject, along with his personal experience, would impress everyone in the audience.

What Evan did not think through, however, was how to organize his ideas for his speech to achieve specific results for this particular audience. He did not plan an introduction to capture the attention of the audience, rather he dove right into the topic assuming everyone shared his enthusiasm for landscaping. Evan also failed to think through how he should structure his ideas. So, he shifted from point to point resulting in looks of confusion on the faces of his classmates. He tried to adapt by offering more detailed explanations of certain technical points, but his classmates just seemed to lose interest. As Evan returned to his seat, he wondered, "How could all of my careful preparation have failed me?"

Although Evan gave appropriate thought to the technical information he needed to present, he did not consider adequately how to organize his ideas in a manner that would be interesting and informative for his audience. The ability to organize one's ideas effectively is central to producing a high quality speech. In fact, listeners demand coherence from speakers. They lose patience when speakers shift unpredictably from idea to idea. Listeners are not like readers who can reread a previous page if they have trouble understanding an idea. Listeners only have a speaker's oral message. In a sense, a speech is like a movie and a speaker is like a director. Speakers, like directors, must make sure listeners can follow the plot of a message from beginning to end (Lucas, 2011).

INTRODUCTION

In this chapter, the process of organizing your speech will be described. We start by focusing on the main points a speaker selects and then looking at alternative approaches to ordering them. We then look at how to create effective introductions and conclusions. Finally, we cover the outlining process.

SELECTING AND NUMBERING YOUR MAIN POINTS

A speaker's main points comprise the central features of the speech. Given the importance of the main points to accomplishing the speaker's purpose, they should be selected and phrased carefully, and be arranged in an order likely to accomplish the speaker's objective. You might think it is logical to work on your introduction first, however, most speakers find it easier to begin with the main points of the speech. Here are the main points of a student speech about the benefits of exercise:

Specific Purpose:	To inform my audience of the major effects of a program of regular exercise.
Central Idea:	A program of regular exercise controls weight, combats health conditions and diseases, improves mood, and boosts energy levels.
Main Points:	I. A program of regular exercise controls weight.
	II. A program of regular exercise combats health conditions and diseases.
	III. A program of regular exercise improves mood.
	IV. A program of regular exercise boosts energy.

These four main points form the initial structure of the body of the speech. If there are four major effects of a program of regular exercise, then logically there can be four main points in the speech.

How do speakers effectively select their main points? One starting point is the specific purpose statement. Let's say a speaker's specific purpose is "To inform my audience of the development, technology, and benefits of photovoltaic cells (solar energy) for the production of electricity." Clearly, this speech will have three main points. The first will deal with the development of solar energy for electricity production, the second with the technology behind solar energy, the third with the benefits of solar energy. In outline form, the main points could be written as follows:

Specific Purpose:	To inform my audience about the development, technology, and benefits of photovoltaic cells for electricity production.
Central Idea:	Developed as an alternative to coal for electricity production, solar energy uses sophisticated technology and provides significant economic and environmental benefits.
	I. Photovoltaic cells were developed commercially during the 1980s as an alternative to coal for electricity production.
	II. Photovoltaic cells produce electricity by converting sunlight into electricity.
	III. Photovoltaic cells provide significant economic and environmental advantages to producing electricity in comparison to coal.

It is also important to decide how many points to develop in your speech. In the speeches you will be giving in class, your time guidelines will range from three or four minutes to seven minutes. In this relatively short time span, you should plan on having at least two main points, but no more than four. Including more than four main points in a short speech gives a listener too many main points to remember, and it limits the support material you may include to back up each point.

ORGANIZING YOUR MAIN POINTS

Once you have selected your main points, you need to decide the order in which you will present them during your speech. Again, in order to select the most appropriate organizational pattern, you need to consider your topic and your specific purpose. The most common patterns of organization selected for speeches are: chronological, spatial, causal, problem-solution, and topical. Let's take a brief look at each of these patterns:

Chronological Order

A speech should be arranged chronologically if the speaker wants to describe a process that unfolds over time or a historical event. So, the events that led up to the financial crisis of 2008, the evolution of Major League Baseball, or the preparation and serving of a gourmet meal could all be developed using a chronological pattern. For example, consider how one student provided an historical account of the evolution of England's monarchy using a chronological pattern:

Specific Purpose: To describe the evolution of England's monarchy during the House of Lancaster.

Central Idea: England's House of Lancaster was influenced by the reign of three Kings: Henry IV, Henry V, and Henry VI.

Main Points:
    I.   The reign of King Henry IV, 1399–1413

    II.   The reign of King Henry V, 1413–1422

    III.   The reign of King Henry VI, 1422–1471

The chronological pattern of speech organization can also be used to perform a task. For example:

Specific Purpose: To inform my audience of the steps required to prepare Mulligatawny Soup.

Central Idea: To prepare Mulligatawny Soup requires selecting the ingredients, food preparation, and following a published recipe.

Main Points:
    I.   Selecting the ingredients

    II.   Food preparation (cutting, chopping, and measuring ingredients)

    III.   Finding and following a published recipe

The chronological pattern works particularly well for informative speeches.

Spatial

Speeches organized spatially follow a specific direction pattern. For example, the main points can move from top to bottom, left to right, front to back, inside to outside, north to south, or east to west. For example:

Specific Purpose: To describe for my listeners the topography of the five major regions of Vermont.

Central Idea: Vermont is comprised of five major regions, each having a unique topography.

Main Points:
    I.   Southern Vermont and the Lower Connecticut River

    II.   The Upper Connecticut Valley and the River Towns

    III.   Central Vermont and the Majestic Green Mountains

    IV.   The Lake Champlain Valley

    V.   Northern Vermont and the Northeast Kingdom

As with the chronological pattern, the spatial pattern is particularly appropriate for informative speeches.

Causal

Causal speeches are organized by describing a cause-and-effect relationship between points. When selecting this pattern of organization, a speaker is attempting to explain why something happens. There are two different approaches a speaker may select when developing a causal pattern. First, the speaker can present the causes and then describe the effects. Second, the effects can be presented first; then the speaker can outline the causes. Consider the following examples:

Specific Purpose: To inform my audience of the causes and effects of the Great Recession of 2008–2009.

Central Idea: Banking deregulation, subprime loans, and the credit derivative market brought about the Great Recession of 2008–2009, leading to a meltdown of the financial markets and massive unemployment.

Main Points:

    I.   *Cause:* Banking deregulation led to financially risky investments by commercial banks

    II.   *Cause:* A subprime loan market gave billions of dollars in loans to homebuyers without the means to make loan payments

    III.   *Cause:* An unregulated credit derivative market sold trillions of dollars in insurance on risky debt worldwide

    IV.   *Effects:* Meltdown of the financial markets and massive unemployment

Because causal reasoning can be applied in different ways, it is appropriate for both informative and persuasive speeches.

Problem-Solution

Problem-solution speeches begin by describing a problem that exists in society. An important part of the speaker's responsibility in the first point is showing how significant the problem is. Then, in the second point, the speaker develops a solution to the problem.

Specific Purpose: To persuade my listeners that public health education programs are needed to reduce the incidence of drunk driving in the U.S.

Central Idea: Drunk driving is a serious problem in the U.S. that requires action by the government, health care practitioners, and educators.

Main Points:

    I.   Drunk driving leads to the death and injury of thousands of innocent people in the U.S. every year.

    II.   Public health education programs designed by health care practitioners and educators, and funded by the government, can significantly reduce this problem.

The problem-solution pattern is most appropriate for persuasive speeches.

Topical Pattern

A topical pattern of organization is used when a speaker divides his or her speech into logical and consistent subtopics. Each of these subtopics becomes a main point in the speech. The subtopics should be selected based on research conducted by the speaker. The subtopics should be selected based on their relevance to the specific purpose and the general idea of the speech. For example:

Specific Purpose:	To persuade my audience to conduct careful research to guide their purchase of a new car or truck.
Central Idea:	New vehicle buyers should consider objective ratings of a vehicle's safety, reliability, performance, and comfort.

Main Points:	I.	New vehicle safety ratings
	II.	New vehicle reliability ratings
	III.	New vehicle performance ratings
	IV.	New vehicle comfort ratings

Let's consider another example of a topical pattern of organization:

Specific Purpose:	To inform my audience about different fishing techniques.
Central Idea:	Different fishing techniques are required for lakes, streams and rivers, and the ocean.

Main Points:	I.	Fishing techniques for lakes
	II.	Fishing techniques for streams and rivers
	III.	Fishing techniques for the ocean

Topical patterns of organization can be applied to many different topics, and this organizational pattern can be used for informative and persuasive speeches. Speakers frequently use this pattern of organization.

SUGGESTIONS FOR PREPARING MAIN POINTS

Use Parallel Wording for Each Main Point

Let's consider two approaches to wording main points for an informative speech on the major effects of high levels of sugary drink consumption.

Ineffective

I. High levels of sugary drink consumption leads to weight gain.

II. Type 2 diabetes is linked to sugary drink consumption.

III. To reduce tooth decay, avoid sugary drink consumption.

Effective

I. High levels of sugary drink consumption leads to weight gain.

II. High levels of sugary drink consumption leads to Type 2 diabetes.

III. High levels of sugary drink consumption leads to tooth decay.

The more effective approach to wording main points uses parallel wording, meaning the speaker uses a consistent pattern of wording for each point. When main points are worded this way they are easier to understand and remember.

Balance the Amount of Time You Devote to Each Main Point

Main points are a very important part of any speech. As you develop your main points, you want to make sure each point receives sufficient emphasis to be clear and to accomplish your objective with the audience. Let's say a speaker discovers the proportion of time devoted to each of his or her three main points is as follows:

I.   80 percent

II. 10 percent

III. 10 percent

Such a breakdown may suggest you only have one main point (I). Another possibility is points II and III have not been developed adequately. This does not mean that you need to devote equal time to each main point; however, the proportion of time spent on each point should be roughly balanced. Importantly, the amount of time spent on each point is linked to the amount of support material a speaker uses.

Connectives

Connectives are the words, phrases, or sentences that connect speech ideas, and enable the speaker to move smoothly from one point to the next. Without connectives, your audience may find it difficult to follow the progression of your ideas.

Connectives enable speakers to move smoothly from one point to the next.

Transitions

Transitions are words or phrases that show you have completed one idea and are moving on to another. Transitions keep the audience attentive as you shift from one part of the speech to the next.

   You should think of transitions as verbal signposts that tell the audience where they are, and where they are headed. Here are several examples:

The first recommendation I would like to address…
You are forewarning your listeners that more ideas will follow.

Now that we have reviewed the past, let's look at the future
This statement signifies a movement in time.

Next, I'll turn from addressing the problem, to reviewing solutions
You are communicating to your audience that you are following a problem-solution pattern.

Internal Previews

Internal previews let the audience know what you are going to discuss next. Frequently, internal previews are used in the body of the speech to outline the details of a main point, previewing for listeners what they will hear next. For example:

In discussing the process of community organizing, we'll first look at how a diverse group of people can establish a sense of camaraderie, and then we'll examine the process of taking collective action.

Internal Summaries

Internal summaries reiterate your preceding point or points. They are especially important if you have been speaking about ideas that are complex or abstract. The internal summary consolidates and restates your ideas, which can help your listeners remember your message. For example:

In this presentation I have emphasized two aspects of effective child rearing. The first and foremost job of parents is to show their children unconditional love. Second, they need to encourage their children to develop their own unique talents.

INTRODUCTIONS

The first impression you make on your audience is important. A poor opening may lose the attention of your audience. Moreover, a successful introduction is crucial to your self-confidence. The introduction of the speech has four basic purposes: (a) gain the attention of the audience, (b) relate the topic to the audience, (c) establish the speaker's credibility, and (d) preview the body of the speech. Let's look at each of these purposes in detail.

Audience members need to be drawn into your topic to motivate them to listen. To start your speech by saying, "Today, I'm going to talk about drunk driving," does not spark interest in the information that is to follow. In addition, consider the fact that on the day you are to speak you will probably be one of six to eight students who will be presenting speeches. An audience can become fatigued quickly if their interests are not sparked early in each presentation.

Several years ago, a student gave a speech on increasing the penalties associated with drunk driving. Erin began the speech recounting her experience getting in a car with a friend who was drunk and behind the wheel. The drive began with both of them laughing about how much fun they had at the bar. Laughter turned to terror as the car swerved while her friend was singing to a song blaring on the radio. Erin described what it felt like as the car crashed into a highway divider and then was hit in the rear by another vehicle. She described her emotions as she was placed in the ambulance. Although she suffered a concussion, she was released from the hospital the next day. As Erin told her story every member of the class listened, gripped by the details of her experience. She had captured their attention and they remained focused on her speech to the end.

Erin's introduction represents one way to capture the attention of an audience. Stories can captivate an audience and draw them into your speech. They also show your motivation and interest in addressing a particular topic. You can also tell a story based on another person's experiences. Walter Fisher, a communication professor who is an expert on narratives, observes that humans are storytelling creatures (Fisher, 1984). We love telling stories and we love listening to them.

Other ways of gaining the attention of the audience include beginning your speech with a startling statement, a humorous anecdote, or an interesting quotation. A student speaker addressing the importance of cancer screening used a startling statement to gain the attention of the audience.

> Imagine sitting at a table with nine of your closest family members about to share a holiday meal. You all raise your glasses to toast the occasion, and you look at their smiling faces. Think of your feelings at this moment. Now, recognize that based on a report by President Obama's cancer panel, four of you will be diagnosed with cancer at some point during your lifetime and two of you will die from the disease (United Press International, 2010).

Humorous anecdotes or observations can also be made to open a speech. You need to consider your use of humor carefully, however, because sense of humor varies from person to person. Trying out your humorous opening in front of others is a good safeguard. As an example of a successful humorous opening, consider Conan O'Brien, late night talk show host, in his opening comments during a commencement address given at Dartmouth University in May of 2011.

> I've been living in Los Angeles for two years and I've never been this cold in my life. I will pay anyone here three hundred dollars for Gore-Tex gloves. Anybody. I'm serious. I have the cash. Before I begin I must point out that behind me sits a highly admired president of the United States and decorated war hero. While I, a cable television talk show host, has been chosen to stand here and impart wisdom. I pray I never witness a more damning example of what is wrong with America today. Graduates, faculty, parents, relatives, undergraduates, and old people that just come to these things, good morning and congratulations to the Dartmouth class of 2011 (Trendhunter, 2013).

Opening with a well-recognized quotation could also work well in a speech introduction. The quotation may be from a famous writer, speaker, politician, business leader, or popular culture icon. The quote may be from a statement made in public, or from a poem, song, or film. Consider, for example, giving a speech on learning from the mistakes one makes early in a career to eventually become successful. To open the speech, you could quote Booker T. Washington, African-American educator, author, orator, and advisor to Presidents of the United States: "Success is to be measured not so much by the position that one has reached in life as by the obstacles which he has overcome."

The first impression you make on your audience is important.

After gaining the attention of the audience through your opening comments, you need to relate the speech to the audience. Doing so assures the audience that there is a relationship between them and your topic. Erin's opening story to begin her speech on drunk driving laws was followed by the observation that anyone's life may be touched by drunk driving given its prevalence in the U.S. The student speaker focusing on cancer screening asked audience members to think of loved one's potentially facing a cancer diagnosis. Connecting the audience to the topic can even be accomplished in challenging situations. Consider giving a speech to a group of retired men on equal pay for women. How can you make a connection between them and your topic? You could ask them how they would feel if they received less pay for the same work because of their gender. You could also ask them how they would feel if their wives, children, or grandchildren received lower pay although they worked as hard, or harder than, their male coworkers. Connecting your audience to your topic gives them a reason to listen.

The third part of the speech introduction is to establish your credibility to speak on your topic. This involves describing your interest, experience, research or credentials pertaining to the topic. For example, if you were to give a speech on the importance of community service, you could describe your experiences at a local soup kitchen, and why you have found this service to be so personally meaningful. Or, if you were to give a speech on cardiopulmonary resuscitation (CPR), you could state that you have received your certification from the Red Cross to perform this technique in emergency situations. When you build your credibility in the introduction your audience has a reason to listen, and you increase your believability.

The final part of the speech introduction is to preview the body of the speech. For example, "Today I am going to talk about why you should become a bone marrow donor by explaining how simple it is to become a donor, how vital it is for recipients, and how donors and recipients locate each other." Stating your main points gives your audience a clear idea of what your focus is and how your speech will be structured.

When preparing your speech introduction, it is also important to keep a few guidelines in mind. First, the introduction should be kept relatively brief, representing about 10 to 15 percent of your speaking time. So, a six-minute speech should have an introduction of approximately 60 to 90 seconds. Second, you should look for possible introductory material throughout the process of conducting researching for your topic. Third, work on the wording of your introduction until you are very familiar with it, and can deliver it smoothly with minimal glances at your notes.

CONCLUSIONS

Your closing words are your last opportunity to drive home your ideas and leave a final impression with your listeners. So, you need to work on your conclusion with as much effort as your introduction. The conclusion of the speech has three purposes: (a) signal the ending, (b) summarize your main points, and (c) reinforce your central idea. Let's look at each of these three purposes in detail.

Signal the Ending

The first purpose of the conclusion is to **signal the ending** of your presentation. By providing such a signal you set the audience up for your closing comments, and your final clinching statement reinforcing your central idea. Verbal signals can be accomplished very simply. For example, you could say, "In conclusion, I'd like to focus on the main idea I've concentrated on today."

Alternatively, you could say, "Let me reinforce the three main points I've advanced today." If you want to encourage students to participate in a campus election for student government, you could transition to the conclusion by saying, "Today we have seen how important it is for every member of this class to participate in our student government election."

More artful signals for a speech ending are possible when a speaker has carefully built to a peak of interest by use of voice. Specifically, some speaker's use their tone, pacing, intonation, and rhythm to build momentum in a way that signals the end of the speech. One example of this form is the **crescendo** ending, a term borrowed from music. In symphonies, a crescendo occurs when one instrument after another joins in until the entire orchestra is involved. Applied to speaking, a crescendo occurs when a speech builds in force until it reaches a pinnacle of intensity. Martin Luther King, Jr. delivered one of the best examples of this type of ending the night before he was assassinated in April 1968. The speech was given in Memphis, Tennessee and it is commonly called "I've Been to the Mountaintop." In his closing remarks King affirmed with great emotion and power that the civil rights movement would move on despite threats of violence against him.

Invest as much effort in your conclusion as in your introduction.

> Like anybody, I would like to live a long life. Longevity has its place, but I'm not concerned about that now. I just want to do God's will, and he's allowed me to go up to the mountain, and I've looked over and I've seen the Promised Land. I may not get there with you, but I want you to know tonight that we as a people will get to the Promised Land. So, I'm happy tonight. I'm not worried about anything; I'm not fearing any man. Mine eyes have seen the glory of the coming of the Lord.

Another artful way of signaling the conclusion is called the **dissolve** ending. This approach is akin to a song ending in a way that engenders deep emotions among listeners. As Sarnoff (1970) explains, singers accomplish the dissolve when "the song seems to fade away while the light on the singer shrinks gradually to a smaller and smaller circle until it lights only the face, then the eyes. Finally, it is a pinpoint, and disappears with the last note of the song" (p. 190). A speaker can accomplish this same effect through use of voice and choice of words. General Douglas MacArthur gave an excellent example of this approach in his final farewell to the cadets of the U.S. Military Academy:

> In my dreams I hear again the crash of guns, the rattle of musketry, the strange mournful mutter of the battlefield. But in the evening of my memory always I come back to West Point. Always there echoes and re-echoes: duty, honor, country.
>
> Today marks my final roll call with you. But I want you to know that when I cross the river, my last conscious thoughts will be of the Corps, and the Corps, and the Corps.
>
> I bid you farewell.

The crescendo and dissolve ending require considerable effort, and artistic use of language and voice. Speakers must practice diligently until the wording, use of voice, and timing are just right. The effort will be worth it because of the response it will generate.

Summarize Your Main Points

The second purpose of the conclusion is to **summarize your main points.** Just as you preview the main points in the introduction, you need to summarize your main points in the conclusion. An effective summary serves the purpose of reinforcing the central idea and main points one last time for your listeners. Referring back to our car buying speech, you could summarize your main points by saying, "So, remember, before you go to a car dealership and listen to a sales pitch, you should know which car you want to buy based on its ratings for safety, reliability, performance, and comfort."

Reinforce Your Central Idea

The final function of a conclusion is to reinforce your central idea in the minds of your audience. There are many ways to accomplish this. Let's consider five of the most frequently used: (a) striking statement, (b) highlight the central idea, (c) quote, (d) refer to the introduction, and (e) challenge the audience to act.

A striking statement crystallizes your central idea through artful expression and powerful words. The audience is left with a deep understanding of your commitment to your ideas, and there is no doubt about what they should take away from the speech. Many speeches have become memorable because of their powerful closings. One such speech was given by Manal al-Sharif, a Saudi women's rights activist who was imprisoned after posting a YouTube video of her driving a car in a nation forbidding women from doing so. In a speech delivered to the Oslo Freedom Forum she used the following striking statement:

> The struggle is not about driving a car. It is about being in the driver's seat of our destiny (Alsharif, 2012).

President Bill Clinton's 1992 inaugural address also ended with a striking statement. Because his speech was fourteen minutes long, his striking statement was lengthier than typical, but appropriately so given the content.

> And so my fellow Americans, as we stand at the edge of the 21st century, let us begin with energy and hope, with faith and discipline, and let us work until our work is done. The scripture says, "And let us not be weary in well-doing, for in due season, we shall reap, if we faint not."
>
> From this joyful mountaintop of celebration, we hear a call to service in the valley.
>
> We have heard the trumpets. We have changed the guard. And now—each in our own way, and with God's help—we must answer the call (Americans Challenged to Embrace Change and Sacrifice, 1993).

Clinton's speech is memorable because of his artful use of metaphor, contrasting mountains with valleys, and linking joyfulness to service. He asks us to listen to the trumpets signaling the changing of the guard, and our need to answer the call. Many speakers will find it challenging to be as artful as the two speakers referenced here, however, within each of us there is a unique, artful voice that can emerge with effort and commitment.

Ending with a Quotation

Quotations are a very effective way of ending a speech. Effective quotes allow you to reinforce your main idea using the words of others who have spoken or written powerfully on an idea connected to your topic. President Jimmy Carter gave a speech to the American public on October 1, 1979, ending with a moving quotation from former President Abraham Lincoln. The speech ended as follows:

> The struggle for peace—the long, hard struggle to bring weapons of mass destruction under the control of human reason and human law—is the central drama of our age.
>
> At another time of challenge in our nation's history, President Abraham Lincoln told the American people: "We shall nobly save, or meanly lose, the last best hope on earth."
>
> We acted wisely then, and preserved the nation. Let us act wisely now, and preserve the world (Carter, 1979).

The quote President Carter selected precisely fit the theme of his speech. He then linked the quote to the decisions and actions that needed to be made by the American people in 1979.

Refer to the Introduction

One way to tie together your speech in a memorable way is to refer back to an idea from the introduction to close your speech. Doing so reinforces your central idea, and gives your speech a sense of symmetry. Earlier in the chapter we read about a speaker who asked the audience to envision sitting at a table during a holiday celebration with nine cherished family members. Of the ten people seated at that table, four are likely to be diagnosed with cancer during their lifetime. This speaker could end the speech in the following manner.

> Let's return to that holiday meal I asked you to envision earlier, sitting with cherished family members. This time imagine having a conversation in which each of you commits to asking one another once a year, "Did you have your cancer screening this year?" Just asking that simple question could save a loved one's life, it could even save your own.

Referring back to the introduction ends the speech in a powerful manner, and it makes clear what the speaker wants the listeners to take away from the presentation.

Challenge the Audience to Act

In a persuasive speech, an important goal of the speaker may be to challenge the audience to act in ways supportive of his or her central idea. One very effective use of this technique was made by then Senate candidate Barack Obama at the 2004 Democratic National Convention in Boston:

> Hope in the face of difficulty, hope in the face of uncertainty, the audacity of hope: In the end, that is God's greatest gift to us, the bedrock of this nation, a belief in things not seen, a belief that there are better days ahead.
>
> I believe that we can give our middle class relief, and provide working families with a road to opportunity.
>
> I believe we can provide jobs for the jobless, homes to the homeless, and reclaim young people in cities across America from violence and despair.
>
> I believe that we have a righteous wind at our backs, and that as we stand on the crossroads of history, we can make the right choices and meet the challenges that face us.
>
> America, tonight, if you feel the same energy that I do, if you feel the same urgency that I do, if you feel the same passion that I do, if you feel the same hopefulness that I do, if we do what we must do, then I have no doubt that all across the country, from Florida to Oregon, from Washington to Maine, the people will rise up in November, and John Kerry will be sworn in as president. And John Edwards will be sworn in as vice president. And this country will reclaim its promise. And out of this long political darkness a brighter day will come (Transcript: Illinois Senate Candidate Barack Obama, 2004).

Senate candidate Obama's words were artfully crafted. He was hopeful of change in America, brought forth by the actions of the American people, and he encouraged Americans to act in support of the ideas advocated by John Kerry and John Edwards. Although Kerry and Edwards did not win the election, many Americans were inspired by President Obama's message. With this speech, he was thrust to the forefront of the Democratic Party in a wave that led to his party's nomination for president four years later.

THE FORMAL OUTLINE

A **formal outline** is a final outline in complete sentence form. This outline should be given to your instructor before you go to the front of the classroom to deliver your speech. The formal outline includes the following components:

- The title
- The specific purpose
- The central idea
- The introduction of the speech (outlined or written out in full sentences)

- The body of the speech in outline form
- The conclusion of the speech (outlined or written out in full sentences)
- A bibliography of sources cited during the speech

Title

The **title** of the speech reflects the essence of the speaker's topic, generates listener interest, and entices the audience to listen. A good title will be brief, descriptive, and creative. Consider the following:

Unsafe Drinking Water and Your Local Coal Plant

Addicted to Gaming

Laws Against Public Smoking

Remembering the Holocaust

Driving in a Snowstorm

Specific Purpose Statement

The **specific purpose statement** is a precise statement (informative or persuasive) of what the speaker intends to achieve with his or her topic. The specific purpose should be appropriate for the audience's interests, knowledge, and beliefs. Consider the following examples.

My audience will be able to explain the religious significance of Eid-al Fitr in the Islamic faith.

My audience will be able to identify common herbal remedies for minor medical problems.

My audience will be able to describe the most common retirement savings plans.

My audience will be able to identify three arguments supporting why more women should major in information sciences.

Central Idea

The **central idea** is a one-sentence synopsis of your speech explaining to the audience exactly what your speech is about. The central idea identifies each of the main points developed during the speech. Some examples of central ideas are:

Living a healthier lifestyle through diet, aerobic exercise, and yoga.

Tobacco should be declared an addictive drug like heroin because it causes emphysema, heart disease, and cancer.

How smartphones allow us to live in the information age, while also decreasing our ability to think in a complex world.

Introduction

The introduction captures the audience's attention, orients the audience to the topic, establishes credibility for the speaker, presents a thesis statement or central idea and provides a preview statement identifying the main points of the speech. The preview statement is usually the last component of an introduction. The speech introduction should comprise about 10 to 15 percent of your total speaking time.

Body

The body of the speech is the first part of the outline that a speaker should develop. In planning the body of the speech, select and state the main points. You must have at least two main points in the body of the speech, and at least two pieces of support material for each main point, So, if there is a *I* there is a *II*, if there is an *A* there is a *B*, and if there is a *1* there is a *2*. Remember, each main point should be clearly independent of the other main points, and support your specific purpose and central idea. Second, determine the best organizational pattern (chronological, spatial, causal, problem-solution, topical). Third, select and develop evidence to support the main points: examples, narratives, testimony, statistics, research findings, quotations, etc. Also remember to orally cite the source of any evidence presented in your speech (even if based on personal experience). Finally, use transitions to help the listeners understand how ideas are related to one another. Transitions are connectives between major or minor ideas in a speech.

OUTLINE OF THE BODY OF A SPEECH

I. Write a simple and complete sentence stating your first main point. Your main point must support your central idea.
   A. Write a simple and complete sentence supporting (I).
      1. Cite evidence and source
      2. Cite evidence and source
   B. Write a simple and complete sentence, parallel with (I A) and supporting (I).
      1. Cite evidence and source
      2. Cite evidence and source
   [Transition: Write a verbal transition by using a few words to connect (I) and (II)]
II. Write a simple and complete sentence stating your second main point. Your second main point must support your central idea and be parallel with (I).
   A. Write a simple and complete sentence supporting (II).
      1. Cite evidence and source
      2. Cite evidence and source
      3. Cite evidence and source
   B. Write a simple and complete sentence, parallel with (II A), and supporting (II).
      1. Cite evidence and source
      2. Cite evidence and source
   C. Write a simple and complete sentence, parallel with (II A and B), and supporting (II).
      1. Cite evidence and source
      2. Cite evidence and source
   [Transition: Write a verbal transition by using a few words to connect (II and III).]
III. Write a simple and complete sentence stating your third main point. Your main point must support your central idea, and be parallel with (I and II).
   A. Write a simple and complete sentence supporting (III).
      1. Cite evidence and source
      2. Cite evidence and source
   B. Write a simple and complete sentence, parallel with (III A) and supporting (III).
      1. Cite evidence and source
      2. Cite evidence and source

Conclusion

The conclusion should pull the speech together for the audience by signaling the end, summarizing your main points, and reinforcing your central idea. The conclusion should leave an impression that is both forceful and favorable toward your topic.

Bibliography

Using APA (American Psychological Association), place a list of cited sources, arranged alphabetically by author, at the end of your speech outline. The following are samples of APA style for books, magazines, journal articles, and online sources.

Books

Richmond, V.P., Wrench, J.S., & McCroskey, J.C. (2012). *Communication Apprehension, Avoidance, and Effectiveness* (6th ed.). Boston, MA: Pearson.

Wallechinsky, D., Wallace, A.D., Basen, I., & Farrow, J. (2006). *The Book of Lists: The Original Compendium.* New York: Bantam Books.

Magazine Articles

Henry, W.A., III. (1990, April 9). Making the grade in today's schools. *Time, 135,* 28–31.

Hoffer, R. (1995, August 21). Mickey Mantle: The legacy of the last great player on the last great team. *Sports Illustrated,* 18–30.

Journal Articles

Ingram, R. (2006). Sound solutions for rising healthcare costs. *Vital Speeches, 79,* 746–751.

Kenny, D. (2007). Student plagiarism and professional practice. *Nurse Education Today, 27,* 14–18.

Newspaper Articles

Estrich, S. (1995, May 9). An apt compromise on affirmative action. *USA Today,* p. 9A.

Schultz, S. (2005, December 28). Calls made to strengthen state energy policies. *The Country Today,* pp. 1A, 2A.

Online Sources

Adams, S. (2013, October 11). The 10 Skills Employers Most Want in 20-Something Employees. *Forbes.* Retrieved March 10, 2014, from http://www.forbes.com/sites/susanadams/2013/10/11/the-10-skills-employers-most-want-in-20-something-employees/

Pew Research Center for People and the Press. (2012, June 4). Partisan Polarization Surges in Bush, Obama Years. *Pew Research Center for People and the Press.* Retrieved March 2, 2014, from http://www.people-press.org/2012/06/04/partisan-polarization-surges-in-bush-obama-years/

Now that we have considered the guidelines for constructing an effective formal outline, let's look at an example of a formal outline.

SAMPLE OUTLINE

Title: Anorexia Nervosa: A disease that can happen to anyone

Specific Purpose: To inform my audience about the disease anorexia nervosa

Thesis Statement or Central Idea: Anorexia Nervosa affects a person both physically and mentally.

Introduction:

Attention-getting Device:

"During the day I have been swaying between wanting to be normal and live a full normal life, and feeling that I have to be more dedicated to the cause that is starving myself. I hate it. I look at pictures of myself when I was incredibly thin (seventy pounds) and I think, "Oh my god I didn't realize I was that thin," quickly followed by, "I wish I looked like that now," and I don't. I don't want to look ill, but there's something in me that wants to be "the thinnest." I guess it's tied up with beauty and youth. I have some new work starting soon, and I want to look beautiful and skinny for it. And with Christmas coming up, I get so panicky thinking about how I'm going to cope. If I feel fat when I sit down at the dinner table on Christmas day, it will make it all so unpleasant. I wonder do other people feel physically uncomfortable in their own bodies?"

A young woman posted these words on the blog, The Anonymous Anorexic (2010).

[Transition: Why should we focus on Anorexia?]

According to the U.S. Department of Health and Human Services, one out of every one hundred young adults between the ages of twelve and twenty-five has been diagnosed with anorexia nervosa. Of that 1 percent, 44 percent are of the typical college age.

According to the National Association of Anorexia Nervosa and Associated Disorders, anorexia is the third most chronic illness among young adults.

Credibility:

I have been interested deeply in anorexia nervosa since my best friend was diagnosed with the disease three years ago, and I have done extensive research on this topic, giving me insights that are both personal and based on medical expertise.

Thesis:

Anorexia Nervosa affects a person both physically and mentally.

Preview:

Today I am going to discuss what anorexia is, what the causes are, and what some of the damaging effects can be.

[Transition: Let's begin by defining the disease.]

Body

  I. What is Anorexia Nervosa?

    A. McAnarney and colleagues, in the Journal of Adolescent Health, define anorexia nervosa as a psychological disorder characterized by a resistance to maintain a healthy weight, a distorted body image, and an intense amount of distress associated with gaining weight.

B. The National Eating Disorders Association (NEDA) identifies two subtypes of this disease: anorexia involving restricted food intake, and anorexia involving purging or purposeful vomiting.

    1. A person with anorexia who restricts food intake will severely limit the amount of calories they consume, and after eating they will often compulsively exercise to burn off those calories.

    2. A person with anorexia who purges also restricts their food consumption and exercises excessively, but they also purge or purposefully vomit after eating. This is the more dangerous of the two subtypes including such complications as tearing of the esophagus, gastric rupture, or cancer of the larynx due to acid reflux.

[Transition: Now that we know what Anorexia Nervosa is, let's consider some of its causes.]

II. What are the causes of Anorexia Nervosa?

A. It's difficult to pinpoint exactly what causes anorexia nervosa, but according to the Mayo Clinic, the many different causes can be separated into three subgroups: biological, psychological and emotional health, and societal factors.

    1. According to WebMD, a website that posts information written only by medical professionals, a person's genetics can make them more prone to developing an eating disorder.

      a. The suggestion of a potential genetic link comes from research finding that people, who have siblings or a parent with an eating disorder are more likely to develop anorexia.

      b. The U.S. Department of Health and Human Services also sponsored a study involving a drug that was given to stimulate dopamine production (a hormone and neurotransmitter that is naturally released when we eat). When the drug was given to women without eating disorders, they experienced a sense of satisfaction. When it was given to women with eating disorders, they felt anxious.

    2. The presence of psychological and emotional disorders can also contribute to the development of anorexia, according to Lock and LeGrange, authors of a recent book on eating disorders.

      a. If a person is dealing with depression, they are much more prone to developing an eating disorder because they are already unstable psychologically. People with depression also have low self-esteem and issues with the pursuit of perfection, both characteristic traits of anorexia.

      b. Other psychological and emotional causes include (but are not limited to) troubled relationships with friends and family, anger management difficulties, and other forms of reckless behavior.

    3. Societal factors indirectly influence why some people develop anorexia.

      a. The media places a large amount of stress on both men and women to have an ideal body shape that emphasizes thinness, causing some individuals to work toward an unhealthy and unrealistic body shape.

      b.   Societal support for this emphasis on thinness occurs when people equate thinness with happiness, worth, success, and popularity.

[Transition: The final area I want to discuss is the damaging effect of anorexia.]

III.   What are some of the significant effects of anorexia?

    A.   The first effect of anorexia is the bones, according to WebMD

       1.   Because anorexia typically occurs during the teenage years, the bones are particularly at risk. Critical bone mass development takes place during these years, helping to sustain the teenager through adulthood.

       2.   When teens severely limit food intake during this crucial time of bone development they risk early onset osteopenia or osteoporosis.

    B.   Anorexia also places stress on the heart, according to WebMD

       1.   One impact of a prolonged bout of anorexia is arrhythmia, or an irregular heartbeat.

       2.   The heart also loses muscle mass, becoming smaller and weaker, struggling to keep the person alive.

    C.   The Mayo Clinic reports that anorexia can lead to other mental illnesses including depression and obsessive-compulsive disorder.

    D.   Finally, anorexia may lead to lesser physical effects such as dry and brittle hair and nails, increased hair on the body (other than the head), and jaundiced skin (Mayo Clinic).

[Transition: So, let's consider briefly what we've learned today.]

Conclusion

Review of Main Ideas:

Based on considerable medical research, anorexia is an incredibly serious disease that afflicts many young people in the U.S.

I've explained what anorexia is, what some of the causes of anorexia are, and some of the detrimental effects of this eating disorder.

Concluding Remarks:

My hope is for all of you to remember that anorexia is serious, and can affect anyone. No one is immune to it, so look carefully for the signs because it can happen to your brother or sister, your best friend, and even you.

Bibliography

Anonymous Anorexic. (2010). The Anonymous Anorexic. Retrieved March 24, 2014, from http://theanonymousanorexic.blogspot.com/

Lock, J., & LeGrange, D. (2005). *Help your teenager beat an eating disorder.* New York, NY: Guilford.

Mayo Clinic. (2012). Diseases and conditions: Anorexia nervosa. Retrieved March 10, 2014, from http://www.mayoclinic.org/diseases conditions/anorexia/basics/definition/con-20033002

McAnarney, E.R., Zarcone, J., Singh, P., Welsh, S., Litteer, T., Hongyue, W., & Klein, J.D. (2011). Restrictive anorexia nervosa and set-shifting in adolescents: A biobehavioral interface. *Journal of Adolescent Health, 49,* 99–101.

National Association of Anorexia Nervosa and Associated Disorders (ANAD). (2014). Retrieved March 10, 2014, from http://www.anad.org/get-information/about-eating-disorders/eating-disorders-statistics/

National Eating Disorders Association. (2005). What is an eating disorder? Retrieved March 10, 2014, from http://www.nationaleatingdisorders.org/nedaDir/files/documents/handouts/WhatIsEd.pdf

U.S. Department of Health and Human Services. (2011). Anorexia's brain chemistry. Retrieved March 10, 2014, from http://www.hhs.gov/news/healthbeat/2011/06/anorexias_brain_chemistry.html

WebMD. (2012). Anorexia Nervosa Health Center. Retrieved March 10, 2014, from http://www.webmd.com/mental-health/anorexia-nervosa/default.htm

Evaluation of Sample Outline

Using the criteria described in this chapter for constructing an effective formal outline, this outline receives a favorable evaluation. The speaker gains the attention of the audience with a personal story from a person struggling with anorexia nervosa. Using someone's own words personalizes the topic for the audience. The speaker also establishes the significance of the topic by detailing the number of people who have this disorder. If the audience is comprised of adults who are typical college age (18–24), another link is made between the audience and the topic. Next, the speaker establishes her credibility by sharing the story of her friend who had the disorder, and explaining the extensive research she has done on this subject. The speaker then provides an internal preview of the main points of the speech, and uses a transition to link to the first main point.

Each main point is phrased using parallel wording in the form of questions. Each subpoint is worded clearly and backed up with varied support material in the form of statistics, examples, and empirical research findings. Quality sources are cited throughout the speech. Transitions are provided between each main point, and between the final main point and the conclusion.

In the conclusion, the speaker reaffirms the importance of this topic, and summarizes the three main points. The speech ends with the speaker making a final connection to the audience, reminding them that anyone can develop an eating disorder.

The Speaking Outline

USE THE SAME OUTLINE FRAMEWORK USED IN THE FORMAL OUTLINE

Your speaking outline should use the same outline framework as your formal outline, including the same symbols and indentation pattern. This will allow you to see clearly exactly where you are in your speech at any given moment, You can look down at this outline from time to time to ensure you are covering the right points in the correct order.

KEEP THE OUTLINE BRIEF

The more detailed your notes, the more tempted you will be to read your speech rather than maintain eye contact with your audience using an extemporaneous style. Your speaking outline should contain only key words or phrases that help you remember your main points, subpoints, and connectives. The only parts of the speech you may want to write out fully are your introduction, quotations, statistics, and your conclusion. Of course if you do not need to write out your introduction and conclusion to deliver them confidently, you should not do so. The best rule of thumb is keeping your notes to a minimum to allow you to focus on connecting with your audience through effective eye contact, and speaking conversationally through an extemporaneous style.

GIVE YOURSELF PROMPTS FOR DELIVERING YOUR SPEECH

A speaking outline may also serve the purpose of helping you deliver the speech in the most effective manner. For example, there may be certain ideas or phrases that you want to emphasize. You can prompt yourself to show this emphasis in your speaking outline by writing pause, speak slowly, or speak loudly. This technique can be helpful for both novice and experienced speakers.

SUMMARY

In this chapter, we described the process of organizing your speech through different organizational patterns, using connectives, developing introductions and conclusions, and outlining.

First, we overviewed various approaches to organizing the main points of the speech. The five patterns we discussed were chronological, spatial, causal, problem-solution, and topical. Recommendations were also made to use parallel wording for each main point, and to spend a balanced amount of time on each main point.

Second, we emphasized the importance of using connectives to link ideas and thoughts in your speech. In this section of the chapter we covered the use of transitions, internal previews, and internal summaries.

Third, the purposes of speech introductions and conclusions were detailed. The introduction of the speech has four basic purposes: (a) gain the attention of the audience, (b) relate the topic to the audience, (c) establish the speaker's credibility, and (d) preview the body of the speech. The conclusion of the speech has three purposes: (a) signal the ending, (b) summarize your main points, and (c) reinforce your central idea.

Finally, we covered the outlining process. Speakers should follow a standard outline template in which they identify using full sentences, the main points, subpoints, supporting material, and transitions. We also discussed the difference between the formal outline and the speaking outline.

By following the recommendations presented in this chapter, you will be able to present a well-organized speech with interesting support material that is remembered by your audience.

REFERENCES

Alsharif, M. (2012). Driving for Freedom: My Speech in Oslo Freedom Forum. Retrieved March 26, 2014, from http://manal-alsharif.com/2012/05/08/driving-for-freedom/

Americans Challenged to Embrace Change and Sacrifice. (1993, January 21). *The San Francisco Chronicle*, A12.

Carter, J. (1979). U.S. Response to Soviet Military Force in Cuba. *Vital Speeches of the Day, 64*, 4.

Fisher, W. (1984). Narration as Human Communication Paradigm: The Case of Public Moral Argument. *Communication Monographs, 51*, 1–22.

Lucas, S.E. (2011). *The Art of Public Speaking* (11th ed.). New York, NY: McGraw Hill.

Sarnoff, D. (1970). *Speech can change your life*. New York, NY: Dell Publishing.

Transcript: Illinois Senate Candidate Barack Obama (2004, July 27). *The Washington Post*. Retrieved March 26, 2014, from http://www.washingtonpost.com/wp-dyn/articles/A19751-2004Jul27.html

Trendhunter. (2013, August 14). 12 humorous speeches by comedians. Retrieved March 25, 2014, from http://www.trendhunter.com/course/funny-speeches

United Press International. (2010, May 6). 41 percent of Americans will get cancer. Retrieved March 25, 2014, from http://www.upi.com/Health_News/2010/05/06/41-percent-of-Americans-will-get-cancer/UPI-75711273192042/

CHAPTER 4

Delivery

Although President Barack Obama has both supporters and detractors, few question his skills as a speaker on a national stage. As linguist Geoff Nunberg observes, the President has mastered a certain cadence that is very effective. "He turns to the right to make his first point with a rise, then he turns to his left with a fall to close." The way he moves helps to hold the audience's attention. In addition, his limited pitch range enables him to convey passion without exhibiting it. Finally, much of the excitement President Obama generates in large gatherings has had to do with voters attending his events with the idea that he will deliver excitement. "If you come with the idea or hope of being engaged, or sufficient numbers of people come with the hope of being engaged, it is engaging," Nunberg says (New York Observer, 2008).

The President's normally flawless delivery was not in place, however, on October 3, 2012, the night of the first presidential debate with candidate Mitt Romney. Rather, he seemed frazzled. He clearly was not having a good time on stage. "His head was down when Romney was talking. His responses were halting at times. He often nodded (as if showing approval), or smirked when Romney was talking" (Blake, 2012). None of these were by themselves huge moments, but the totality suggested a candidate who wasn't terribly comfortable. And he wasn't. Romney came across as strong and forceful. The President was passive and lackluster. There were even times he looked tired and irritated. Although some thought the President won the debate on substance, most thought Romney ultimately won because of style (MacAskill, 2012).

These contrasting observations about President Obama and candidate Romney as speakers show the importance of delivery. A polished and enthusiastic delivery engages and lifts an audience. If a speaker does not practice his or her delivery, or is unable to project interest and enthusiasm for the topic and occasion, the audience will drift away and not evaluate the speech positively.

An effective delivery conveys a speaker's ideas clearly without distracting the audience. There should be a certain amount of formality while also displaying the attributes of a good conversation, meaning the speaker should be direct, spontaneous, animated, and lively while showing vocal and facial expressiveness. In this chapter, we look at general rules and methods of delivery, and the speaker's use of voice and body. The importance of practicing delivery is discussed, as well as answering audience questions after the speech ends.

GENERAL RULES OF DELIVERY

BE ENTHUSIASTIC — If you are interested in your topic, your audience will be as well

Think about listening to a speaker who appears to be bored with the information he or she is presenting. Standing stiffly, showing little animation, speaking in a monotone voice, and not making sufficient eye contact with the audience, is a sure way to lose their interest. By contrast, enthusiasm is contagious, igniting the audience's attention by showing your interest in the topic and occasion. So, when choosing a topic for your speech, consider issues, ideas, or experiences you find interesting or exciting. If you are excited about your topic, it is much easier to display that excitement during your presentation.

Our words carry the content dimension of our message, but we communicate with more than our words. Our nonverbal behaviors communicate the affective and emotional dimensions of our message. That is why we will focus on nonverbal behaviors (voice and body) in this chapter.

BE NATURAL — The delivery shouldn't call attention to itself

Speech delivery is not a science, so there is no recipe for success. Rather, effective delivery is an art, involving our uniqueness as a communicator. What works for one person may not work for another. The effective delivery is one that is natural. So, you should approach an upcoming speech with the attitude that you are about to have a conversation with your audience. Not only will this assist you in adopting a more natural style of delivery, it will help you reduce any anxiety you may be feeling. Although a natural delivery may be difficult to accomplish in your first or second speech, the more you practice, and the more familiar you are with your topic, the better you will be able to present a speech in a conversational manner.

BE CONFIDENT — If you are confident, your audience is more likely to be convinced by your message

A key to effective delivery is appearing confident to your audience. The majority of speakers experience some anxiety prior to or while giving a speech. What separates effective speakers from ineffective ones is being able to control or mask their anxiety. Although you may be experiencing butterflies on the inside or an accelerated heart rate, the audience is not able to see this while you are standing in front of them. Because you have practiced your speech, you should be confident in your delivery. Instead of thinking about how you must look to your audience, focus your attention on the message you are delivering and to the feedback you are receiving from the audience. This will help you be more confident in how you are delivering your speech.

METHODS OF DELIVERY

There are four basic methods of delivering a speech: (1) manuscript, (2) memorized, (3) extemporaneous, and (4) impromptu. Let's look at each one.

Manuscript

Speakers who write out their entire speech word-for-word, and read from it when addressing an audience, are employing the manuscript method of delivery. Reading directly from a manuscript is the most formal type of delivery. There are instances, however, when it is very appropriate to employ this approach. Examples include the President's State of the Union Address, a lawyer approaching a microphone to make a statement to the press about her client, or a police chief explaining the status of a high profile murder investigation. In these types of situations, absolute accuracy in wording is necessary. Every word of such speeches will be analyzed by the media and by colleagues. A person's opponents may exploit any weakness, error or omission in the statement, raising the stakes for accuracy and precise wording.

Although a manuscript provides the speaker with the exact wording to be used, delivering such a speech requires skill. This speech should be practiced ahead of time, making sure you clearly and correctly pronounce every word, and that you speak neither too quickly nor too slowly. Pauses should be placed in appropriate places, and you should practice including these pauses in the presentation. The speech should not be presented in a monotone voice; rather your voice should reflect the appropriate affect and emotion for the topic. You should also practice delivering the speech

When absolute accuracy is called for, reading from a manuscript is appropriate.

as often as possible so you are very familiar with the overall message, and the exact wording you will use. This will allow you to establish sufficient eye contact with the audience. In this way you will come across as talking with your audience rather than reading to them. Finally, make sure the text is legible so you can glance easily from the manuscript to the audience and back to the manuscript until completing the speech.

Memorized

Although any speech can be memorized, it is most customary for short speeches to be memorized such as toasts, congratulatory comments, acceptance speeches, or brief speeches of introduction. Since we all have different abilities to memorize, you need to give yourself adequate time to memorize a speech. Your memorization needs to be so thorough that you can come across conversationally, allowing you to concentrate on communicating with the audience rather than trying to remember the words. Speakers who do not give adequate time to memorization often wind up staring at the ceiling, looking out the window or at a blank space on the wall, as they search for words. This is as ineffective as reading a manuscript in a monotone voice without any audience eye contact.

Extemporaneous

The extemporaneous style of delivery is the most widely used in different public speaking situations. Extemporaneous speaking involves the use of a brief speaking outline to assist the speaker in delivering his or her message. As you practice the speech, you will notice that you use slightly different wording each time. Eventually, that practice will direct you to the best way to present each idea. The more comfortable you are speaking from the outline, the more conversational you will come across, and the more comfortable you will be in responding spontaneously to the audience's reactions during the speech. This form of delivery also maximizes the eye contact you will have with the audience because you will be able to glance briefly at a few words or a sentence representing an idea, and then look at your audience as you communicate that idea to them. Finally, because your speaking notes are in outline form, it is easier for you to find your place if you forget exactly where you are in your speech, or what the next idea should be.

There are some disadvantages to the extemporaneous style. If a speaker must be careful that each word be exact, a manuscript or memorized speech might be more appropriate. Or, if you have no time to prepare, an impromptu speech may be preferable, as we will explain in the next section. You will find, however, that under most circumstances, the extemporaneous method is the best choice.

Impromptu

The impromptu method of delivery is used when there is no time available for advanced preparation. An example of this type of situation would be if a person were asked at a wedding reception to say a few words about the bride and the groom at the spur of the moment. In such a situation there is no time for the speaker to plan, prepare, or practice what is going to be said. Your skill in delivering an impromptu speech lies in your background, knowledge, and experience on a particular topic. So, you would find it easier to give an impromptu speech about a friend who has just been married, than it would be to introduce a manager visiting your place of work from another city, especially if you have had few interactions with this person.

We have all had experience with impromptu speaking. If you've ever been asked to answer a question during a job interview that surprised you, or provided directions to a person who is lost, you have had experience with this type of speaking. Impromptu speaking gives speakers experience in thinking quickly, and forming essential arguments or points spontaneously. If you find yourself in a situation where you are asked to give an impromptu speech, consider the following guidelines:

1. Restate the point you have been asked to address (perhaps jotting down a few words to structure your thoughts).

2. State the point you want to make.

3. Support your point using statistics, an example, a narrative, or testimony.

4. Summarize.

Sometimes, impromptu speeches may be given while seated at a chair. Other times you will be asked to stand in front of the room. If the latter is the case, walk calmly to the front of the room, face the audience, take a deep breath, establish eye contact, and begin. To further develop your skills with this type of speaking, write down ten or twenty topics you like to talk about on small pieces of paper that you fold up. Pick one, stand up and follow the four guidelines described above. Repeat this process until you feel comfortable giving a brief impromptu speech.

USING YOUR VOICE

Given the unique physiology of our speaking mechanism, including our larynx (voice box) and vocal cords, no two people have the same voice. James Earl Jones has a deep resonant voice, while Jerry Seinfeld has a high-pitched nasal voice. Clint Eastwood speaks with a raspy voice, while Catherine Zeta Jones has a soft and alluring voice. What our voice sounds like is very difficult to control, however, there are aspects to our voice that we can control: volume, pitch, rate, pronunciation, and articulation.

Volume

In large speaking venues, a speaker may use a microphone so everyone may hear a speech. When this is the case, it is important for the speaker to practice ahead of time using the microphone so his or her voice is not too soft or loud given the level of amplification used by a particular sound system.

When giving your speeches in class, you will not use a microphone. So, the main considerations are how to adjust your voice given the size and acoustics of the room, and the presence of any background noise. A speaker who speaks too loudly may overwhelm an audience, giving them the feeling they are being yelled at. A speaker who speaks too softly makes it difficult for the audience to hear every word or understand the message. After you begin your speech, make sure to look at the people seated in the back of the room. If they show signs of straining to hear you (puzzled expression, leaning forward in their seats), you need to talk in a louder voice.

Speakers should also give attention to varying their volume occasionally. Volume variety can vary the affect or emotions a speech produces. Emphasis or emotion can be shown, for example, by either speaking more softly or more loudly at different points in the speech.

Pitch

Pitch refers to the highness or lowness of our voice. Pitch can also be looked at as reflecting the musical quality of our voices as we vary our pitch while speaking much the same way we produce different notes by striking different keys of a piano.

Changes in pitch are called *inflections*. We use different inflections to reveal whether we are making a statement, asking a question, being sincere or sarcastic. Our inflections also give life to our voice revealing whether we are happy, sad, angry, enthusiastic, relaxed, tense, interested or bored. In conversation, most of use inflections instinctively, if not, a person has a monotone voice. Nervousness sometimes results in a person speaking in a monotone voice. So, when you practice your speech, make sure your pitch varies naturally as it does during conversations with friends and family. So, show your interest and enthusiasm for your topic, as well as your emotions, through how you vary your pitch.

Rate

In the U.S., people typically speak at a rate of between 120 and 150 words per minute. If you speak too slowly during a speech, your listeners may become bored. If you speak too rapidly, it may be difficult for listeners to follow your ideas, and you are more prone to make errors in pronunciation or articulation, problems we explain in the following two sections. Also important to keep in mind, nervousness often increases the rate at which we speak.

When practicing your speech, ask your friends if you are speaking too slowly or too rapidly. If you do not have an audience for your practice sessions, use the video camera on your phone or computer to record yourself while speaking to determine if you need to adjust your speaking rate. Also, monitor your speaking rate when you give your speech in class, mentally telling yourself to slow down or speed up based on your perceptions of how the speech is progressing, or based on the reactions of your audience. Finally, on your speaking outline make notes of the places where you may want to slow down, speed up, or pause.

Few people have voices as distinctive as James Earl Jones's, but we can control some aspects of our voices.

Pausing influences the rate of speaking, and it can be used effectively to influence how a message is received. At the end of a thought or unit of a speech, a pause signifies the ending, and perhaps your transition to the next unit. A pause also helps a dramatic statement sink in. When pausing, however, remember, not to use filler words such as "uh" or "um."

Pronunciation

We all mispronounce words from time to time. Our mistakes are magnified and may cause some embarrassment when they occur in a public setting such as a speech. Consider the following incorrect and correct ways of pronouncing words that many people mispronounce.

Word	Mispronunciation	Correct Pronunciation
Antarctic	An-ar-tic	Ant-arc-tic
Ask	Aks	Ask
February	Feb-u-ary	Feb-ru-ary
Federal	Fed-ral	Fed-er-al
Hierarchy	Hi-arch-y	Hi-er-arch-y
Regardless	Ir-re-gard-less	Re-gard-less
Liable	Li-bel	Li-a-ble
Nuclear	Nu-cu-lar	Nu-cle-ar
Often	Of-ten (hard t)	Of-en (soft t)
Orient	Or-i-en-tate	Or-i-ent
Prescription	Per-scrip-tion	Pre-scrip-tion
Probably	Prob-ly or Prol-ly	Prob-ob-ly
Supposedly	Su-pos-ab-ly	Su-pose-ed-ly

Of course, we don't know when we are mispronouncing a word. So, we should always take notice when we hear a person pronounce a word differently than we do, and question whether or not we are making the correct choice. One of the reasons we should try to practice our speeches in front of family or friends, is to pick up on possible pronunciation errors we are making. Alternatively, if you have any doubts about the pronunciation of a word, check the dictionary.

Articulation

Articulation problems occur when a speaker does not perform a specific speech sound in a clear and distinct manner. They are most often linked to laziness in how the speaker uses his or her lips, tongue, jaw, and soft palate to produce clear and precise sounds. Saying "fur" instead of "for," "dint" instead of "didn't," "dunno" instead of "don't know," "hafta" instead of "have to," and "wanna" instead of "want to," are all examples of articulation errors. As explained earlier, giving your speech ahead of time to family or friends, or recording your speech when alone and listening to your articulation, will help you to identify and correct any problems.

USING YOUR BODY

The speaker's body should be used in ways that are natural, purposeful, and supportive of the message that is delivered. Here we consider three elements of using your body during a speech: (1) movement, (2) gestures, and (3) eye contact.

Movement

When it is your turn to speak, walk slowly to the front of the room, focusing on being calm and confident even if you feel some butterflies. If there is a podium or lectern, do not lean on it. Arrange your notes carefully. Pause before starting. Establish eye contact with your audience, and then begin.

A speaker's movement, gestures, and eye contact should support the message that is delivered.

While delivering your speech, focus on keeping your posture erect, but relaxed. Your feet should be pointed toward your audience, with your weight evenly distributed. If delivering a speech from a podium or lectern, consider some movement during your presentation. For example, moving to the side or to the front of the podium to get closer to the audience. As a general rule, you should only plan on taking a step or two to one side or the other; otherwise your movement could become distracting.

Novice speakers make some common errors in body movement. When nervous, some speakers pace back and forth, shift their weight from foot-to-foot, play with their note cards, or stand rigidly with an expressionless face. One time I had a student who braided and unbraided her hair during her entire speech, unaware of her actions until I mentioned something afterwards. Again, the key to using your body effectively is either getting feedback from friends and family as you rehearse your speech before giving it in class, or by videotaping yourself.

When you do give your speech in class, the final consideration is movement at the end. After saying your last words, hold eye contact for a few seconds, as your audience members applaud (hopefully). Wait to see if your classmates or instructor have any questions or comments, and then return to your seat. Even if you feel relief at the end, refrain from saying, "Wow, I'm glad that's over!"

Gestures

Gestures refer to how a speaker moves his or her hands or arms while speaking. Gestures can add to the impact of a speech if used in a natural and expressive manner. Importantly, some of us gesture more than others, so we should never force performing a gesture because it will not come off naturally. Most of us gesture naturally and spontaneously in a conversation, so we should let our natural instincts guide how we gesture during a speech. In your rehearsals in front of friends and family, or upon viewing yourself speaking in a video clip, attention should be given to distracting or unnatural gestures. The key to gesturing effectively is to concentrate on communicating with your listeners. If you do this, your gestures will emerge naturally, just as they do in conversation.

There are also certain uses of your hands and arms that you want to avoid when speaking. Common mistakes made by novice speakers are: keeping your hands in your pockets, keeping your arms crossed, holding your hands behind your back or in front of your body.

Eye Contact

In the U.S., we make many assumptions about a speaker based on the eye contact made during a presentation. Think of how many times we've heard someone say, "Look at me while I'm talking to you." A speaker who avoids eye contact may be perceived as nervous, unprepared, or dishonest. Eye contact also connects the speaker to the audience, encouraging the audience to become involved in the presentation, and making the speaker more personable.

When addressing an audience the size of your public speaking class, you should usually look briefly from person-to-person, making sure to include everyone. For larger groups it is more effective to scan the audience rather than trying to engage the eyes of each person individually. A good rule of thumb all speakers should follow is looking at your audience 80 to 90 percent of the time you are speaking.

PRACTICING YOUR DELIVERY

We've all heard the saying, "Practice makes perfect." Although expecting perfection may be too high a standard, systematic practice can improve anyone's performance. Consider the following steps when practicing your speeches:

1. **Give your speech aloud (using full voice) using your preparation outline.** This will allow you to hear how your speech sounds. Do you sound conversational? How long is your speech? Does it fall within the time guidelines given by your instructor? Do your supporting materials accomplish what you wanted them to accomplish? How do your introduction and conclusion sound? By addressing these questions you can decide if you are ready to progress to the next step or if you need to revise.

2. **Convert your preparation outline into a speaking outline** to minimize your reliance on this outline so you can maintain eye contact with your audience as much as possible. Use the same visual outline framework as you did in your preparation outline so you can clearly see each part of the speech, and how those parts connect to one another. The speaking outline needs to be easy to read as well as provide cues to guide your delivery.

3. **Using the speaking outline, practice the speech aloud at least four times.** Work on presenting the speech in an extemporaneous style. Give the speech from beginning to end each time you practice it, including all of your support material, and your visual aids if you are using any. If you make mistakes the first couple of times, don't stop and start at the beginning, rather work through the mistake, just as you would in a real public speaking situation. After a few practice sessions, you should find yourself becoming comfortable with your extemporaneous style as you refine how you word your ideas.

4. **You are now ready to work on refining your delivery.** Practice the speech while looking in a mirror, checking for eye contact and gestures, assessing your volume, pitch, and rate of speaking, as well as how you vary these dimensions of your voice. Most importantly, if possible, try it out with family and friends, asking for their honest feedback.

5. **Finally, give your speech under conditions closely approximating those you will experience in class.** Some students even give practice speeches in an empty classroom in the days preceding their actual speech.

Importantly, do not procrastinate in preparing and practicing your speech. Giving yourself adequate time to prepare and practice your speech increases your confidence, reduces your anxiety, and improves your likelihood of performing to your full potential.

ANSWERING AUDIENCE QUESTIONS

After giving presentations, speakers are frequently asked questions by members of the audience. We've all seen speakers answer questions, whether it is after a televised press conference, or after we listen to a speaker on campus. When a speaker handles a question well, he or she can strengthen the impact of the speech on the audience. Speakers who are not prepared for questions, or address them clumsily, will lose much of the credibility they built during the presentation.

Preparing for the Question-and-Answer Session

Given the importance of handling questions effectively after a presentation, a speaker should prepare ahead of time for questions that may be raised by audience members. Of course, you cannot anticipate every question an audience member may pose, but you should be able to anticipate the most likely questions.

DEVELOP ANSWERS TO POSSIBLE QUESTIONS

If you practice your speech in front of family or friends, what questions do they ask? Write down their questions, and develop your answers, first by creating a preparation outline, then a speaking outline.

When giving a persuasive presentation, you should always anticipate some opposition to some of your ideas. How will you address such questions? Working out your response ahead of time will allow you to respond articulately without sounding defensive.

PRACTICE THE DELIVERY OF YOUR ANSWERS

Just as you practice the delivery of your speech, you should practice the delivery of your answers. An important part of what you should work on is keeping your answers brief and to the point. Simple questions rarely require more than thirty seconds to address, and more complicated ones shouldn't require more than a minute or two.

Managing the Question-And-Answer Session

There is an art to managing the question-and-answer session. Take the opportunity to watch a press conference to see professionals address questions in ways that reinforce their message, and respond to the needs of the person posing the question. To help you manage your Q-and-A session effectively, consider the following suggestions:

APPROACH EACH QUESTION WITH A POSITIVE ATTITUDE

Look at each question you receive as a sign of genuine interest from a listener who wants to learn more about your ideas and your topic. If you thought you made a point clearly, but a listener asks for clarification, reiterate or develop your ideas further. If you are asked a critical or even a hostile question, above all, do not become defensive or argumentative. Respond in the same manner as you would to a supportive question, respecting your audience member's right to hold an opinion different from your own.

LISTEN CAREFULLY

Listen carefully to the entire question, so you may respond to it fully and appropriately. Do not assume you know the direction a question is going in before the question is completed, because you may not offer an effective response. If you are posed with an unclear or complicated question, either rephrase it to see if you understand it, or ask the audience member to repeat it because you are uncertain about what they are asking you.

DIRECT ANSWERS TO THE ENTIRE AUDIENCE

When a question is asked after your presentation, look directly at the person asking the question. When giving your answer, however, speak to the entire audience. If your answer is directed only at the questioner, the rest of the audience may not stay engaged in the question-and-answer session.

BE HONEST

You should never "bluff" your way through an answer. If you do not know the answer to a question, admit it! You do not need to know everything there is to know about a topic. You could say, however, "That's a really interesting question. I will look into it, and get back to you when I find the answer."

SUMMARY

In this chapter, we focused on different components of speech delivery: general rules of delivery, methods of delivery, using your voice, using your body, practicing your delivery, and answering audience questions.

The three general rules of delivery are: be enthusiastic, be natural, and be confident. When you are enthusiastic, your audience recognizes this topic is important to you, and they will not be bored by your presentation. When you are natural in your delivery, there is nothing distracting in your use of voice or body, and your audience will be able to focus on your message. When you are confident, you are able to focus your attention on your message, and the feedback you receive from the audience.

There are four basic methods of delivering a speech: manuscript, memorized, extemporaneous, and impromptu. Speaking extemporaneously is the focus of most public speaking classes. When speaking extemporaneously, you use a brief speaking outline, choosing the exact wording as you deliver the speech.

The elements of voice most essential to public speaking are volume, pitch, rate, pronunciation, and articulation. Volume is how loudly or softly one speaks. Pitch refers to the relative highness or lowness of one's voice or the musical quality of how we vary pitch to communicate meaning. Rate reflects how many words we speak per minute during a presentation. Regarding these three dimensions of voice, we discussed the helpfulness of occasionally varying volume, pitch, and rate to affect meaning or show emotion. Finally, we considered the importance of pronouncing words correctly, and articulating them correctly during speeches.

Movement, gestures, and eye contact are the most important areas of using your body during a presentation. Effective use of gestures and bodily movement may enhance your message, and eye contact establishes a personal connection between the speaker and the audience.

Practicing your speech in a systematic manner allows you to deliver your speech to your fullest potential; helping you to improve each time you rehearse it. We also emphasized the importance of giving yourself sufficient time to prepare systematically, so you can build your confidence before your actual presentation.

If a question-and-answer session is included after a presentation, a speaker should anticipate possible questions, develop answers to them, and practice the delivery of those answers. Then, during the actual question-and-answer session, the speaker should listen carefully to the questions, direct answers to the entire audience, and always be honest in providing responses.

REFERENCES

Blake, A. (2012, October 4). Six reasons Mitt Romney won the first debate. Retrieved April 2, 2014, from
    http://www.washingtonpost.com/blogs/the-fix/wp/2012/10/04/six-reasons-mitt-romney-won-the-first-debate/

MacAskill, E. (2012, October 4). Mitt Romney comes out on top as Obama stumbles in first debate. Retrieved April 2, 2014, from
    http://www.theguardian.com/world/2012/oct/04/romney-obama-first-presidential-debate

New York Observer, (2008, February 13). What makes Obama a good speaker? *New York Observer*. Retrieved April 2, 2014, from
    http://observer.com/2008/02/what-makes-obama-a-good-speaker/

CHAPTER 5

Informative Speaking

Upon reviewing her public speaking syllabus, Angelique realized her outline for her informative speech was due in two weeks. Sitting at her laptop, she attempted to come up with a list of possible topics. Frustrated, she was unable to come up with a single idea. So, she looked at her textbook's chapter on informative speaking and she became even more confused. The goal of informative speaking is to provide your audience with new and interesting information, but Angelique did not feel like she had any ideas that would be interesting for her classmates. She then emailed her professor, telling her of the difficulties she was having coming up with a topic. Her professor invited her to come to her office the next day.

Professor Minh greeted Angelique warmly when she arrived at her office, inviting her to sit down. Minh asked, "What ideas do you have at this point?" "That's the problem, I don't have ANY ideas," said Angelique. Minh suggested they start by making a list of things Angelique found interesting. "What do you enjoy doing in your free time?" Minh asked her. "Well, I enjoy rollerblading, playing soccer, and building a website about my family genealogy," replied Angelique. Minh then asked her about contemporary issues that concerned her, and Angelique said she recently became interested in e-cigarettes and poverty in the U.S. Finally, Minh asked Angelique to list three people she found interesting. Angelique said Mia Hamm, J.K. Rowling, and Beyonce.

Minh looked at Angelique and said, "All of your interests could be turned into really interesting informative speeches. If *you* are interested in these activities, issues, and people, you can create a speech that will be interesting for the class. Just select one of these interests, start your research, and then organize your ideas."

INTRODUCTION

How do you know what you know? How do you know how to play soccer, drive a car, cook a pot roast, or write a research paper? Over the course of our lives, our parents, teachers, coaches, supervisors, and friends have helped us increase our knowledge. In many cases, the way information was passed onto us was an informative presentation of one kind or another. A coach shows us how to strike a soccer ball with our foot in order to score a goal. A teacher instructs us in the process of researching, organizing, and writing a formal research paper. A supervisor teaches us how to scrape and clean a grill, or how to give a sales pitch.

When you complete your college education, you will be cast in the role of passing information onto your children or other relatives, fellow workers, or community members. The purpose of this chapter is to describe the process of constructing and presenting informative speeches. We will cover five aspects of informative speeches: (a) purposes of informative speaking, (b) types of informative speeches, (c) organizing the informative speech, (d) methods for presenting information in the informative speech, and (e) guidelines for informative speaking.

PURPOSES OF INFORMATIVE SPEAKING

The first purpose of informative speaking is to spark a *desire for information* among your listeners. To create such a desire, speakers need to arouse their listeners' interest or need for information. One way a speaker can accomplish this is by showing how this information will improve their everyday lives. Audience analysis is critical in order to link your topic to your listeners' interests. For example, many college students in their late teens or early twenties may not be interested in listening to a speech entitled, "Retirement Housing Options." However, since many of them are either working now, or will soon be working, they may be interested in a speech titled, "Investing in Your Twenties So You Can Retire as a Millionaire." Consider the following introduction to create a desire for information among young listeners on the importance of investing early in retirement:

> How many of you have started saving toward your retirement? I see only a couple of you have started saving. But let me ask you this. How many of you would like to retire with a portfolio worth millions allowing you to live a comfortable life, and travel the world? Well, if you begin investing as little as 10 percent of your income in your twenties, and increase that by 5 to 10 percent per decade, that dream may be a reality (Brown, 2013). If you wait until you're thirty, it may be too late. Today, I will describe for you what it takes to retire rich.

The second purpose of informative speaking is to *increase your listeners' understanding of the topic*. Again, by conducting an appropriate analysis of the audience, you find how much they are likely to know about your topic, and then you select and present information that will add to their knowledge base. Consider the following recommendations to help your audience understand your topic:

1. Audience members understand main ideas and generalizations more than specific facts and details. So, you need to state explicitly and repeat your main ideas and generalizations.

2. Audience members are more likely to understand simple words and concrete ideas than complex words and abstract ideas. Replace complex words and abstract ideas with simple words and concrete ideas.

3. In your introduction, show clearly how the topic is related to your audience members. If you do not capture their attention early in the speech, you may never gain it.

4. Encourage listener involvement by asking your listeners to raise hands, stand up, answer a question, or offer an opinion. You increase learning when you ask audience members to both listen and do something.

The third purpose of informative speaking is to *help your listeners remember*. How can you help your listeners to remember important information? One technique is to state in your introduction what you want them to learn from your presentation. A second technique is to identify which ideas are your main ones, and which are subordinate. You may also identify which ideas are generalizations they should remember, and which are details to support the generalizations. A third technique is to repeat your most important ideas two or three times during your presentation.

The final purpose of informative speaking is to *help your listeners apply information*. For example, one student gave a demonstration speech on how to make the world's best paper airplane (Struckbyanarrow, 2008). As he demonstrated the process of folding the paper, he had each class member follow along so each person had a plane at the end of the speech. Other students have invited their classmates to try out a new dance step by moving to music. You can also ask the audience to apply the information you have presented after your speech concludes. For example, ask them to talk to others about your topic, try out the recipe you have demonstrated, or do their own Google search on your topic.

Informative speaking provides your audience with new and interesting information.

TYPES OF INFORMATIVE SPEECHES

In our opening scenario, Angelique had a difficult time at first coming up with an idea for her informative speech. Her professor provided her with a very effective strategy for identifying possible topics, generating an inventory of personal interests. So, consider asking yourself four questions as you search for a possible topic:

1. Who are three people I find to be influential, interesting, or controversial?

2. What are three activities I enjoy or do well?

3. What are three events I either remember or believe are important in our history?

4. What are three issues or concepts I find interesting or intriguing?

By answering these four questions, you will discover that you have several ideas that could work very well for an informative presentation.

There are different ways of classifying informative speeches. The most common types are: (1) speeches about people, (2) speeches about objects, (3) speeches about events, (4) speeches about processes, and (5) speeches about concepts.

Speeches about People

If you create a list of people you find to be interesting, influential, or controversial, you will probably identify a lengthy list of possibilities for your speech. Such speeches may describe a person's positive or negative professional or societal contributions, or their influence in history. For example, you could give a speech about the role of Elizabeth Cady Stanton on the women's rights movement in the U.S. in the late nineteenth century. In choosing a person to talk about, a speaker should identify accomplishments or facts about that person's life that your audience members are not likely to have prior knowledge about. So, instead of giving a speech about Bill Clinton's presidency, focus on his work for the Clinton Foundation, an organization that convenes businesses, governments, non-governmental organizations, and individuals to improve global health and wellness, increase opportunities for women and girls, reduce childhood obesity, create economic opportunity and growth, and help communities address the effects of climate change (Clinton Foundation, 2014). Some examples of famous people that could be the focus of an informative presentation:

Mother Teresa	Omar Vizquel
Bernie Madoff	Stephen Hawking
Claude Monet	Elizabeth Warren
Rachel Maddow	Rush Limbaugh

In addition to specific persons, you could also give an informative speech about people who belong to a specific category. For example, a speech might focus on school bullies in middle school, and the two theories most often used by psychologists to explain their aggressive behavior. Other examples of categories of people could be:

homeless people	Nobel Laureates
civil rights activists	jazz musicians
death row inmates	NBA coaches
lung cancer survivors	community organizers

Speeches about Objects

Objects include anything that is tangible and stable in form. Speeches about objects could focus on a piece of sports equipment, a building, a place, a consumer product, or a prescription drug. For example, you could give a speech about the parts of a downhill ski including the base, sidewall, edges, and bindings. Another interesting speech could be the construction, dimensions and special features of the Freedom Tower in New York City. Your classmates might also be interested in hearing about the history and features of the Tesla electric car. Other possible topics include:

New York Stock Exchange	Lake Michigan
coral reefs	the human liver
political cartoons	nanotechnology
Rock and Roll Hall of Fame	Grand Canyon

Whatever object you will select, you will not be able to tell your class everything about it. An effective informative speech on an object focuses on a specific aspect of it. For example, an informative speech could focus on the most important features to look for when buying a GPS navigation device, how the human liver processes alcohol, or how warming oceans change coral reefs. These statements are precise, and they focus attention on a specific purpose that tells your listeners what they will learn from your speech.

Speeches about Events

An event may be an occasion that people find interesting, or one that provokes memories or emotions. The Super Bowl, for instance, is an event that draws the attention and interests of tens of millions of Americans each year. The bombings at the Boston Marathon, and the Sandy Hook school shooting are events that provoke vivid memories and strong emotions. Events can also be thought about along a time continuum. This means you could give a speech on an event that happened in the past such as the Great Recession of 2008–2009. A speech could also be given on an event that is happening now such as the current status of statewide Medicaid expansion decisions in the U.S. Finally, a speech could be given about a future event such as the 2016 presidential primaries. Other possible topics for events include:

Special Olympics	Passover
Wheatland Music Festival	Komen Detroit Race for the Cure
Canada's Boxing Day	Gulf of Tonkin Incident
wedding planning	tsunamis

As with all informative speeches, the speech about an event needs to have a specific purpose or goal to focus the audience's interests, and allow the speaker to stay within the time guidelines established by the instructor. Speeches about events should focus on particular characteristics of the event, and then develop those characteristics either chronologically or topically. For example, a speech on Halloween in Akron could focus on trick-or-treat traditions, adult activities on Halloween evening, and special neighborhood festivities. A speech on tsunamis could focus on the ocean-based earthquakes that cause them, the waves produced from these earthquakes, and the impact of the waves when they reach coastal areas. Although both speeches are about events, the Halloween speech is topical, while the tsunami speech is chronological.

Speeches about Processes

A speech about a process explains the series of actions that produce a particular result or product. So, speeches about processes provide details on how something is made or done, or how something works. A speaker could explain how a silicon chip works, or demonstrate how to bake an apple pie. Other examples of informative speeches about processes would be:

how tornadoes develop	how to write an effective cover letter
how U.S. coins are made	how to choose a study abroad program
setting up a home aquarium	how magicians perform tricks
Hindu wedding rituals	how to make peanut butter pie

The examples described above point to the fact that there are two types of process speeches. The first explains a process so your audience will understand it better. In this type of speech you want your audience to know the steps of a process and how these steps relate to one another. For example, a speech on Hindu wedding rituals could focus on pre-wedding rituals, rituals during the wedding ceremony, and post-wedding rituals. In order to increase listener understanding of these rituals, they would first be described, then the meaning behind the ritual would be explained. The second type of process speech explains a process so audience members know the steps to perform that process themselves. So, a speech on how to set up a home aquarium could involve the speaker demonstrating certain steps in front of the class, as well as showing pictures or brief clips of performing specific steps. The speaker's goal is enabling the audience to actually perform this process themselves.

Speeches about Concepts

A speech about a concept focuses on ideas, beliefs, theories, or principles. Because these speeches are more abstract than the other types of informative speeches, they can be more difficult to develop in a way that meets listeners' interests. One possible speech about a concept would be to inform your audience about the basic principles of the Jewish faith. Another possibility would be to inform your audience about the principles of materialist feminism. Your audience might also be interested in learning about the different philosophies of education in Europe and the U.S. Other examples of concept speeches would be:

string theory	postmodernism
Scientology	human rights
Jainism	the necessary and proper clause
general theory of relativity	courage

How can speakers help their listeners better understand an abstract concept? First, avoid technical language that is only familiar to experts. Second, define key terms linked to your topic as clearly as possible. Finally, use examples and comparisons to more generally known ideas to illustrate your concept.

Each of the five types of informative speeches may be about the same topic because a speaker can approach that topic in different ways. For example, if you want to speak about Scientology, you could give a speech about its founder, L. Ron Hubbard. An object speech could focus on the writings of Hubbard, considered to be sacred among believers. An event speech could describe how believers celebrate the birthday of Hubbard, one of the most important holidays in Scientology. A process speech could focus on the purification rundown, "a detoxification process followed by Scientologists to rid the body of the harmful effects of drugs, toxins, and other chemicals that lodge in the body and create a biochemical barrier to spiritual well-being" (Hubbard, 2014). Finally, a concept speech could describe the basic tenets of Scientology. Once you decide the type of speech you want to give, you can work on organizing the body of the speech in a way that helps your listeners to better understand your topic.

ORGANIZING THE INFORMATIVE SPEECH

Once you have selected a topic, decided what type of informative speech you want to give, and conducted your research, you are ready to organize your ideas. Organization is critical to gaining and maintaining the attention of your listeners and to helping listeners understand your speech. Although different methods of organizing speeches may be used, below are effective patterns for the informative speech.

Cause-Effect Pattern

When a speaker uses a cause-effect pattern, he or she explains the cause or causes of some phenomenon, event, or situation followed by a discussion of the consequences, results, or effects. For example, a speaker could focus on the economic causes and effects of high inflation. Although most speeches follow a cause-effect pattern, an effect-cause sequence may also be followed. For example, in her first point, Eman could describe the current effects of the Great Recession of 2008–2009 on the U.S. economy. Her second point could then detail the major causes of that recession.

Cause-effect speeches can address many interesting topics. One important consideration is recognizing that complex problems often have multiple causes, generating multiple effects. For example, a speech on climate change would need to detail the causal factors of burning fossil fuels and deforestation in relation to CO_2 levels in the atmosphere, and methane emissions from animals, rice paddies, and arctic seabeds. The major effects of the increase in CO_2 levels is a warming planet resulting in a melting of ice worldwide, a rise in sea levels, species extinction, more droughts and floods, more catastrophic storms, less fresh water availability, and an increase in diseases such as malaria. The key to an effective cause-effect speech is making explicit the connections between the causes and effects so they are obvious to the audience.

Chronological Pattern

The chronological pattern sequences events in the order in which they occur. This speech illustrates for the audience what occurs at each step and how a process or sequence of events unfolds over time. For example, consider a speech on recovery from rotator cuff surgery. The first point could document the process of performing a series of exercises to regain a normal range of motion with the arm, using the shoulder joint. The second point could describe the exercises needed to regain strength in the arm, using the shoulder joint. The third point could describe the activities and exercises that should be performed to keep the shoulder joint healthy once recovery is complete. This speech is chronological because strength exercises can only begin after a patient regains a normal range of motion, and activities and exercises to maintain a healthy shoulder joint can only be followed once strength returns to the arm.

A chronological pattern can be used for any speech that considers the past, present, and future of any idea, issue, plan, or project. For example, consider the following examples: (a) how the Goodwill organization began, (b) a history of the *Today* show, (c) the past, present, and future of space exploration, (d) the history of the University of Michigan, or (e) the evolution of the Republican Party. The chronological pattern can also be used to describe the life of a person. For example, a speaker could give a speech on the life accomplishments of Dave Thomas, founder of Wendy's restaurants.

Spatial Pattern

The spatial relations pattern assists the audience in visualizing how things are related in space, position, or in location to one another. Many of you took a tour of your campus and listened to an informative presentation by your tour guide prior to deciding to enroll. During that tour, the guide explained where various buildings were located, what functions or activities happen in each building, and how to travel from one section of campus to another. The tour guide also pointed out the key buildings such as the library, the student recreation and wellness center, Kolbe Hall, the football stadium, and the basketball arena.

An informative speech on the interior design of a private residence might include drawings or photographs to illustrate the spacing of objects, personal mementos, and pictures on shelves or mantels. The arrangement of furniture to create interaction zones, and the placement and structure of an audio-visual entertainment center may also be described and illustrated through diagrams or photographs. Other examples of topics that would benefit from a spatial pattern include: (a) plant placement when landscaping the front yard of your home, (b) arranging your office, (c) how to follow a road map when your GPS stops working, (d) designing a gourmet kitchen, and (e) exploring the Grand Canyon.

Topical Pattern

The most common form of organization for the informative speech is the topical pattern of organization. The topical pattern focuses on the categories, qualities, advantages, disadvantages, qualities or types of persons, places, or things. Speakers use this pattern of organization when they want their audience members to adopt a certain point of view toward a topic. Also, all of the main points included in this type of presentation should be of relatively equal importance. For example, you could give a speech informing your audience about three new women's sports added to your

There are different ways of presenting information in an informative speech.

university's athletics programs to meet NCAA Title IX regulations. Your three main points could focus equally on each of the three new teams: softball, golf, and field hockey. A speaker could also give an informative presentation on the benefits of regular aerobic exercise at the student recreation and wellness center: (a) cardiovascular health, (b) weight maintenance, and (c) social interaction.

Dr. June Osborn, co-chair of the United States National Commission on AIDS, gave a speech at the Iowa Academy of Science in Cedar Falls, Iowa. Using the topical pattern of organization, she discussed some important facts about AIDS.

1. The human immunodeficiency virus is a necessary—and sometimes a sufficient—condition to cause AIDS

2. The virus is transmitted through blood, sharing IV needles, sex, birth to an infected mother, or nursing from an infected mother

3. People know more about this virus and its pathogenesis than about any other infectious agent

4. AIDS will not be the last novel microorganism to beset humans (DeFrancisco & Jensen, 1994).

METHODS FOR PRESENTING INFORMATION IN INFORMATIVE SPEECHES

There are different ways of presenting information in an informative speech to help the audience better understand your topic. Here we describe four different ways of presenting information: defining, describing, explaining, and demonstrating.

Defining

Miscommunication occurs between people when they assign different meanings to words. Denotative meanings are the commonly understood, dictionary definitions associated with a word. Connotative meanings are the personal and sometimes emotionally charged meanings people associate with specific words or concepts. Suppose you are giving a speech on the topic of "spousal abuse." Many of your audience members may have a similar definition of the term. There may be additional connotative meanings, however, that some audience members may have based on stories they have heard or on personal experiences they have had.

Offering definitions can be helpful to make sure your audience members know the meaning you want them to attach to a word or term. Alternatively, you could define something the audience is unfamiliar with by comparing it to something they are familiar with. Explaining the origin of a word may also work well. Some samples of speech topics that may require a speaker to provide definitions include: (a) what does it mean to have "autism spectrum disorder"?, (b) investing in "blue chip stocks," and (c) understanding "geothermal energy."

Describing

Many informative speeches require the speaker to describe a person, place, object, event, or experience by providing the audience with specific details that create a distinct visual image. To do so, the speaker can use adjectives, colorful language, and visual imagery. The speaker should also think about activating the senses of the listeners by describing aspects of an object's size, weight, color, texture, or smell. You could even describe your feelings about a person, place, event, or experience. Good description requires concrete language, and being as precise, accurate, and specific as possible.

For example, consider giving a speech on "a day in the life of a homeless person." You could describe the struggles of finding a warm place on a cold night. When a homeless person fails to find a bed, they often shiver under highway overpasses covered only with scraps of cardboard or pieces of cast off cloth. You could describe how homeless people describe their hunger pangs when they go without a nutritious meal for days at a time, not knowing when there next good meal may be. The emotions linked to losing one's pride when having to extend one's hand for money from a stranger could complete the imagery for your audience about what it is like to be homeless. Other speeches that would lend themselves to rich description would be: (a) how hormones affect human behavior, (b) driving a Lamborghini, (c) Detroit: the city's past, (d) airport security: can it get any worse, and (e) the 4 C's of buying a diamond: carat, clarity, color, and cut.

Explaining

Explaining is necessary when a speaker needs to tell listeners how something works, why something happens, or how something should be evaluated. This method of presenting information is especially useful for explaining social, political or economic issues, as well as historical events, theories, principles, or laws. Speakers may also offer a critique of art, music, literature, drama, film, or speeches. One example of a speech of explanation would be to explain the decision to lease a car, including explaining the contract between the dealership and the buyer, the benefits of leasing versus purchasing, and the disadvantages of leasing versus purchasing. Other examples of speeches of explanation include: (a) what stock investments are best for the young investor, (b) how to earn money selling merchandise online, (c) understanding the national debt, (d) why we need to reduce military spending, and (e) how to write poetry.

Demonstrating

Demonstrating involves showing your audience how something works, how to do something, or why something occurs. This approach is similar to describing or explaining, but the focus when you demonstrate is helping your audience visualize your topic. Speakers demonstrate when words alone are not sufficient in getting the point across to the audience. One way of demonstrating is using your body to show how to do something. A speech on performing CPR, displaying karate moves, or dancing to hip-hop would all involve the use of the speaker's body. A variety of presentational aids may also be integrated to demonstrate a process to an audience. Assembling the ingredients for a recipe, showing how to prepare or work with the ingredients, following the steps of a recipe, and showing the finished product would be interesting for an audience to follow. Diagrams, video clips, slides, overhead projections, living models, physical objects, handouts, or computer graphics may also be used to demonstrate.

Demonstration speeches are often enjoyable for both the audience and the speaker. Importantly, the speech should involve more than demonstrating a process or an activity. Background research needs to be conducted to add information to the body of the speech, and add interest to the presentation. For example, recently a student demonstrated the process of playing a djembe, a type of African drum. Before actually playing the instrument, this student described the evolution of the drum, its physical components, how and in what ways its produces sound, and when it is played in African villages. He then played different types of beats and produced tones of different pitches, inviting his classmates to join along in producing beats while striking their hands on their desks. Other examples of speeches where demonstrating is relevant are: (a) how to make tom yum soup, (b) how to fillet a fish, (c) how to build a sandcastle, (d) how to accessorize your outfits, and (e) how to do yoga.

GUIDELINES FOR INFORMATIVE SPEAKING

All of the previous chapters of this book relate to constructing and presenting an informative speech. Selecting a topic and a specific purpose, analyzing the audience, choosing support materials, organizing the speech, using language to convey meaning, speaking ethically, and delivering the speech all must be done effectively for an informative speech to be a success. Now let's consider five additional guidelines that will help you accomplish your goals as a speaker: (a) relate the topic to the audience, (b) relate the speaker to the topic, (c) present new and interesting information, (d) help your audience visualize, and (e) build on information that is already familiar.

Relate the Topic to the Audience

The first main job of a speaker is to get the audience interested in what you have to say. Then, you need to keep them interested. A speaker can accomplish this in a number of ways. Part of gaining the interest of the audience is using language vividly. For example, you could open your speech with, "I want to talk about habanero chili peppers." A more effective way of gaining interest would be the following:

> Imagine your mouth on fire, the pain of a thousand needles on your tongue. Your eyes are watering in a stream of tears. Your face is flushing and you are sweating from every pore. Are you sick? No. You just ate your first habanero chili pepper, one of the hottest peppers in the world. I'm here to tell you why I love habaneros and why you can use them to spice up meals to new heights of flavor.

This introduction draws in the listeners by connecting to their senses. The speaker asks the listeners to place themselves in this situation of eating an incredibly hot chili pepper, using vivid language to get them to think about what they would feel. He then challenges them to put aside their skepticism and consider how these chili peppers could spice up their meals. Speakers should not just do this in the introduction. Whenever you can, put your listeners into the body or conclusion of the speech by using the words "you" and "your."

Relate the Speaker to the Topic

What makes you qualified to talk about your topic? If listeners do not know the answer to this question, why should they listen to you? If a person introduces you to an audience, that person could talk about your background, experiences, or qualifications to talk about a topic. Since you will not be introduced to your classmates before you speak, you need to show how you are connected to the topic in the introduction. For example, you could say that you have been a fan of horror films for years and have seen hundreds of these films across all twenty-four genres. If you were to speak about hang gliding, you could talk about the first time you jumped off a cliff and glided to the ground and how you have remained addicted to the sport for the last three years. A speaker who wishes to give a speech on the Indian Village neighborhood in Detroit might mention in the introduction that her great-grandparents were among the first residents of this neighborhood, and each generation of her family has lived there since. In each of these instances the speakers establish a relationship between themselves and their topic. A personalized introduction also builds the speaker's credibility to address the topic.

Present New and Interesting Information

Informative speakers need to present audience members with information that is new and interesting to them. Effective audience analysis is helpful in determining the level of experience or prior knowledge your listeners have before listening to your speech. You do not want to overestimate or underestimate what your audience knows. Find out what our classmates know about your topic by talking to them or by distributing a brief survey. Also, if you are talking about a topic that your classmates have some knowledge of, conduct research to find unique and interesting facts and sources of information to illustrate your points. If you capture and maintain your audience's attention through presenting new and interesting information, they will remember your speech.

Help Your Audience Visualize

Whenever possible you should help your audience to visualize the ideas you are sharing with them. Use colorful language, and develop narratives describing a personal experience you have had. Use adjectives to describe, and to compare and contrast. Provide examples and use metaphors to link familiar ideas and concepts to ones that are less familiar. Use presentational aids to bring ideas, experiences, and objects to life. Consider the following description of a severe thunderstorm capable of producing a tornado:

> Dark heavy clouds roll across the sky. Rain pelts the pavement. The air smells electric. Flashes of light ignite descending from cloud to ground. Thunder cracks. I feel the vibration; then my ears pop. The rain stops and I see a cloud not far away begin to swirl, taking a V-shape as it touches the ground beginning its path of destruction.

Description takes your audience to where you were when having an experience. Less dramatic but just as effective in helping the audience to visualize information is using visual aids. Instead of just identifying the statistics regarding rising health care costs, a speaker could show the audience a line or bar graph illustrating the increases that have occurred over the last ten years. When an audience can visualize your message, it is more meaningful to them, and they are more likely to retain it.

Build on Information That Is Already Familiar

One way to help your listeners understand something new is to relate that thing to something the audience already knows. After establishing a common frame of reference for the audience, they will be better prepared to understand or follow the new information. Suppose you were to give a speech on the game of cricket, a bat and ball game originating in England in the sixteenth century. You could start by explaining the similarities between American baseball and cricket, including that it is a bat and ball game between two teams. The game is divided into innings where one team is at bat attempting to hit the ball and score runs while the other team attempts to catch batted balls and prevent runs. Once common ground is established, the uniqueness of the game of cricket can be discussed including the number of outs per inning, the number of fielders, the way the ball is pitched, and how runners are declared out. Importantly, by building on the familiar, you will have an easier time gaining your audience's attention, and enhancing their retention of what you have said.

SUMMARY

As you prepare to research, organize, and deliver your informative speech, there are several points to keep in mind to assist you in giving a high quality presentation. These include:

- **The purposes of informative speeches:** Spark a desire for information among your listeners, increase your listeners' understanding of the topic, help your listeners to remember, and help your listeners to apply information.

- **The types of informative speeches:** Informative speeches are about people, objects, events, processes, and concepts.

- **Organizing the informative speech:** Informative speakers may use cause-effect, chronological, spatial, and topical patterns of organization.

- **Methods of presenting information in informative speeches:** Speakers may define, describe, explain, and demonstrate.

- **Guidelines for informative speeches:** Speakers should relate the topic to the audience, relate the speaker to the topic, present new and interesting information, help their audience visualize, and build on information that is already known.

REFERENCES

Brown, A. (2013, January 29). A guide to jumpstarting a retirement plan in your 20s. *Forbes*. Retrieved April 4, 2014, from http://www.forbes.com/sites/abrambrown/2013/01/29/a-guide-to-jumpstarting-a-retirement-plan-in-your-20s/

Clinton Foundation. (2014, April 4). The Clinton Foundation. Retrieved April 4, 2014, from http://www.clintonfoundation.org/

De Francisco, V. L., & Jensen, M. D. (Eds). (1994). *Women's voices in our times: statements by American leaders.* Prospect Heights, IL: Waveland Press, Inc.

Hubbard, L. R. (2014, April 4). What is the purification rundown? Retrieved April 4, 2014, from http://www.scientology.org/faq/scientology-and-dianetics-auditing/what-is-the-purification-rundown.html

Struckbyanarrow. (2008, March 9). The world's best paper airplane. Retrieved April 4, 2014, from http://www.instructables.com/id/The-worlds-best-paper-airplane.-The-world-length-r/

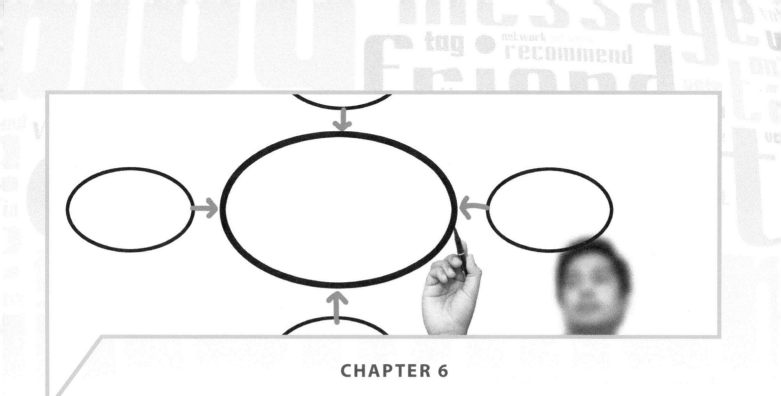

CHAPTER 6

Selecting Your Topic

Roberto paced around his dining room for fifteen minutes trying to think of possible topics for his informative speech. His instructor told him to come to class with at least three topics, and his mind was completely blank. He went to get some water to drink and then sat at the dining room table with a legal pad, trying to jot down topics he found interesting. Another fifteen minutes passed with nothing to show for it. Then he remembered an exercise recommended by his instructor to brainstorm topics by categories he found interesting. He started thinking about recent news stories he found interesting when browsing the Internet. The last three stories he read were about domestic terrorism, the impact of climate change on the supply of fresh water, and states in the U.S. that have passed restrictive voter identification laws. As he thought about these stories he realized they were very interesting to him, and he wanted to learn more about them. Roberto had just taken the first step in speech preparation—selecting a topic.

INTRODUCTION

Outside of the classroom context, when you give a speech, you will usually be asked to speak on a specific topic, one that you have specific knowledge on. For example, your supervisor may ask you to give a presentation on a new software program you have discovered that allows you to download and convert videos from video-streaming sites. Or your daughter wants you to talk to her fourth-grade class about your career as a criminal defense attorney. Perhaps in your neighborhood there is a controversy surrounding widening and paving a gravel road that leads to a lake at the end of your lane. You are asked by your neighbors to give a brief presentation to the county road commission about the environmental impact of the proposed road changes because of your years of experience as an environmental advocate.

In your public speaking class, however, you are not directed to speak on a topic selected by your instructor. Rather, you have the freedom to select your own topic. For some students this is a creative opportunity to consider all of the topics they find fascinating. For others, searching for a topic is a challenge that frustrates them as they go down various roads only to come up short of a topic that sustains their interest. In this chapter, we consider the four-part process of selecting a topic: (a) brainstorming for topics, (b) identifying the general purpose, (c) identifying the specific purpose, and (d) developing the central idea.

BRAINSTORMING FOR TOPICS

Brainstorming is a creative technique of spontaneously generating a list of ideas. To generate the largest possible list, defer judging or critiquing an idea—just jot down whatever comes to mind, no matter how odd, silly, or irrelevant it may seem. The goal is to come up with as many ideas as possible, and then to work with some of those ideas until you find a topic that interests you and will be of interest to your audience.

When brainstorming, jot down whatever comes to mind.

As you begin the brainstorming process, think about topics you know a lot about, because people tend to speak best about those subjects with which they are most familiar through reading, exposure to media, or personal experience. Alternatively, you could think about topics you have some knowledge on, but not enough for an entire speech. However, if these are topics you have always wanted to learn more about, your personal interests will motivate you to do a good job when conducting research for the speech. Finally, for persuasive speeches, you could think about topics for which you have strong opinions or beliefs. Having considered different starting points for identifying possible speech topics, let's now look at two approaches to brainstorming: taking a personal inventory and clustering.

Taking a Personal Inventory

What experiences have you had that are interesting? What are your interests in terms of what you like to read or do for fun? Do you have any hobbies? What special skills do you have that you could demonstrate? Are there certain beliefs that you have that would be interesting to share with the class? What issues concern you in contemporary society? Each of these questions can prompt a list of possible topics and help you to arrive at your eventual speech topic.

Clustering

Another technique is called **clustering.** Take a sheet of paper and divide it into different columns. Then, in each column, write down the first five or six thoughts or items that come to mind. Consider the following:

People	Places Lived/ Traveled	Issues of Concern	Events	Special Skills	Nature
Oprah Winfrey	South Carolina	gun control	World Series	cooking Indian food	tornadoes
Oscar Pistorius	Toronto	recycling	Rosh Hashanah	managing credit card debt	hurricanes
Pope Francis	Colorado	climate change	Cinco de Mayo	using Photoshop	earthquakes
Nancy Pelosi	Yosemite National Park	campus crime	Special Olympics	writing a winning resume	glacier erosion
Paul Ryan	my neighborhood	affirmative action	Mardi Gras	playing guitar	lightning

You can come up with as many categories as you can think of. The more categories and the more items you list, the more likely you will identify several possible topics to pursue. Then identify subcategories that will aid your topic development or move you in a more specific direction. Let's look at some possibilities from the lists generated above:

World Series	Climate Change	Nancy Pelosi
1st World Series	rising sea levels	Affordable Care Act
the Tigers win in 1984	droughts	House Speaker
1994: no World Series	food production	same-sex marriage
Will the Tigers win again?	natural disasters	minimum wage
the curse of the Bambino	fresh water supply	tax policy

The items on these sublists could become the main points of a speech or represent a more specific speech topic. For example, a speaker could give a speech on Nancy Pelosi's views on three topics: the Affordable Care Act, same-sex marriage, and the minimum wage. Alternatively, a speaker could solely address her positions on the Affordable Care Act: providing affordable health care to millions of uninsured Americans, controlling rising health care costs, and improving health care outcomes. Importantly, many students have found clustering to be very helpful in suggesting possible topics and in overcoming the frustration of feeling stumped and directionless.

IDENTIFYING THE GENERAL PURPOSE

Once you select your topic, you need to identify the **general purpose** of your speech. The majority of speeches have one of two purposes—to inform or to persuade.

When your general purpose is to inform, you need to spark a desire for information among your listeners, increase your listeners' understanding of the topic, help your listeners remember important information, and help your listeners apply information. Informative speeches may be about people, objects, events, processes, and concepts. When presenting information, speakers engage in the processes of defining, describing, explaining and/or demonstrating. In effect, you are acting as a teacher for your listeners, giving them information they did not have before your presentation.

When your general purpose is to persuade, you seek to change your listeners' beliefs or actions concerning your topic. Persuasive presentations address questions of fact, value, or policy. Some questions of fact can be answered absolutely, such as: What women's basketball team won the NCAA championship in 2014? Other questions of fact can only be answered speculatively: Will the U.S. unemployment rate be lower or higher next year? Questions of value involve facts, but they also require making judgments. Take the issue of waterboarding, an enhanced interrogation technique used by the CIA when questioning suspected terrorists. A speaker could pose the question: Is it ethically justifiable to waterboard, a technique that simulates the experience of drowning? Questions of policy focus on specific courses of action. For example, consider the issue of climate change. A speaker could pose the following question: What steps should be taken by the federal government to mitigate climate change? When speaking persuasively, your main goal is to get listeners to accept your point of view, believe something, or do something as a result of your presentation.

IDENTIFYING THE SPECIFIC PURPOSE

Once you have determined your general purpose, you must narrow down your topic by identifying the **specific purpose** of your speech. The specific purpose focuses on a particular aspect of your topic, and it should be stated as a single infinitive phrase that makes clear exactly what you hope to accomplish in your speech. For example, let's say Duane wanted to give a speech on an activity he enjoys—playing tennis. He played tennis for four years on his high school tennis team, and he has continued playing recreationally at a local indoor tennis facility while in college. This gave him a topic, and since the assignment was to give an informative speech, he had a general purpose, which he wrote down:

Topic: Playing tennis

General purpose: To inform

This is a good start, but how is Duane going to discuss this topic? He could focus on playing competitive tennis or on a well-known tournament such as Wimbledon. He could talk about the different strokes a player can make and what type of ball movement is produced by each stroke. He could also talk about Arthur Ashe, one of the world's top tennis players from the late 1960s through the mid-1970s. Whatever topic Duane selected, he knew it had to be interesting for his audience, and it had to be narrow enough to be covered in a six- to seven-minute time frame. He came up with the following specific purpose:

Specific purpose: To inform my audience of the three health benefits of playing recreational tennis.

Duane's specific purpose statement is clear and it is related directly to the audience. If he had left out the phrase "my audience," he may have lost track of how to include information and ideas that would be of interest to his classmates. He also makes clear what he wants his audience to know at the end of his speech—the three health benefits of playing recreational tennis.

SUGGESTIONS FOR WRITING THE SPECIFIC PURPOSE STATEMENT

When writing a **specific purpose statement,** a speaker must keep in mind to write a full infinitive phrase (not a question) that avoids figurative language, is limited to one idea, and is not too vague or general. Let's consider a few examples of ineffective and effective specific purpose statements.

WRITE THE SPECIFIC PURPOSE STATEMENT AS A FULL INFINITIVE PHRASE, NOT AS A FRAGMENT

Ineffective: Curry chicken.

Effective: To inform my audience about how to make curry chicken.

The ineffective specific purpose statement does not identify what the speaker hopes to accomplish. He or she could focus on the health benefits of curry chicken, different variations of the dish, or why listeners should try this dish. The effective statement clarifies for the listeners what they will learn from the speech.

WRITE THE SPECIFIC PURPOSE AS A STATEMENT, NOT AS A QUESTION

Ineffective: What is Cinco de Mayo?

Effective: To inform my audience of the celebrations occurring in Saginaw during Cinco de Mayo.

The ineffective statement may spark interest among listeners, however it does not specify the direction that the speech will take or what the speaker hopes to accomplish.

AVOID FIGURATIVE LANGUAGE IN THE SPECIFIC PURPOSE STATEMENT

Ineffective: To persuade my audience that our college's proposal to address student parking concerns is a real bummer.

Effective: To persuade my audience that our college needs to revise its parking proposal to more adequately address student concerns.

The ineffective specific purpose statement does not give the audience an indication of what the audience should take away from the speech, other than the speaker's vague dissatisfaction with the college's proposal. Also, figurative language such as "bummer" does nothing to clarify the speaker's purpose.

LIMIT THE SPECIFIC PURPOSE STATEMENT TO ONE IDEA

Ineffective: To inform my audience about the federal government's proposals to ban all cigarette advertising and to prohibit smoking around all college campus buildings.

Effective: To inform my audience about the federal government's proposal to ban all cigarette advertising.

Or

Effective: To inform my audience about the federal government's proposal to prohibit smoking around all college campus buildings.

The ineffective specific purpose statement contains two ideas, each of which could be a speech in its own right. This does not mean that a specific purpose statement cannot include the word "and." The use of "and" is appropriate when the speaker connects two parts of a unified topic. For example: To inform my audience about the causes and effects of clinical depression.

A SPECIFIC PURPOSE STATEMENT SHOULD NOT BE TOO VAGUE OR GENERAL

Ineffective: To inform my audience about how the federal deficit should be reduced.

Effective: To inform my audience about how a national sales tax can help to reduce the federal deficit.

There are many proposals that experts have suggested for reducing the federal deficit. The ineffective specific purpose statement is too vague, giving the audience no idea what the focus of the speech will be. The effective specific purpose statement is clear and concise, specifying exactly what the speaker will discuss.

CRITIQUING THE SPECIFIC PURPOSE STATEMENT

For some speakers an effective specific purpose statement can be written minutes after identifying a topic. For others, the process may be time consuming, requiring some research before a specific purpose is identified. When you do arrive at a specific purpose statement, you should critique it to determine if you can (a) accomplish your purpose in the time allotted for the speech, and (b) meet the interests and needs of your listeners. Considering the following four questions will lead to a quality critique of your specific purpose statement:

Can I accomplish my specific purpose in the time allotted for the speech?

Classroom speeches are relatively short, ranging from four to eight minutes. Most people speak at a rate of 120–150 words per minute, meaning a six-minute speech will contain 720 to 900 words. If a speaker selects a highly complicated topic, it will be difficult to develop in four to eight minutes. Consider the following examples:

To inform my audience about the events leading up to the U.S. war in Afghanistan.

To inform my audience about the principles underlying nanotechnology.

To persuade my audience to convert to Jainism.

Each of the topics identified above could be the focus of a presentation, however, each would take much more than eight minutes. Speakers are much better off identifying a limited purpose that can be achieved in the time allotted by the instructor.

Is my specific purpose relevant to my listeners?

Renting vacation villas in Tuscany might be interesting for very wealthy audience members. And the development of calculus by Isaac Newton might be interesting to those with a highly developed background in mathematics. Neither topic, however, is likely to hold interest for a general audience of college students. You need to think about the backgrounds, experiences, and interests of your listeners in order to develop an effective specific purpose statement.

Making sure your specific purpose statement is relevant to your listeners does not mean limiting yourself to what college students think about or do day-to-day. Most college students' interests are wide-ranging, and most are also intellectually curious, so just use your common sense in identifying a topic and developing a specific purpose statement. If you are genuinely interested in the topic, that is a good starting point. Then, if you are not sure about how relevant that topic might be to your listeners, find a way to connect it to goals, values, and interests they might have. Doing so requires effective audience analysis.

Is my specific purpose too trivial for my listeners?

Speakers also need to avoid topics that are too trivial to pique listeners' interests. You may think it is important to trim cuticles, but your classmates may not be interested in listening to you talk about the process for six minutes. Here are some additional examples of topics that most listeners would find too trivial for a speech:

> To inform my audience about the parts of a computer bag.

> To inform my audience about how to throw a football.

> To persuade my audience that café mocha is better than vanilla latte.

Is the specific purpose too technical for my listeners?

An overly technical speech can put your listeners to sleep as easily as taking an Ambien at midnight. Although you may be interested in the financial derivatives market, most of your listeners may not be. If you find yourself having to define multiple technical words and ideas, you might not have a topic that meets your listeners' interests and needs. Here are some examples of topics that would be too technical for most classroom speeches.

> To inform my listeners about the principles underlying quantum mechanics.

> To inform my audience about the usefulness of management information systems.

> To inform my audience about writing computer code to hack into restricted websites.

WRITING THE CENTRAL IDEA

The specific purpose details what you want to accomplish in your speech. The **central idea** is a precise statement of the main ideas or points that will be developed in the speech. The central idea identifies what you want your audience to take away from your speech, and it is expressed in a clear, declarative sentence. The term thesis statement is also used to refer the central idea.

Your topic gives the most general insight into your speech (America's cities). Your specific purpose statement reveals more precise insight into your speech ("To inform my listeners of the three major financial problems facing America's cities"). By stating exactly what the three major financial problems are, the central idea sums up the entire speech in a single sentence. Let's consider a few examples, including the initial topic, the general purpose, the specific purpose, and the central idea.

> **Topic:** Animal Research
>
> **General Purpose:** To persuade
>
> **Specific Purpose:** To persuade my listeners to support the use of animals for medical research.
>
> **Central Idea:** Using animals for medical research speeds the development of drugs to treat illnesses, helps physicians perfect new surgical techniques, and increases cancer survival rates.

In this instance, the speaker starts with a broad topic (animal research) that can go in many different directions. The speaker then narrows the topic, moving from the general purpose, to the specific idea, to the central idea. The central idea gives the audience clear information about the content of the speech. Animal research will be justified by looking at the role such research plays in speeding up the development of new drugs to treat illnesses, helping physicians perfect new surgical techniques, and increasing survival rates for cancer. Let's look at another example:

Topic: Alpine Skiing

General Purpose: To Inform

Specific Purpose: To inform my audience of the strategies skiers use in three different alpine races.

Central Idea: To inform my audience of the racing strategies skiers use in the downhill, giant slalom, and slalom.

In this example, the speaker starts off with a topic linked to her general interest in skiing, and she knows she want to inform her audience about the sport. In her specific purpose statement she narrows her focus to the strategies skiers use in different alpine races. Finally, she specifies in her central idea that she will discuss the strategies racers use in the downhill, giant slalom, and slalom.

The central idea sums up your speech in one sentence.

The central idea reveals much more about the content of the speech than the specific purpose. The reason for this is after arriving at a specific purpose a speaker needs to conduct research to decide what the main points will be. Let's look at how this process plays out with a speaker in a public speaking class.

Sam is an environmental science major with an interest in climate change and he decided this would be a good topic for his informative speech. After giving the topic some thought, she came up with the following specific purpose statement: To inform the audience of the seriousness of climate change. Then Sam started to research her topic.

An article in *Newsweek,* which she located through a Google search, explained how climate change would impact food production. Continued increases in temperature would shorten growing seasons, increase the length and severity of droughts, increase the impact of pests on crops, and decrease the fish population.

Next, Sam found the latest report by the U.N.'s Intergovernmental Panel on Climate Change, an organization that recently shared the Nobel Peace Prize with Al Gore. Current projections are that increases in temperature over the next one hundred years will increase the sea level by four to thirty-six inches. Currently one hundred million people live within three feet of the sea level (Nature Conservatory, 2014). All of these people would be displaced by a three-foot increase in the sea level. Furthermore, the land covered by the sea and needed for the new homes of displaced residents, further reduces land available for agriculture.

Sam then decided to interview her favorite environmental science professor who argued that continued global warming was going to accelerate the frequency and intensity of catastrophic weather events, impacting the lives of millions of people worldwide. He then identified for Sam several climatological reports predicting how catastrophic storms will impact people living on every continent.

After reading all of the information she collected, Sam was ready to develop her central idea: Climate change must be mitigated as soon as possible because it is going to adversely impact food production, displace hundreds of millions of people, and increase the frequency and intensity of catastrophic storms.

GUIDELINES FOR WRITING THE CENTRAL IDEA

Like the specific purpose statement, the central idea should: (1) be written in a full sentence, (2) not be phrased as a question, (3) avoid figurative language, and (4) not be vague or too general. Let's look at three examples of how to change ineffective central ideas into effective ones:

Ineffective: Problems with the Atkins Diet

Effective: Although the Atkins Diet produces weight loss, it may also lead to serious health problems such as high cholesterol, kidney disease, and an unhealthy metabolic state.

The first central idea is too general. What are the problems associated with the Atkins Diet? The second central idea both acknowledges that the diet may produce weight loss and that it carries specific serious health risks.

Ineffective: New Orleans is wonderful place for a vacation.

Effective: New Orleans has many attractions for tourists, including diverse architectural styles, delicious food, and high quality musical entertainment.

The first central idea is too general and it uses figurative language. What does wonderful mean to a listener? The second central idea specifies the features of the city that may be interesting for tourists.

A good central idea sums up in a single sentence, the main points that will be presented in a speech. The central idea emerges after the speaker has formulated the specific purpose and conducted research on the topic.

SUMMARY

The first step in selecting a topic is to think about topics you know a lot about or topics you have always wanted to learn more about. If you become stuck in identifying a topic, we recommended two brainstorming techniques: taking a personal inventory and clustering.

The second step in selecting a topic is identifying a specific purpose statement, a single infinitive phrase focusing on a particular aspect of or approach to understanding your topic. Suggestions for developing a specific purpose statement include forming a full infinitive statement (as opposed to a fragment or a question), avoiding figurative language, limiting the statement to one idea, and not using vague or overly general language. Finally, we recommended critiquing your specific purpose statement by considering whether you can accomplish it in the time allotted for the speech, assessing its relevance for your listeners, and evaluating it for possibly being too trivial or technical.

The third step in selecting a topic is developing your central idea. The central idea is a precise statement that sums up the main ideas or points a speaker will cover in a speech. The central idea emerges after a speaker has conducted research on his or her topic. Like the specific purpose, the central idea should be phrased as a full infinitive statement (as opposed to a fragment or a question), avoid figurative language, and not use vague or overly general language.

REFERENCES

Nature Conservatory. (2014). Climate change impacts: Rising seas, higher sea levels. Retrieved April 9, 2014, from http://www.nature.org/ourinitiatives/urgentissues/global-warming-climate-change/threats-impacts/rising-seas.xml

CHAPTER 7

Researching Your Topic

Abdul had been diagnosed with type 2 diabetes. He went to his family physician after several months of feeling fatigued, urinating frequently, having increased thirst and hunger, and blurred vision. His physician told him that the best way to treat his condition was to monitor his blood sugar levels, eat healthy, and start a program of regular exercise (Collazo-Clavell, 2014). Abdul was very concerned about his diagnosis, and he wanted to find out as much information as possible about type 2 diabetes. When he arrived home, he told his wife about his visit to the doctor. She recommended that he talk to her cousin, Rahman, who also had the illness. When he talked to Rahman, he was relieved to find out that he had successfully kept his blood sugar levels within an acceptable range for the past two years by losing weight and walking briskly at the local gym for an hour a day. Abdul also went to the library and met with a reference librarian who helped him find several books and recent articles on type 2 diabetes. He also went to the Mayo Clinic website and found more information. Abdul began to feel confident that he could manage his illness by losing thirty pounds and following the recommendations of his physician.

The steps followed by Abdul are same steps you should follow in searching for information for your speeches. You can talk to experts, friends, or family members who have experience with your topic. You can also find published material in the form of books, articles, or government documents. Web documents produced by reputable businesses, government agencies, organizations, or public-interest groups may also prove useful.

INTRODUCTION

In this chapter we will describe the process of researching your speech topic. First, we look at the process of conducting library research, focusing on consulting librarians, using your library's online catalog, and consulting periodical databases, newspapers, and reference works. Second, we consider searching for information on the World Wide Web by using Internet search engines. We also provide recommendations for evaluating documents on the World Wide Web. Third, we describe the process of conducting personal interviews for research purposes. Finally, we offer suggestions for conducting high-quality research in the most efficient manner possible.

CONDUCTING LIBRARY RESEARCH

Although the Internet is a valuable research tool, you should always consider using the resources available at your campus library. At the library you will be able to talk with experienced librarians who will help direct your research as well as be able to consult the online catalog, periodical databases, newspapers, and various reference works.

Librarians

Too many students waste valuable time perusing the library's online catalog or searching the Internet, coming across countless sources that could be included in a speech, but not knowing if they are finding the best or most pertinent information about their topic. That's what librarians are for! Furthermore, they love helping students. All reference librarians have one or more areas of expertise. So the first librarian you approach may recommend that you talk to another who is an expert in the topic you are pursuing for your speech. Librarians also have extensive training in library use and research methods. You should always consider speaking to a librarian about research for your topic because they will point you in the direction of high-quality information and sources.

The Online Catalog

The online catalog lists all of the books, periodicals, and other resources owned by the library. You may search for books by author, title, subject, or keyword. The catalog will also inform you whether the book you want is available or if it has been checked out. When you do find an available book, you need to find and write down the **call number,** which tells you the section of the library where the book may be found. When you find the correct section, you can then search the shelves until you find exactly where the book is located.

Periodical Databases

A regularly published magazine or journal is called a periodical. Periodicals are one of the most common sources of information for student speeches. Periodicals include popular magazines such as *Time, Newsweek, Business Week,* and *U.S. News & World Report.* Specialized academic journals may be relevant to your topic as well, such as *Journal of the American Medical Association, Nature, Basic and Applied Social Psychology, American Sociological Review, Academy of Management Journal, Journal of Marketing,* and *Communication Monographs.*

When using one of your library's online periodical databases, you type in the subject you want information on in the search box, hit enter, and articles on your subject will appear on the screen. The full citation of the article will appear including the author, title of the article, the magazine or journal, the date of publication, and the pages of the article. If your library has online access to the article, you will be able to call up the full text of the article. If your library does not have online access, you may ask a librarian if they can order a copy of the article from another library.

The most useful general article database at the University of Akron is *Academic Search Complete.* To get access to this database, type http://www.uakron.edu/libraries in your browser, then click on the Academic Search Complete link. This database gives you access to authoritative research and published sources, most of which is not available freely on the Internet.

Newspapers

Newspapers may also be consulted for information that is relevant to your topic. You can search newspapers for current events or examine older issues for historical information. For topics focusing on local issues, you can find articles in the *Akron Beacon Journal* or the *Cleveland Plain Dealer.* For coverage of national and international issues, some of the best U.S. newspapers are *New York Times, Washington Post, Christian Science Monitor, USA Today, Boston Globe, Detroit Free Press, Chicago Tribune, Los Angeles Times, Atlanta Journal Constitution, Wall Street Journal,* and *Dallas Morning News.* For these national newspapers as well as international newspapers, you may consult *Lexis/Nexis Academic,* a database that gives you access to articles from more than 700 newspapers, including full text articles.

Reference Works

In the reference section of your library, you will find a variety of reference works that may be helpful in your search for information pertaining to your speech. Reference works that might prove helpful for your research include encyclopedias, almanacs, books of quotations, and biographical volumes.

ENCYCLOPEDIAS

General encyclopedias provide a compilation of information about all branches of human knowledge. Since they summarize knowledge in all areas, they can be an excellent place to begin your research. Many general encyclopedias may also be accessed online. *Encyclopedia Britannica* and *Encyclopedia Americana* are two of the more commonly used general encyclopedias. Certain topics may also be researched by consulting specialized encyclopedias such as *Encyclopedia of African American History; Asian American History and Culture: An Encyclopedia; Oxford Encyclopedia of Latinos and Latinas in the United States; Oxford Dictionary of Art; Encyclopedia of Religion; Encyclopedia of Physical Education, Fitness, and Sports;* and *McGraw Hill Encyclopedia of Science and Technology.*

The library offers access to the online catalog, perodical databases, newspapers, reference works, and experienced librarians.

ALMANACS

Almanacs are published annually and they contain an incredible amount of current information on almost every conceivable subject. The most valuable almanac is *The World Almanac and Book of Facts,* called a "treasure trove of political, economic, scientific and educational statistics and information" by *The Wall Street Journal* (Altschiller, 2008). Among the many things you can find are the winners of the past year's academy awards, the most watched television shows in the U.S., college and professional sports records and annual champions, the literacy rate in Belize, and the natural resources of Malaysia.

BOOKS OF QUOTATIONS

A well-chosen quotation reinforces your ideas. A speaker chooses a quote because it offers a concise, memorable phrasing of an idea. A quotation can serve to boost your credibility because it implies the person you are quoting agrees with your idea. Finding the right quote to reinforce your ideas may demonstrate your domain knowledge and preparation, add variety to your logical arguments, create a sense of anticipation, suspense, and drama, or add humor to your speech (Dlugan, 2012). The best-known collection of quotations is *Bartlett's Familiar Quotations,* a book containing over twenty-five thousand quotations from historical and contemporary people. Other well-known books of quotations include *The Oxford Dictionary of Quotations, The New Penguin Dictionary of Quotations, The Oxford Dictionary of Literary Quotations, The Penguin Concise Dictionary of Biographical Quotations,* and *The Oxford Dictionary of Humorous Quotations.*

BIOGRAPHICAL VOLUMES

Sometimes speakers need to find out information about people who have been covered in the news. There are a number of biographical volumes that contain brief information about the life and careers of present day men and women. The most useful biographical volumes include *International Who's Who, Who's Who in America, Who's Who Among Asian Americans, Who's Who Among African Americans, The Latino American Who's Who,* and *Who's Who of American Women.*

SEARCHING THE WORLD WIDE WEB

The World Wide Web is a global set of documents, images, videos, and other resources, logically interrelated with hyperlinks and referenced with Uniform Resource Identifiers (URIs). URIs symbolically identify services, servers, and other databases, and the documents and resources that they can provide. Hypertext Transfer Protocol (HTTP) is the main access protocol of the World Wide Web. We access the World Wide Web through browser software such as Microsoft's Internet Explorer, Mozilla Firefox, Apple's Safari, or Google Chrome. These browsers allow us to navigate from one web page to another by way of hyperlinks

There are methods for efficiently finding information on the World Wide Web.

embedded in the documents we locate (Heywood, 2010). In this section of the chapter, we describe the general process of using search engines to locate information on the World Wide Web. Then, we look at a few government websites that contain information that would be helpful for many speeches.

Although there are a number of different search engines or browsers, the most widely used is Google. How can you efficiently use a search engine such as Google to find the information you need for your speech? The answer to follow a research strategy that will allow you to find specific, high-quality information.

Let's say you are interested in giving a speech on hydraulic fracking, the process of fracturing rocks by pressurized liquid in order to extract underground gas or oil (Lubber, 2013). If you simply enter the term "fracking" in the Google search box, you will get a list of every document on the World Wide Web that contains that word—over 6.7 million. How can you narrow the available documents in a way that makes your research more efficient and produces information that is interesting for your audience? One approach is to make your search more specific. If your primary interest in fracking is that it causes water pollution, type in fracking + "water pollution." The + sign limits the search to items that contain the keywords *fracking* and *water pollution*. Importantly, the term *water pollution* is put in quotation marks in the search box. Not doing so would result in finding every document containing the separate words: *fracking, water,* and *pollution* (generating a list of more than seven million items). Your interest is in the specific impact of fracking on water pollution, so you need to put that term in quotation marks.

A search of fracking + "water pollution" still yields too many items, approximately 216,000. One approach you could take at this point is to search specifically in Google Scholar. This will direct you to scientific research studies that focus on the practice of fracking and possible water pollution. Entering fracking + "water pollution" in Google Scholar yields a more manageable list of 937 items. You could narrow your topic further, however, in ways that would be interesting for your audience and yield the most current information. If you enter the terms fracking + "water pollution" + Michigan + 2014, 180 items are identified. You now have a much more manageable set of articles that are recent and that focus on fracking in your home state.

Government Websites

Government documents and publications will be useful for speeches on many topics. You can get information from the federal government or from state or local agencies. The following three websites provide the most comprehensive information:

- **Statistical Abstract** (www.census.gov/compendia/statab/). The U.S. Census Bureau compiles the information reported on this website. Here you will find statistical information on economic, political, and social aspects of American life.

- **USA.gov** (www.usa.gov). All U.S. government information on the Internet is contained on this website, including more than 250 million web pages from local, tribal, state, and federal governments.

- **World Factbook** (www.cia.gov/library/publications/the-world-factbook/). The Central Intelligence Agency (CIA) compiles information about every country in the world. Topics include people, economy, communication, transportation, and government.

EVALUATING DOCUMENTS ON THE WORLD WIDE WEB

When you go to the library and locate books, magazines, and journals, you can be certain that the information is likely to be accurate and of high quality. That is because each of these publications follows a process of editorial, expert, or peer review to determine whether it should be published. On the Internet, however, you cannot be so certain of the quality of what you find. Anyone with access to the Internet can post ideas or opinions in personal blogs, publish an online newsletter, or create a website devoted to a particular topic. So, let's look at three ways to evaluate documents posted on the World Wide Web.

Authorship

When looking at a document on the World Wide Web, the first thing to look for is an author's name. If you cannot find a name there is no way to evaluate the source. If a name is provided, what are the qualifications of this person to address this topic? Does the author establish his or her expertise? Does it seem that the ideas or claims made by the author are objective, or do you detect some bias?

If author expertise is not clearly established, you can type the author's name in the Google search box. You can then find out if the author has suitable credentials, has published quality work on the subject, and whether he or she is affiliated with a reputable organization, research institute, college, or university.

Sponsorship

Businesses, government agencies, and public-interest groups post many of the documents we find on the web. When this is the case, you need to consider whether the sponsoring organization is objective concerning the topic they are addressing, or whether they have some vested interest that slants their views. For example, in the year 2001, the world's second largest oil company, BP, advertised its new identity as a leader in moving the world "beyond petroleum," touting its $45 million purchase of the Solarex solar energy corporation. But in this ad, BP did not announce that this purchase was less than 1 percent of the $5 billion they planned to spend over the next

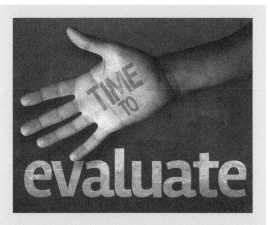

On the Internet, you cannot be certain of the quality of the information you find.

five years for oil exploration in Alaska, only one of the places they drill worldwide (CorpWatch, 2001). Why did BP do this? Their advertising is meant to reach environmentally-conscious people who might be more likely to purchase BP oil if they believe the company is engaging in "green technologies." The amount of their investment, however, is nothing in comparison to the billions of dollars they spend every year on oil exploration, an environmentally damaging activity.

The last three letters of a website's URL can also help you judge the credibility of the information that is presented on it. Government agencies and educational institutions use the letters .gov and .edu. The information published on these websites is usually accurate and objective. The letters .org and .com can be used by profit-making as well as nonprofit organizations. The interests of these organizations should be scrutinized because they may be trying to advance views that serve their economic or ideological interests.

You can also click on the *About* link on the homepage of the sponsoring organization's website. Here you can find information about the purpose, philosophy, or political interests of the organization. If there is no *About* link, that may suggest that the organization does not want questions to be raised about its objectivity or about the expertise of its members.

Recency

Whenever you are considering using information from a web document, you should look for a copyright or publication date, or the date the document was last revised. This information is usually at the top or bottom of the document. You should always try to find the most recent information on your topic, especially if you are focusing on an issue that is of relevance today. If a source is not dated, you should not cite it. Rather, find another document that does provide a date you can cite.

INTERVIEWING

Another potential source of information for your speech is speaking to a person who is an expert or has substantial experience concerning your topic. Most people enjoy talking about their work or experiences with others, so you should be able to identify one or more people who will be willing to meet with you. Students have interviewed professors, university administrators, business executives and other business professionals, police officers, government officials, health care professionals, engineers, attorneys, and many other professionals who have specialized experiences that may be helpful to include in your speech. Let's look at three parts of the interview process: preparing for the interview, conducting the interview, processing the interview.

Preparing for the Interview

In order to have a successful interview you need to prepare. By following these five steps, you should be able to conduct a successful interview.

DEFINE THE PURPOSE OF THE INTERVIEW

You have completed your library and Internet research, but you still have questions about your topic. You decide that the best way to get answers to these questions is to speak with someone who has personal experience. For example, let's say you are giving a presentation on binge drinking among college students. You then come across a story in the campus newspaper about a professor who studies public communication campaigns to educate college students about the dangers of binge drinking to discourage them from drinking excessively.

SELECTING A PERSON TO INTERVIEW

Who should you interview? You want to be certain to select a person whose experiences will add insight to your topic. It is also helpful if the person you select has had interesting experiences that your classmates would enjoy hearing about. For example, let's say you know of a soldier who has served two tours in Afghanistan and he has been part of a team to locate and defuse improvised explosive devices (IEDs). His experiences would be fascinating to share with the class. Your university also keeps information about faculty experts in the arts and humanities, physical sciences, business, economy, political issues, law, health care, mass media, education, politics, and the economy. You may find out how to contact faculty experts at the following link (http://www.uakron.edu/im/online-newsroom/expert-sources.dot).

ARRANGING THE INTERVIEW

Once you identify the person you wish to interview, you need to set up a time and place for the interview. You can do this through calling the person's office or workplace or through email. Make sure to give the person at least a few days to find time in their schedule to talk to you. Also, be certain to describe the purpose of the interview so your interviewee will be prepared to answer your questions. Finally, give the interviewee an idea about how much time you will need. You should not ask for more than fifteen or twenty minutes. If you would like more time, consider asking, "How much time would you be able to spare for this interview?"

RECORDING THE INTERVIEW

You can digitally record the interview if your interviewee agrees to be recorded. Recording your interview allows you to quote your interviewee accurately. If you do not have a recorder, or if your interviewee does not want to be recorded, make sure to bring a pen and paper so you may write notes about their responses.

PREPARING QUESTIONS

You want to make sure your questions are specific, clear, and necessary, meaning you are seeking information that cannot be found easily by just looking up the answer. Some "yes" or "no" questions can be asked, but most should ask your interviewee to describe their professional experiences as they pertain to your topic, research they have conducted, or opinions they have. You want to work on the wording of your questions so the interviewee knows exactly what you are looking for, and you should list the questions in the order you will ask them.

Conducting the Interview

Preparation is essential to conduct quality interviews. You also have to be alert and flexible, however, because a person might answer a question in an unexpected fashion or take the interview in a direction you did not anticipate. By concentrating on everything your interviewee says, you will get the most out of your interview. Consider the following recommendations to conduct a successful interview.

DRESS PROFESSIONALLY AND ARRIVE ON TIME

You do not have to dress like you would for a job interview, but a good guideline would be to dress in business casual attire. This shows your seriousness and professionalism. You also need to make sure you arrive a few minutes ahead of the scheduled interview.

OPENING COMMENTS

Introduce yourself, shake hands, and thank the interviewee for agreeing to meet with you. When a professional person takes time out of their busy day to talk with you, it is important to begin by showing your appreciation. Also, be prepared for your interviewee to ask you a couple of questions before you start, such as why you are interested in your topic and what you plan to focus on in your speech.

RESTATE THE PURPOSE OF THE INTERVIEW

Before posing your first question, remind your interviewee of the purpose of your interview. Doing so reminds your interviewee of the line of questioning you are going to pursue, and it helps them to choose the best experiences and information for potential inclusion in your speech.

SET UP THE RECORDER

If your interviewee agreed to be recorded, set up your recorder, placing it on the desk or table you are sitting at. Practice with your recorder so you can set it up as quickly as possible. Turn the recorder on, and start with your first question.

Potential interviewees may be professors, business executives, police officers, government officials, attorneys...

PRACTICE ACTIVE LISTENING

Show an interest in your interviewee's responses. If you hear something you want to get word-for-word, and you are not recording the interview, write down the comments, asking the interviewee to repeat the comments if necessary. You also want to listen carefully so you can ask good follow-up or probing questions. Your interviewee may also bring up an important point that you did not anticipate in developing your list of questions. By listening carefully, you may think spontaneously about asking some questions that open up this new area for discussion.

ENDING THE INTERVIEW

After your interviewee answers your last question, turn off the recorder (if necessary), thank him or her, shake hands, and leave the office.

After the Interview

After the interview is over there is still work to do. You need to thank the interviewee, review and develop your notes, and transcribe your notes or digital recording.

THANKING THE INTERVIEWEE

As soon as possible, thank the interviewee for spending time with you and thoughtfully answering your questions. You may do this through a thank-you note or email.

REVIEW AND DEVELOP YOUR NOTES

While the interview is still fresh in your mind, sit down with your notes and develop your understanding of what your interviewee shared with you. This is especially important if you did not record your interview. If you wait too long it may be difficult for you to recapture what your interviewee said. If you recorded your interview, there may still be reasons to review and develop your notes. Perhaps your interviewee said something that sparked a new thought concerning your topic. By developing your notes you will be better able to direct your subsequent library or Internet research.

TRANSCRIBE YOUR NOTES OR DIGITAL RECORDING

Transcribe your notes by fully developing the ideas or phrases you copied down while conducting your interview. This will help you decide how to best incorporate your interviewee's responses into your speech. If you digitally recorded the interview, you should also produce a verbatim transcript to ensure that you quote your interviewee accurately (or at least transcribe the portions of the comments you will include in the speech).

SUGGESTIONS FOR DOING RESEARCH

Some people genuinely enjoy researching topics they find interesting; others find research a tedious process. No matter what your perspective is on doing research, there are a few suggestions to consider to make your research more productive.

Start Early

The biggest mistake a speaker can make is to wait too long to start the research process. The longer you wait, the more pressure and tension you will experience. You also reduce the likelihood of finding quality support materials for your presentation. The more time you give yourself to do research, the more likely you will find quality information, and the more time you will have for constructing and practicing your speech.

Keep a Running Bibliography

As you conduct research, you will come across books, magazine and journal articles, and Internet documents that look like they might have information that could be included in your speech. Every time you identify a potential source, enter the full citation in your running bibliography, even though you are not certain that you will use each source. You should probably identify at least twenty sources in your running bibliography in order to find seven or eight that you will actually be able to use. Only the sources that you actually use and cite are then listed in the bibliography that you hand in to your instructor.

You keep a running bibliography to prevent you from coming across a source, not writing down the full citation, and then not being able to reproduce the search process that found that source at a later date. Keeping a running bibliography makes sure you follow a productive and efficient research process.

When you are preparing your bibliography, remember to follow APA style. You can consult the APA manual or go to Purdue University's Online Writing Lab (http://owl.english.purdue.edu/).

Take Careful Notes

As you read information from your various sources, keep notes summarizing, paraphrasing, or directly quoting what an author said. For each note, identify the specific subject the author is addressing (subject heading), and an abbreviated author and title for the reference (full citation is in your running bibliography). Then write your note about the source. Each time an author makes a different point, you should enter it as a separate note, even if it is from the same source. Doing so will allow you to more efficiently organize your speech. When you print out your notes, you can organize them by the different topics or areas that are covered. So a single source may be referenced in different places in your speech. Keeping separate notes for each point makes it easier to see how ideas develop or may be pieced together.

SUMMARY

In this chapter, we focused on the process of conducting research for your speeches. We started by describing the process of conducting library research. The helpfulness of meeting with a librarian was discussed, as well as the process of using your library's online catalog. In the library you will find research on your topic in periodical databases, newspapers, and various reference works.

The second section of the chapter described the process of finding information on the World Wide Web. We described the process of using search engines or browsers to find high-quality information for your speeches in the most efficient manner possible. We also identified three government websites that have information that may be included in many different types of speeches. In order to evaluate the quality of the information you find on the web, we recommended evaluating the expertise and objectivity of the author, the objectivity or bias of the sponsoring organization, and the recency of the posting.

Sometimes, speakers find that interviewing experts or people with significant experience pertaining to their topics is helpful. Such people can offer unique information or insights into your topic, they may have interesting stories to tell, and they might have well-developed opinions. In order to conduct a quality interview, we described the process of preparing and conducting the interview, as well as what needs to be done after you complete the interview.

The final section of this chapter offered three suggestions for doing research for your speeches. We recommended starting the research process early, keeping a running bibliography, and taking careful notes.

REFERENCES

Altschiller, D. (2008, September 13). Reference Books. *The Wall Street Journal*. Retrieved April 11, 2014, from http://online.wsj.com/news/articles/SB122125935106030191

Collazo-Clavell, M. (2014). Type 2 diabetes. *Mayo Clinic*. Retrieved April 11, 2014, from http://www.mayoclinic.org/diseases-conditions/type-2-diabetes/basics/treatment/con-20031902

CorpWatch. (2001, March 22). Greenwash Fact Sheet. Retrieved April 11, 2014, from http://www.corpwatch.org/article.php?id=242

Dlugan, A. (2012, December 4). How to use quotes in your speech: 8 benefits and 21 tips. *Six Minutes: Speaking and Presentation Skills*. Retrieved April 11, 2014, from http://sixminutes.dlugan.com/speech-quotes/

Heywood, A. (2010, May 17). Web Content Management and Design. Retrieved April 11, 2014, from http://imd208blog.blogspot.com/2013/03/types-of-internet-services-there-are_22.html

Lubber, M. (2013, May 28). Escalating Water Strains in Fracking Regions. *Forbes*. Retrieved April 11, 2014, from http://www.forbes.com/sites/mindylubber/2013/05/28/escalating-water-strains-in-fracking-regions/

CHAPTER 8

Supporting Your Ideas

Maya was team captain of her college's soccer team. When considering a topic for her informative speech, she thought a focus on Title IX would be a good idea. Title IX is the federal law preventing sex discrimination by schools receiving federal funding. After searching for information online and at the library, she found out there are three primary ways schools can demonstrate their compliance with this law. The explanations were somewhat technical and would take up most of the time for her presentation. Her research was all but done!

Then Maya began to think about what her audience would find interesting about this topic. The specific details about how schools demonstrate compliance with this law may not hold their interest. What could she do? After giving the matter some more thought, Maya decided to focus on how Title IX was addressed at her college. She came across articles published in the campus newspaper describing the impact of Title IX when it was first instituted on campus. She then interviewed three women who participated on the basketball, swimming, and golf teams at the college. Maya then reflected on what she had learned about leadership and about being a contributing team member as a result of her participation on the soccer team.

The evidence and ideas Maya selected for her speech would be much more interesting for her classmates to hear. Her focus was not on colleges and universities in general with respect to Title IX. This was a speech about their own college. The stories she shared were about athletes they watched and read about in the school paper. Her personal experiences linked her to the topic and showed her expertise to address it.

INTRODUCTION

Selecting high-quality support materials for the main points of your speech is a critical part of the speech preparation process. Support materials help your listeners to understand your message, hold their attention, and show them that you have conducted adequate research on your topic.

In this chapter we describe different types of supporting materials you may use in your speeches: definitions, examples, statistics, testimony, narrative, and analogy. We also give guidelines for using support materials effectively.

DEFINITIONS

One assumption sometimes made by speakers is that their listeners will define ideas and words the same way they do. In fact, that assumption is one of the most common reasons for misunderstandings between people. For example, you prepare a speech on landscaping because you have worked as a landscaper the last three summers, and you really enjoy your work. You even subscribe to two different landscaping magazines. Can you assume that everyone in your audience knows what landscaping is? Some of your classmates may have grown up in large urban areas with few green spaces surrounding their apartment buildings. These classmates may never have considered what a landscaper does. Other classmates may have lived in rural areas; however, their families may not have believed in altering the natural beauty of the surrounding land. A brief definition of landscaping may help the audience to better understand your speech from the outset. As part of your introduction you could say, "Landscaping is a process of beautifying the grounds surrounding a home by contouring the land and planting flowers, shrubs, and trees" (Morris, 1976, p. 736). Any time a specific term is critical to understanding your speech, you should consider whether this term is common knowledge or a term some classmates may not understand. If the latter is likely, a definition should be provided.

EXAMPLES

An **example** provides support for or illustrates a general claim made by a speaker. If a speaker does not make adequate use of examples, his or her ideas may seem vague or impersonal. Examples give life to a speech and make your ideas more specific and personal. If you want to describe how difficult it is to park on campus, you could talk about your experiences this morning:

> I pulled into the parking lot twenty minutes before class. I saw someone pull out of a space close to the Com building where I had my first class. I accelerated toward the space as another car whipped around the corner and pulled in ahead of me. I then went to the far end of the lot where I can sometimes find a spot on a busy day. No such luck today. Then another car pulls out about a hundred feet away. I think I can get this one until another car beats me to it, again. After ten minutes of this game of hunting for a spot, I find one, pick up my laptop, and run to my first class.

This example gives life to the process of finding a parking spot on campus. It gives details of time, place, and action. We can almost see ourselves in the same situation, driving from one section of a parking lot to another, competing with our classmates so we can get to class on time. A person listening to this story may also gain a sense of the same frustration he or she feels hunting for a parking spot on a busy day. Importantly, research has demonstrated that when speakers use vivid, concrete examples they strongly impact their listeners beliefs and intended future actions (Tal-Or, Boninger, Poran, & Gleicher, 2004).

A **brief example** is a short statement made to support or illustrate a point. Let's say a speaker wishes to support the point that Americans are increasingly at risk of losing their privacy because of the intrusion of technological surveillance in our lives. The following would be an effective brief example to support this point:

> After Microsoft bought Skype for $8.5 billion in 2011, they obtained a patent for "legal intercept technology" making it possible to "silently copy communication" between speakers. Do you want Microsoft to see and hear everything you say or do when you chat on Skype? (Gallagher, 2012).

An **extended example** gives a speaker the opportunity to tell a story vividly and dramatically. If developed carefully using rich and descriptive language, it can pull listeners into your speech. Consider the following extended example by Matt Bai (1997) in *Newsweek* magazine. Bai's article focused on charges of corruption leveled against Washington, D.C. police chief, Larry Soulsby:

> Larry Soulsby's critics often said he was asleep on the job. But it was where the Washington, D.C. police chief actually slept that did him in. The man who was supposed to reform D.C.'s struggling force was sharing a luxury apartment with a fellow cop who had allegedly secured it at a discount by pretending it was for official police business.
>
> Recently, Soulsby, who spent twenty-four years on the capital's force, has seemed to be the Chief who knew too little: he'd been shocked to find out that half his homicide cops hadn't solved a single

murder all year, and he had no idea that he's picked a convicted wife-beater for an anti-crime post. Soulsby is like Columbo, but the light bulb never goes off. Last week was the final blow. He stepped down—hours before his roommate was indicted for embezzlement and extortion (Bai, 1997, p. 42).

The preceding example is effective because it highlights interesting facts using descriptive language about a corrupt police officer. The way Bai develops the example draws people into to the story. The example is specific, personal, and lively.

A speaker does not need to use factual examples in a presentation. A **hypothetical example** describes an imaginary or fictitious event or person. Consider the following hypothetical example:

Imagine yourself at a beautiful beach, lying on your back as the sun warms your body. At the surf's edge, the water gently touches your feet. The sound of the waves is lulling you to sleep when your moment of tranquility is broken suddenly by a cry off in the distance. A young child has ventured off too far in the ocean. He is struggling to stay afloat, his arms flailing wildly. Would you know what to do?

This hypothetical example could be used effectively to set up a presentation on life-saving techniques. Just because you have not encountered a real situation in which you have had to save someone's life, does not mean you cannot establish a clear image in the minds of audience members regarding such an event. Again, the success of your example is based on how clearly you can portray a situation, incorporating as many details as possible to paint a vivid picture for your listeners.

STATISTICS

Speakers use **statistics** to express information in numeric form. One common cliché used by many is, "Numbers don't lie." Although numbers may give accurate insights into various issues, problems, and topics, they can also be manipulated or distorted. Consider a product that is advertised as 75% fat free to entice consumers into buying it as a healthy food choice. The 75% figure is accurate, but it also means the product contains 25% fat, a level considered unhealthy by all nutritionists if that food product is consumed in large quantities.

Also, consider a recent article written by Shelly Schwartz and published on the CNBC website (Schwartz, 2012). The title of the article was, "The Inflation of Life—Cost of Raising a Child Has Soared." As support for this claim, Schwartz examined statistical information reported by the U.S. Department of Agriculture and made the following observation: "The cost of raising a child from birth to age seventeen has surged 25 percent over the past ten years, due largely to the cost of groceries and medical care." Although the 25 percent increase in costs is accurate, the use of the words *soared* and *surged* is misleading. A 25 percent increase over ten years represents an annual rate of inflation of 2.25 percent approximately the overall inflation rate in the U.S. during that period (American Statistical Association, 2012).

When speakers find statistics that support their ideas, they need to critically evaluate those statistics to determine if they have been manipulated or distorted in some way. The representativeness of the statistics, the correctness or accuracy of the statistical measurement, and the reliability of the source of the statistics are three areas that should be considered.

Speakers use statistics to express information in numeric form.

How representative are the statistics you are considering for inclusion in your speech?

Let's say you wanted to see whether or not students at Central Michigan University would support a campus-wide ban on smoking, extending the current building-wide smoking ban to all public spaces at the university, including parking lots. One day you walk across campus, ask twenty people this question, and twelve say yes. You now would like to claim in your speech that 60 percent of CMU students favor a more stringent smoking ban. Are you justified?

The answer is, of course not! Twenty students is not a sufficient sample to make a claim representing the views of over twenty thousand students. There would likely be other problems with your approach as well. Did your sample accurately represent the proportion of first-year students, as well as sophomores, juniors, and seniors? Did your sample include the same proportion of men and women who are on campus? Did you collect responses across all majors? Were both full-time and part-time students surveyed? Did you include students from the broad range of cultural and religious backgrounds represented on campus? Statistics should accurately represent what they claim to measure.

Are you using statistical measures correctly?

Let's say you want to give your classmates a sense of the price of homes sold in your neighborhood last year. The prices you find are as follows:

$600,000

$180,000

$171,000

$170,000

$165,000

$165,000

$160,000

There are three approaches to reporting **central tendency,** a statistical term reflecting the central or typical value in a collection of numbers: **mean, median,** and **mode.** Let's look at these three approaches to central tendency given the collection of scores reported above.

To report the mean, you sum all of the scores and then divide by the number of items. The median is the middle number in a collection of scores, and the mode is the most frequently occurring score. Here are the results for your collection of scores representing houses sold in your neighborhood.

Mean = $230,142.85

Median = $170,000

Mode = $165,000

In this case the mean score is skewed by one very expensive house. To report the price of $230,142.85 as representing the cost of the typical house sold in your neighborhood would be reporting a price that is higher than all but one home. In this case, the median or mode would allow you to report a more accurate representation of the typical price of a house sold in your neighborhood last year.

Let's consider another example. The mean salary of all faculty members at a university is $83,426. However, ten medical school professors who earn an average of $1 million a year distort this mean figure. How might different speakers make strategic choices from the options for measuring central tendency? A negotiator representing the university administration would report the mean score, allowing her to claim that faculty members at this university are paid at the second highest level in the statewide university system. A labor negotiator, however, would report the median score showing that the typical faculty member earns $70,610, allowing him to claim that faculty members at this university are paid at the second lowest level in the statewide university system. Both speakers are being truthful, but are they being completely honest? What do you think?

Are your statistics from a reliable source?

Let's say you wanted to give a speech on the environmental impact of toxic waste produced by a local coal plant. Should you consider information reported by the U.S. Environmental Protection Agency (EPA) or the company owning the coal plant? The EPA would clearly be the better choice because it does not have a vested interest in reporting anything other than accurate information. The company owning the coal plant, however, wants to minimize the appearance of any environmental damage they cause in order to minimize public calls for more stringent and costly regulations.

Assessing source reliability is not always simple, however. Complicated issues may offer competing perspectives, each of which has some validity. Consider the statistical information reported by supporters and opponents of the Affordable Care Act, also known as "Obamacare." Each side uses statistics that appear to be accurate, but you also recognize they strategically seek statistical support that represents their own partisan interests.

Being aware of statistical bias is part of what it means to be a critical consumer of statistics. Given the potential for misuse, and the actual practice of manipulation and distortion by many people and organizations, you need to find statistics gathered by objective sources that do not represent partisan interests. For example, let's return to our example of statistics used by supporters and opponents of the Affordable Care Act. Kimberly Amadeo, a writer for About.com, wrote an article entitled, "Obamacare Pros and Cons: Detailed Advantages and Disadvantages of the Affordable Care Act" (Amadeo, 2013). In this article, she reports statistical information reported by the nonpartisan Congressional Budget Office and several other reputable nonpartisan groups. The fact that there are both advantages and disadvantages shows there is an underlying complexity to this new law. Making a personal decision about how to assess this information is aided by the fact that nonpartisan groups collected the information.

Statistics allow us to summarize information in ways that are informative for an audience. There are some helpful guidelines that will help you make good choices about how to include statistics in your presentations. First, *do not overwhelm an audience with statistics.* If an audience is exposed to statistics throughout a speech, they will never be able to remember all of them, and you might even prevent them from remembering the most important statistical information you cite. If you do need to identify multiple numbers because you want to show a statistical trend (e.g., crime statistics over a decade), you could use a visual aid such as a graph. The graph can provide a clear representation of how incidents of crime have changed over time, without having to orally cite each number. Second, speakers should also *identify the sources of their statistics.* Citing your sources allows listeners to evaluate potential bias or partisanship in the person, group, or organization reporting the statistics. In addition, if you turn to high-quality, reliable sources, your listeners will respect the choices you made in doing research for your speech. Third, *provide context to explain your statistics.* Instead of simply saying, "Every day 214,000 acres of rainforest disappear," elaborate with, "Every day 214,000 acres of rainforest disappear, an area equivalent in size to New York City."

TESTIMONY

Imagine you are talking with a friend about trying out a new Indian restaurant in town called The Tandoor Oven. Your friend says, "I went there last Friday. It was fantastic, and I love Indian food. You should definitely go." You trust your friend's recommendation. He is obsessed with the Food Network and is a very good cook as well. You take out your phone, find the number of the restaurant, and make a reservation.

As this story shows, we are frequently influenced by the **testimony** of other people, particularly people we trust. Just as you are likely to be influenced by your friend's recommendation to go to a new restaurant, audience members tend to trust the opinions of people with specific knowledge or experience on specific topics. When you quote or paraphrase such people, your ideas seem more credible, and you are likely to have an impact on your audience. Let's consider the two major types of testimony: expert testimony and peer testimony.

Expert Testimony

In most instances, speakers use expert testimony, incorporating the ideas or opinions of people who are recognized experts in their fields. When you cite experts, it builds your credibility by showing that recognized experts on the subject support your general views or positions on a topic.

Expert testimony can be particularly useful if you plan to address a controversial topic where there are likely to be strong views both supporting and opposing your position. Using the Affordable Care Act as an example once again, let's say you want to give a persuasive speech arguing that it significantly improves the U.S. health care delivery system. There will likely be members of your audience who support your position, but there will also be people who strongly oppose your

We are influenced by the testimonies of people we trust.

argument. In order to improve your chances of have having some influence with those who oppose your position, it would be very important to select expert testimony from a source that is unbiased. As you are doing research, you come across a site called FactCheck.org, a project of the Annenberg Public Policy Center of the University of Pennsylvania. This site presents views by experts who support your position. Their mission statement also shows that they are unbiased in their review of public policy positions and statements made by U.S. politicians. To show this group's commitment to unbiased reporting, you could quote directly from their website:

> We are a nonpartisan, nonprofit "consumer advocate" for voters that aims to reduce the level of deception and confusion in U.S. politics. We monitor the factual accuracy of what is said by major U.S. political players. Our goal is to apply the best practices of both journalism and scholarship to increase public knowledge and understanding. We are a community of scholars at the University of Pennsylvania who address public policy issues at the local, state and federal levels.

Peer Testimony

A second type of testimony comes from our peers. Here we solicit the opinions of people who are like us. The reason we select them is because they have first-hand knowledge and experience on the topic we address in our speech. Listeners often appreciate this form of testimony because it gives a more personal perspective than can be gained from an expert.

Consider a statement made by Aimee Mullins, an American athlete, actress, and fashion model who had her legs amputated when she was one year old. In this statement she shares her views on what disability means to her:

> People presume my disability has to do with being an amputee, but that's not the case; our insecurities are our disabilities, and I struggle with those as does everyone (Rivera, 2011).

Aimee's views are personal and insightful. Her testimony is not linked to being an acknowledged expert on people with disabilities, but as a person whose understanding of disability is informed by her own life. As a result, her statement has an emotional impact that is much stronger than expert testimony.

Suggestions for Using Testimony

There are five issues to consider when including expert or peer testimony: (1) quoting versus paraphrasing, (2) quoting or paraphrasing accurately, (3) using testimony from qualified sources, (4) using testimony from unbiased sources, and (5) identifying the people you quote or paraphrase.

Quoting a person in a speech is much like quoting a person in a paper you write. If the person's quote is relatively brief (three or four sentences), eloquent or witty, and conveys meaning better than you could using your own words, then directly quoting that person is a good idea. In this case it is important to quote the person verbatim, meaning word-for-word. Paraphrasing is the better option if the wording is not particularly eloquent or is somewhat cumbersome. Also, if a quote is longer than three or four sentences, your listeners may lose interest.

Whenever you choose to quote or paraphrase someone, it is important to do so accurately. If quoting, you should do so word-for-word. If paraphrasing, make sure you do not violate the author/speaker's intended meaning of the statement. Finally, do not quote or paraphrase someone out of context to suit your purposes. For example, you prepare a speech that challenges the scientific consensus regarding human-caused (anthropogenic) global warming or climate change. You find an article published on a website, and you quote a statement made by the author:

> Respected geochemist James Lawrence Powell cites two peer-reviewed journal articles that reject anthropogenic global warming (Abrams, 2014).

Although these words were part of the first paragraph of Abrams's article, they were taken out of context. Consider the full quote:

> As geochemist James Lawrence Powell continues to prove, the only people still debating whether or not climate change is "real," and caused by human activity, are the ones who aren't doing the actual research.

In an update to his ongoing project of reviewing the literature on global warming, Powell went through every scientific study published in a peer-review journal during the calendar year 2013, finding 10,885 in total. Of those, a mere two rejected anthropogenic global warming.

The speaker who took Abrams's article and Powell's words out of context totally distorted the intended meaning. This creates a false impression and is highly unethical. When you quote or paraphrase others, you must respect the intended meaning of their words, representing them accurately.

Testimony is a valuable form of support only if the person whose words are quoted or paraphrased is qualified to address the topic. When actor and former U.S. Senator Fred Thompson advises senior citizens to get reverse mortgages, tapping into the equity of their homes, he is not making this recommendation as an expert. However, some people may connect his popularity as an actor or his work as a U.S. senator to expertise on mortgages. This is why the mortgage industry selects well-known people to sell their products. As a speaker, you should also be careful about selecting biased sources. For many years researchers employed by U.S. tobacco companies published research findings claiming that cigarette smoking did not pose a significant health hazard. Unfortunately, financial incentives given to these researchers influenced the findings they reported. So, in order to establish the legitimacy of your expert or peer you must identify your source by name and briefly identify his or her qualifications concerning the topic in question. As an example, let's return to the work done by James Lawrence Powell in his review of studies focusing on climate change. A speaker could quote him in the following manner:

James Lawrence Powell, a respected professor of geochemistry and current President of the National Physical Science Consortium, states that out of 10,885 peer-reviewed climate articles published in 2013, only two reject man-made global warming.

Due to Powell's description as a respected professor of geochemistry and current president of a national physical science organization, listeners are likely to trust his credibility as a qualified, unbiased source on the topic of climate change.

NARRATIVES

A **narrative** may be a brief story or a somewhat longer account told by a speaker to support a main point. Narratives pique listeners' interests because humans are story-telling creatures (Fisher, 1984). People love to tell stories as well as listen to them. Consider the following narrative describing the joys a skier feels when in the mountains of Northern Vermont.

I reach the top of the mountain, taking in the scenery in its entire splendor, the color of the sky, a spectacular azure. Wisps of cotton-like clouds drift lazily across the sky. In the distance, one mountain peak after another, extending over one hundred miles in all directions, their rounded tops covered in white with tipped points of forest green marking countless fir trees. Some thirty miles away I see the shimmering blue water of Lake Champlain. Flashes of white sparkle like diamonds as the sun reflects off the surface of the water. Taking a deep breath, I detect the clean, refreshing scent of pine, emanating from towering fir trees surrounding me. Pausing briefly, I smile as I begin my descent, struck simultaneously by the pristine beauty of my surroundings and my rapid acceleration as I descend steep bumpy trails. I dig my skis' edges into fresh packed powder, carving s-shaped turns rhythmically. Exhilaration turns to peacefulness as I become one with my surroundings. The bottom of the mountain approaches rapidly and all I can think about is getting to the top and starting all over again.

The preceding example uses a variety of specific details that paint a picture for listeners. Fellow skiers may visualize themselves in similar surroundings, thinking of the scenery and feelings they have experienced. People who have not skied may be drawn into the story as well. They gain a clear picture of what it's like to be at the top of a mountain in Vermont on a beautiful day and what it may feel like to rapidly descend down one. Listeners also gain a deeper understanding of this speaker's feelings toward a sport he or she loves.

Narratives can be very effective in capturing the attention of the audience or in illustrating a point. A story can be used as an attention-getter in the introduction, or at a later point in the speech when you want to show how an experience plays out in the real world. After covering complex or technical information, a speaker can tell a quick anecdote lasting five to ten seconds in order to energize the audience. Longer stories can be told when a speaker wants to draw listeners in with a vividly painted picture of an experience.

ANALOGIES

An **analogy** is a comparison based on similarities between two things, one familiar to the audience and the other less familiar. One type of analogy is a **literal analogy.** A speaker might compare the vocal style of Frank Sinatra, an iconic singer, to Landau Eugene Murphy, Jr., a recent winner of *America's Got Talent,* a reality-based singing competition. Alternatively, a speaker could compare France's policies on solar energy to policies followed in the United States. A second type of analogy is a **figurative analogy.** With this type of analogy, the two things that are compared do not belong in the same category. The speaker describes the characteristics of something familiar to the audience as a way to understand a thing that is less familiar. When listeners are exposed to this type of analogy, they can use their existing knowledge to understand new information.

Mervyn King, Governor of the Bank of England from 2003 to 2013, provides us with an excellent example of a figurative analogy. He was speaking to an audience that did not have extensive knowledge of old-fashioned central banking nor modern central banking, so he linked these concepts to something the audience knew—soccer. Everyone in the audience had probably seen coverage of the 1986 World Cup in which England's team played Argentina in the quarter final round. Diego Maradona, one of Argentina's greatest soccer players, scored two goals in this game, clinching the game for his team. The first goal is commonly referred to as the "Hand of God" goal, because Diego used his hand to score (an illegal move), but he was so quick and deceptive the referee did not detect the move. The second goal was voted Goal of the Century by the Federation of International Football Association (FIFA.com, 2002). Here are King's words:

> Maradona's infamous "hand of God" goal, which should have been disallowed, reflected old-fashioned central banking. It was full of mystique and he was lucky to get away with it. But the second goal, where Maradona beat five players, even though he ran in a straight line, was an example of modern practice. How can you beat five players by running in a straight line? The answer is that the English defenders reacted to what they expected Maradona to do. Monetary policy works in a similar way. Market interest rates react to what the central bank is expected to do (Giles, 2007).

One approach to using analogies is to draw upon ideas used by your classmates in their speeches. By taking this approach, you know your classmates will understand the idea you are developing. You will also be expressing goodwill by showing you have learned from one of your classmate's speeches. Another good source for analogies is to draw upon familiar places and traditions on your campus. Such analogies are easy for your fellow classmates to relate to.

SUGGESTIONS FOR USING SUPPORT MATERIAL

Quality supporting materials build audience interest and help them better understand your topic. You can also use supporting material to present or prove certain facts (e.g., human activity is causing climate change). What can you do to select the most effective supporting materials for your speech? Consider the following suggestions.

CITE SOURCES ORALLY DURING YOUR SPEECH

The bibliography or reference page you include with your speech outline lists all of the sources you used in constructing your speech. Your classmates, however, will not have your outline in front of them while you speak. So you need to tell your audience where you got your information and why the source is qualified and credible. For example, a speaker should identify the book, magazine, newspaper, or web document from which information is taken. The author or organization responsible for producing the document should be identified, as well as the qualifications of that source, to produce credible and unbiased information or arguments. Finally, the date the document was published or posted should be identified.

Here is an example of a speaker following these recommendations:

> The Institute for College Access and Success reported on their website in December 2013 that 71 percent of students from U.S. colleges and universities are graduating with some level of debt, with the average borrower owing $26,000.

The listeners of this speech know this information is from an institute that focuses on college access and success for U.S. students, and it is based on a recent study. If they want to read the report that includes these statistics, the listeners can go to the website of the institute.

USE A VARIETY OF SUPPORT MATERIAL

If a speaker uses only one type of support material, listeners may become fatigued and lose interest in the speech. You do not have to use each of the six types of support material described in this chapter, but using two or three different types will sustain the interest of your audience. For example, a personal example in the introduction pulls the listeners into your speech because they now know why the topic is important to you. A carefully developed analogy used later in the speech can help your audience understand an important point concerning an unfamiliar topic. Finally, a startling statistic convinces the audience that the problem you are focusing on is significant.

APPEAL TO DIFFERENT LEARNING STYLES

Educators have long recognized that people have different styles of learning and are more responsive when presented with information conveyed in their personal style. *Active learners* want to know what they can do with the information they receive. *Reflective learners* want to be challenged to think about a topic. *Visual learners* learn best when they can see things visually. *Verbal learners* get more out of written or spoken explanations.

When selecting support materials, speakers should consider how they might meet the needs of people with different learning styles. To appeal to active learners you could involve the audience in an activity that draws on one of your support materials. For example, a student giving a speech on origami (the Japanese art of paper folding) may demonstrate a simple but elegant fold using a sheet of paper provided for classmates, allowing them to follow along. For reflective learners, you could pose a thought-provoking question such as, "What will we do if the predictions of climate scientists are true, and catastrophic storms become the norm all over the world?" For visual learners, graphs or pictures could be incorporated into the presentation. Finally, for verbal learners you could include a vivid extended example.

SUMMARY

In this chapter, we described the process of supporting your ideas during a speech. We first focused on definitions. Speakers define terms to make sure audience members define words and ideas the same way they do. If understanding a specific term is critical to understanding your speech, and some audience members may not be familiar with it, then you should define the term.

Second, we considered the use of examples. Examples give life to a speech, making it more specific and personal. Brief examples are short statements made to illustrate a point. Extended examples give speakers the opportunity to tell a story vividly and dramatically by using rich and descriptive language, pulling listeners into the speech. We also recognized that speakers do not always have to use factual examples, so we looked at the use of hypothetical examples in describing an imaginary or fictitious event or person.

Third, we described the use of statistics. Speakers use statistics whenever they express information in numeric form. Statistics should be presented clearly and simply during a speech. Look out for potential manipulation and distortion by sources that present statistical information. Statistics should also be evaluated for representativeness, source reliability, and correct use of measurement. Guidelines for including statistics in speeches include not overwhelming the audience with statistical information, always identifying the source, and providing context to explain the statistics.

Fourth, we covered the use of testimony, both by experts and peers. When you include expert testimony it builds your credibility by showing that recognized experts on the subject support your general views or positions on a topic. Relying on experts can be particularly useful if you plan to address a controversial topic where there are likely to be strong views both supporting and opposing your position. Peer testimony involves statements by people who are like us. We select our peers for testimony because they have first-hand knowledge and experience on the topics we are addressing in our speeches. Finally, we looked at quoting versus paraphrasing, quoting or paraphrasing accurately, using testimony from qualified and unbiased sources, and identifying the people you quote or paraphrase in your speech.

Fifth, we detailed how narratives may be used in a speech, either as brief stories or longer accounts. People love to both tell stories and to listen to them. Stories can draw listeners into a speech, especially when the speaker vividly paints a picture of an experience.

Sixth, we described the use of analogies, comparisons based on similarities between two things, one familiar to the audience, the other less familiar. We discussed both literal and figurative analogies and their ability to help audience members use existing knowledge to understand new information.

Finally, we offered suggestions for using support materials in speeches. Speakers should cite sources orally during their presentations, use a variety of support materials in each speech, and appeal to different learning styles among their listeners.

REFERENCES

Abrams, L. (2014, March 25). 10,883 out of 10,885 scientific articles agree: Global warming is happening, and humans are to blame. *Salon.com.* Retrieved March 30, 2014, from http://www.salon.com/2014/03/25/10853_out_of_10855_scientists_agree_man_made_global_warming_is_happening/

Amadeo, K. (2013, December 14). Obamacare Pros and Cons: Detailed Advantages and Disadvantages of the Affordable Care Act. *About.com.* Retrieved March 30, 2014, from http://useconomy.about.com/od/healthcarereform/a/Obamacare-Pros-And-Cons.htm

American Statistical Association. (2012, August 1). Misuse of Statistics a National Problem. Retrieved March 28, 2014, from www.magazine.amstat.org/blog/2012/08/01statviewliteracy/8_12/

Bai, M. (1997, December 8). A chief's fall from grace. *Newsweek, 130* (No. 23), 42.

FactCheck.org. (2014, March 30). Our Mission. Retrieved March 30, 2014, from http://useconomy.about.com/gi/o.htm?zi=1/XJ&zTi=1&sdn=useconomy&cdn=newsissues&tm=29&f=00&su=p284.13.342.ip_&tt=65&bt=9&bts=9&zu=http%3A//factcheck.org/2012/06/romney-obama-uphold-health-care-falsehoods/

FIFA.com. (2002, May 30). Diego Maradona goal voted the FIFA World Cup™ Goal of the Century. Retrieved March 30, 2014, from http://www.fifa.com/newscentre/news/newsid=82406/index.html

Gallagher, R. (2012, July 20). Skype won't comment on whether it can now eavesdrop on conversations. *Slate.* Retrieved March 30, 2014, from http://www.slate.com/blogs/future_tense/2012/07/20/skype_won_t_comment_on_whether_it_can_now_eavesdrop_on_conversations_.html

Giles, C. (2007, September 7). Alone Among Governors. *Financial Times.* Retrieved March 30, 2014, from http://www.ft.com/cms/s/0/5f273b40-5d63-11dc-8d22-0000779fd2ac.html#axzz2xSUukrLX

Institute for College Access and Success. (2013, December). Student Debt and the Class of 2012. Retrieved March 30, 2014, from http://projectonstudentdebt.org/files/pub/classof2012.pdf

Rivera, J. (2011, January 5). The inspirational Aimee Mullins. *The Huffington Post.* Retrieved March 30, 2014, from http://www.huffingtonpost.com/jeff-rivera/the-inspirational-aimee-m_b_804774.html

Schwartz, S. K. (2012, May 7). The inflation of life—Cost of raising a child has soared. *CNBC.* Retrieved March 30, 2014, from www.cnbc.com/id/46797268

Tal-Or, N., Boninger, D. S., Poran, A., & Gleicher, F. (2004). Counterfactual thinking as a mechanism of narrative persuasion. *Human Communication Research, 30,* 301–328.

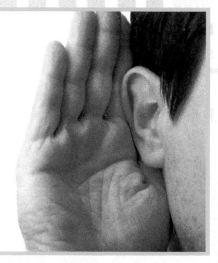

CHAPTER 9

Listening

Chantia walks tentatively to the front of the classroom. She is prepared to present her first speech in her COM 101 class. She pauses briefly, looking up to make eye contact with her classmates. Somewhat predictably, this is what she sees:

Several of her classmates are studying for their psychology midterm. They have textbooks on their laps and notes on the desk. Their eyes dart from the textbook back to their notes, never looking at Chantia. Other students with heads down are scrolling their Facebook page on smartphones as they smile, lost in social media.

Another group of students are seated in the back of the room. They are sleeping off the effects of a long night downtown the night before. One student has her elbow bent with her chin resting in the palm of her hand. Another student's head is tilted back with his mouth wide open, perhaps dreaming of his last visit to the dentist. The rest of the group have their arms crossed and their chins on their chests. Occasionally, their heads jerk upward trying to look awake, but they nod back to sleep within seconds.

The students planning to speak after Chantia are looking over their notecards, glancing away periodically while moving their lips, forming silent words. They are in the room with her, but Chantia's words bounce off them.

Finally, Chantia sees her roommate Carmen. She is listening with all the appropriate nonverbal behavior: alert and attentive appearance, direct eye contact, and apparent note-taking; yet, Chantia is suspicious. Chantia knows Carmen has a date later that evening—one she has been looking forward to all week. Halfway through her speech, Chantia realizes Carmen is not taking notes on her speech; she is writing her date's name over and over again on a piece of paper. Carmen is only pretending to listen to Chantia's speech.

Chantia is justifiably angry but she realizes that she, too, has fallen into each of these categories as an audience member. Listening is a skill too many people do not develop. People who speak in public realize this all too well. Both speaking and listening are essential elements of the public speaking process. In fact, if people stop listening, there is no reason to talk.

Chantia's example illustrates the extent to which so many people are poor listeners and discourteous audience members. If you were having a conversation with a friend, how would you feel if that friend yawned and fell asleep? What would your reaction be if they turned away to look at their notes for an exam or started to post a tweet? You would perceive your friend's behavior as rude. Although most of us would never think of being this rude in a conversation with a friend, when we sit in an audience we can be terribly rude, and this can be painfully obvious to the speaker.

We spend the greatest amount of our communication time listening to others; yet, we receive considerably less formal education in listening than we do in speaking, writing, or reading (Ferrari, 2012; Hardman, 2012; Sanabria, 2004; Westra, 1996). Sadly, the average listener remembers only half of what he or she hears immediately after listening to a message, and a mere quarter of what was said after forty-eight hours (Gibson & Walker, 2011; Liraz, 2013; Nichols, 2009). These statistics may offer explanations for why you perform poorly on a final examination despite being present for all of the class meetings, why married people misunderstand one another's needs, or why a worker is not able to follow a manager's clear directions. Most importantly, this information proves why we need to be better listeners.

INTRODUCTION

Your role as an audience member in this course is just as important as your role as a speaker. For every speech you deliver, you will listen to twenty-five or more speeches. Overall, you will hear between seventy-five and one hundred speeches during the course of the semester. In fact, you will learn more by listening than by speaking, if you listen attentively. Listening is also important in other communication contexts, whether listening to a friend or family member in a conversation, or attempting to understand information presented by a coworker or supervisor in an organization. Listening effectively helps us develop and improve our relationships with others, and it helps us to learn from others. The goal of this chapter is to explain the listening process, disprove the myths of listening, describe the benefits of good listening, decipher the reasons for poor listening, and teach you how to listen critically.

ARE YOU REALLY LISTENING?

Many students equate hearing with listening; yet, hearing and listening are distinctly different activities. Hearing is an automatic physical function in which the ear receives sound. Hearing does not require any specific training or instruction. If an individual experiences a hearing loss, that loss can be diagnosed and often treated by using a variety of electronic hearing devices ranging from simple hearing aids to cochlear implants. Listening is a deliberative process, however, involving more than a physiological response to sound, and it is a skill that can be learned. Wolvin and Coakley (1993) explain, "listening involves the cognitive and affective processing of verbal and nonverbal messages through an intricate internal system which we are just beginning to understand" (p. xi). Specifically, listening involves **hearing, attending, interpreting, understanding,** and **resolving.**

Hearing

The first component in the listening process is hearing. At this stage, the ear receives sound waves, which stimulate neurological impulses to the brain. Any weaknesses in an individual's physical hearing mechanism may cause complications in the listening process. According to Brooks and Heath (1993), human speech frequencies fluctuate from 125 to 8,000 cycles per second, with the majority of words ranging from 1,000 to 7,500 cycles per second, which is acceptable for auditory ability. Although we must be able to hear a message in order to listen, we do not necessarily listen to everything we hear. We often hear things without actually listening, meaning we do not assign meaning to or interpret these things. A person must choose to listen. According to Mintz and Vasile (2000) "...you hear with your ears, but you listen with your brain" (p. 71).

Attention

The process of attention is one of focusing our conscious awareness on specific environmental stimuli (Tubbs, 2012). Unlike the physiological process of hearing, attention requires a conscious choice on the part of the listener. One specific type of attention communication researchers refer to is **selective attention.** The process of selective attention is one in which a listener focuses on certain stimuli in the environment while filtering out others. For example, a person who concentrates her attention on reading a book while listening to music in the background is engaged in selective attention.

Interpretation

To interpret a message is to literally give it meaning. Individuals may take the interpretation process in varying directions, however. When a group of people is exposed to sounds or a specific message from a speaker, each person may attend to different stimuli or interpret those stimuli uniquely. When we interpret, we decode the message by attaching meanings to the verbal and nonverbal symbols produced by the speaker. For example, listeners will attach meaning to a speaker's words as well as his or her tone of voice and facial expressions. If a speaker is giving a speech on euthanasia and is very passionate in how she uses her voice and shows her emotions through facial expressions, a listener may recognize this speaker's commitment to her position on the topic. Alternatively, if some audience members hear "youth in Asia," they may not be prepared to move on to the next step in the listening process— understanding the speaker's message.

Listening skills improve our relationships and help us learn.

Understanding

Once we have interpreted a speaker's message, we begin to fit the message into our own existing framework of knowledge and beliefs. *Interpretation* is based on deciphering a speaker's language; *understanding* is recognizing and discerning a speaker's intent (sarcastic, humorous, thoughtful, etc.). Is the speaker attempting to entertain me, inform me, persuade me, or ask me for help? In other words, what is the speaker's purpose?

Understanding refers to the process of assigning meaning to the words we hear in a manner that corresponds to the meaning intended by the message sender (Tubbs, 2012). As effective listeners, we need to withhold our tendency to judge or evaluate the speaker's message, and focus our listening effort on trying to understand the meaning the speaker has aimed to communicate.

Resolution

Once the message is heard, attended to, interpreted, and understood, the listener must decide what to do with the message. The final step in the listening process is the resolution process. Specifically, the listener must resolve to accept the message, reject it, take action on it, or merely try to remember it, delaying resolution until a later time.

Clearly, we are not consciously aware of going through these five steps each time we listen to a speaker. Yet, understanding that listening is a complex process helps us become more aware of problems that may exist, so we may determine if we are really listening.

LISTENING MYTHS

LISTENING IS EASY

Some people believe listening is like breathing—it comes naturally and subconsciously. However, assuming that because you have been breathing since birth that you breathe well enough to sing like Mariah Carey is probably erroneous. Similarly, just because we have heard others talk to us all of our lives does not mean that we are expert listeners. We assume that because it is easy to relax and listen to our favorite television show, it would be just as easy to listen to a class lecture or a friend talk about the problems he is having with his elderly parents. Instead, we need to recognize that effective listening is a complex process requiring energy and effort. A person is not born a good listener; rather, a good listener is made through hard work.

LISTENING IS A MATTER OF INTELLIGENCE

A second common myth about listening is that listening is a matter of intelligence: "I am smart; therefore I know I am a good listener." Intelligence does not guarantee effective listening. Although many highly intelligent people have been taught effective listening skills, equal numbers have not. Despite their intelligence, some people may fail to listen carefully.

LISTENING DOES NOT REQUIRE PLANNING

A third popular myth is that there is no need to plan for effective listening—it just happens. Of course, most of our listening in day-to-day conversations is unexpected and unplanned. However, if you know in advance that you will be in a listening situation, you should plan ahead. For example, in a public speaking course, students provide each other with feedback. An audience member who understands the speech assignment and the criteria for evaluating the speech will provide the most helpful feedback to his or her classmates. In addition to learning to prepare and present speeches, it is crucial to plan ahead to analyze critically the speeches you hear.

READING AND LISTENING INVOLVE SIMILAR SKILLS

One common misconception people hold is that listening and reading involve similar types of skills. This leads to the assumption that because a person is a good reader, he or she will also be a good listener. However, there is no educational research to suggest that the skills one acquires in reading are transferable to listening situations (Kearney & Plax, 2012). A person can be excellent at reading comprehension, yet choose to be inattentive to most speakers when placed in a listening role. Conversely, a person may be a poor reader but display excellent listening skills as an audience member at a public lecture or as a friend listening to the problems of a next-door neighbor. Since reading and listening involve different types of skills, it is important for teachers to devote instructional time to both activities.

BENEFITS OF BEING A GOOD LISTENER

The process of communication allows people to collaborate through messages to create and participate in social reality. Effective listening is an essential part of this process. People would not be able to create and participate in social reality without listening. In fact, listening is what makes collaboration possible, with each person attending to, comprehending, and interpreting other's spoken messages. So, let's consider the four benefits of being a good listener.

Relationship Satisfaction

To be a good partner in a relationship, one must be a good listener (Bodie, 2011). Listening to a friend, spouse, parent, child, coworker, or supervisor helps to create productive and close relationships (Bodie, in press). Think of how often one person says in the heat of an argument, "You're not listening to me!" In healthy relationships, each person values the listening behavior of the other person. When a relationship is under stress or there is a need for social support, listening is critical (Jones, 2011). Importantly, to be a good listener requires work and the commitment to refrain from judging or evaluating the other person.

Community Activism

If you want to become more involved in your community, you must listen to the needs of other community members. In fact, listening is one of the most important skills for democracy to flourish because social problems can only be resolved when people listen to one another's ideas and arguments (Edwards, Edwards, Wahl, & Myers, 2013). When those who live in a community meet to discuss the issues and problems they have in common, we have the essence of grassroots democracy. This is what it means to be part of an engaged community, and it requires good listening abilities.

Media Awareness

In this Information Age, listening to media is a prominent part of everyone's day. For this reason, it is important to become **media aware,** having the ability to selectively attend to and evaluate media messages. When we work to develop our listening skills, we will be able to make better decisions about how to interpret and evaluate the messages we hear, and we can focus on the messages that most need our attention. Given all of the media choices we have through television and the Internet, we need to make good choices about which media sources are worth our time and effort. Listening critically to media will help us choose wisely (Van de Vord, 2010).

Job Success

One of the most important skills in the workplace is being a good listener (Flynn, Valikoski, & Grau, 2008). In the typical work-day, most of an employee's time is spent listening to others. We may listen to supervisors giving us directions, to coworkers in a department meeting, or to customers asking questions about our organization's products or services. Listening is also important to your success in college. Students listen to their instructors in order to remember, process, and think critically about course material. Just as classroom success is based on one's ability to listen (Cooper & Buchanan, 2010), so is success in the workplace.

REASONS FOR POOR LISTENING

Pseudo-listening

If you are like most students, you have learned how to fake listen. You sit in class and stare directly at the instructor as she or he speaks, but your mind is far away in a pleasant daydream. Or, rather than paying attention to what is being said by your instructor and classmates, you are checking social media on your smartphone, tablet, or laptop. Every so often, you are drawn back to what is going on in class: the instructor or a fellow student makes a witty comment, and while classmates laugh, you smile politely, pre-tending you heard the humorous remark. Perhaps the instructor writes a word or two on the chalkboard or displays a PowerPoint slide, and you respectfully copy the ideas down in your notes. Although you feel somewhat concerned that you are not listening, you tell yourself that you can read the material in the textbook later, or study with a friend before the exam. So back you go to your private little world.

Pseudo-listening is a strategy used to fake our attention with our friends, in classes, and as audience members when our fellow students give their speeches. One of the reasons we fake listen is because it is so difficult to pay attention. According to Goss (1982) the average speaking rate is 125–150 words a minute; however, the brain can process from 400–500 words a minute. Since the listener's mind is working faster than the speaker's rate of speech, we have plenty of spare "brain time"; thus, the tendency to daydream or surf the Internet. To camouflage our lack of focused attention on messages, we have learned to feign our attention by pseudo-listening.

You should avoid pseudo-listening for three reasons: (1) you are rarely fooling anyone, (2) it is habit forming, and (3) you miss a substantial amount of valuable information. It is not uncommon to be caught pseudo-listening. Most of us can recall an embarrassing situation when a teacher called on us and we could not answer the question because we were not paying attention. As coy as many of us believe we are, many speakers are sensitive to the deception of fake listening: a blank expression, an unblink-ing gaze, and a faraway look. Even if you are not exposed, another reason to avoid pseudo-listening is because it is habit forming. Many individuals find it hard to resist daydreaming, surfing the Internet, or checking social media. The reason this occurs is that we have watched so much television, seen so many movies, and spent so much time being stimulated by material on the Internet, that we expect all messages to be fast-moving and entertaining. We feign attention to avoid dull or difficult material. These habits are so deeply ingrained that we go on automatic daydream pilot or start scrolling Facebook messages as soon as a speaker begins to talk. This causes us to miss a lot of interesting and valuable information. If we pretend to listen we will not understand what we hear, and we may pass along partial information or misinformation to others.

Osborn, Osborn, and Osborn (2011) suggest a self-experiment to combat pseudo-listening. As you take notes in your lecture class, put an X in the margin each time you notice your attention wandering. By each X jot down a few words identifying the reason, for example, "thinking about date tonight" or "received a Facebook message." After class, count the number of times you faked attention and note the causes. This exercise will help you identify the reasons your mind wandered and then determine if a pattern of inattention exists.

Pseudo-listening causes us to miss out on valuable information.

Prejudgments

Many of us have strong positive or negative attitudes toward a speaker or message that can diminish our listening ability. Admittedly, all of us have personal prejudices of one kind or another. Personal prejudice confines the translation of a message so that we do not need to consider changing our beliefs or expectations. Whether these prejudices are with the speaker or the message, listening problems will occur when these personal biases prevent us from receiving information accurately. Let's examine more closely some of the prejudgments we may make against the speaker and the message.

THE SPEAKER

Justin attended a state university in Pennsylvania. He signed up for a course called Marriage and Family Counseling. On the first day of class he was surprised to see a Catholic priest walk in and announce that he would be teaching the course. Justin thought to himself, "What does a celibate priest know about marriage? Why should I listen to him?" Justin's initial reaction was to reject the speaker, and he chose not to listen. His choice was unfortunate because the priest taught an excellent course based on the knowledge he gained from counseling couples over thirty years.

Sometimes we reject a speaker before he or she has spoken a word. Perhaps we dislike the speaker's looks, dress, or the organization the speaker represents. All of us have biases that prevent us from receiving messages. For example, if a speaker has high professional status we may accept the message more readily with less questioning and criticism. We are less likely to question the message of a pastor, a physician, an attorney, or a professor when that person is speaking about a topic within their area of expertise. Yet, when a lower-status person, such as a child, makes an intelligent or profound comment, we are likely to say, "Where did you learn that?," "Who told you that?," or "How do you know that is true?"

One of the more remarkable examples of the power of a child's words is a speech given by twelve-year-old Severn Suzuki from Vancouver, Canada. In 1992 Severn, founder of the Environmental Children's Organization (ECO), traveled five thousand miles to the United Nations in New York City to give a speech on why the leaders of the world must take action to stop the damage done to the environment by human beings. She is passionate and persuasive. A video of the speech went viral on YouTube with over twenty-seven million views, and it is popularly known as "The Girl Who Silenced the World for Five Minutes." You may see a video of her speech to the UN on YouTube at http://www.youtube.com/watch?v=TQmz6Rbpnu0. Unfortunately, there were probably some in the audience who did not pay close attention to Severn's words because she was a child. Watch the speech and see what you think. I believe you will conclude that she is a speaker who deserves the attention of listeners around the world.

We also prejudge speakers due to presentational problems. Speakers may talk too fast and be difficult to follow. On the contrary, speakers who talk too slowly may soothe you to sleep. Perhaps the speaker distracts you because she keeps braiding and unbraiding her hair while giving her presentation. Or you can't imagine what the speaker was thinking when he put on that tie this morning.

When you find yourself focusing more on the speaker and less on the message, remind yourself to be a responsible listener. As a listener, you need to remove these distractions—concentrate on what the speaker says, move to a closer vacant seat, and don't go through the motions of pseudo-listening.

THE MESSAGE

Kevin spent weeks preparing an informative speech for his public speaking class. He decided to present his speech on his favorite topic, How to Design an Actor's Website. As an aspiring actor, Kevin believes a high-quality website can be a very effective marketing tool. He also plans to talk about how personal websites can promote careers in other areas. However, once Kevin began to speak, several audience members quickly dismissed his topic.

One audience member, Allison, is a fifty-five-year-old nontraditional student who recently read a book about how technology would destroy human civilization as we know it. Allison has developed strong convictions against the rapid growth and use of technology. She believes the more involved we are with technology, the less likely we are to interact with others face-to-face. When Allison heard Kevin use the words *technology, computer,* and *website,* she reacted to more than just the objective meaning of these words, she responded to emotional meanings as well.

Another audience member, Sam, had heard three prior presentations that year on website design for career marketing. Sam thought, "How many times am I going to hear this speech?" Sam was hasty to suspend listening to Kevin's speech, as she believed she had heard it before.

A third classmate, Taylor, is tired of listening to Kevin talk about his acting career. Taylor wants to be a mechanical engineer. What does anything about an actor's website have to do with him? Taylor decided to check email messages on his smartphone while Kevin spoke.

Just as we make judgments about speakers before they speak, we also make judgments about the message before we attempt to understand it. Listening problems occur when we prejudge the message to be too complex, too trivial, or inconsistent with our previously-held beliefs.

Admittedly, speeches that are full of unfamiliar words or are poorly organized make listening difficult. Often we decide that listening is just "not worth the effort," and we give up. Conversely, when we hear a message that we have heard before, we quickly assume we will not hear anything new on the subject. Finally, we may suspend listening to a speech because we disagree with the speaker's topic or speech purpose. We might even argue silently in our minds instead of listening to the speaker's message. As an effective listener, we need to recognize these barriers and take responsibility in the listening process.

LISTENING AND CRITICAL THINKING

As you work on improving your skills as a listener, you can also become a more critical thinker. People who think critically are able to evaluate the information they are exposed to. Critical listeners are able to assess the accuracy, value, or potential bias in the information or ideas they read or hear. Wolvin and Coakley (1991), in a survey of listening training programs in Fortune 500 Corporations, identified four types of listening that can help us develop our critical thinking skills: appreciative, empathic, comprehensive, and critical. Let's consider each one.

Appreciative Listening involves listening for pleasure or enjoyment. When we listen to our favorite music, watch a stand-up comic, or listen to an entertaining speech, we derive a sense of pleasure from the experience. We may also derive pleasure from listening to stories told by friends and family members, and sharing our stories with them.

Empathic Listening involves providing emotional support for a person we are talking to. If a friend has experienced a personal disappointment and they are sad, we listen with concern and show our support in their time of need. Importantly, in this listening environment it is important that we give the person who needs our help all of our attention. This shows the other person that nothing is more important at this moment than providing support.

Comprehensive Listening focuses on understanding the message of the speaker. When we listen to a professor's lecture, or listen to directions for cooking a favorite gourmet meal, we listen to comprehend so we can apply or use the information in the future.

Critical Listening is for evaluating a message so we can determine whether to accept or reject it. When we listen to a campaign speech by a local politician or a sales pitch by a real estate developer, we critique the message so we can make a good decision based on what we hear.

Each of these four types of listening is important. For the purposes of public speaking, however, we need to focus on comprehensive listening and critical listening. These two types of listening are most often used when listening to speeches in class or lectures by professors. Comprehensive and critical listening are also helpful when we communicate at work or when we hear political messages, and each type of listening is tied closely to critical thinking.

Critical thinking involves a number of distinct skills. First, in order to effectively comprehend an oral message, we need to be able to summarize information, recall key facts, and distinguish main points from minor points. Second, effective critical thinking is displayed when we are able to distinguish fact from opinion, identify weaknesses in reasoning, or evaluate the quality of evidence.

LISTENING CRITICALLY TO SPEECHES

An important dimension of the critical listening process is to critique the speeches that you hear. One purpose of speech criticism is to make a personal decision about whether you should accept or reject the message that is presented by the speaker. Learning to become an effective speech critic can also improve your own ability to speak as you learn to concentrate on effective and ineffective speaking techniques. So, how can you go about performing a competent speech critique?

Critiquing the Introduction

Critical listening begins with an assessment of the speaker's opening comments. One of a speaker's initial goals is to establish favorable attention and interest in the topic. When listening to a speech, you can evaluate the attempt made by the speaker to capture your interest in the topic. For example, did the speaker start the speech with an interesting story or personal example? Why do you think this attempt to capture the interest of the audience was effective or ineffective?

In the introduction of the speech, the speaker should provide a clear, specific purpose that is applicable to the audience. Can you discern the speaker's purpose from his or her introductory comments? If you cannot discern the purpose of the speech in the introduction, what purpose should have been identified for the audience? In addition, the introduction of a speech should preview the main points to be covered in the remainder of the speech. How effective is the speaker in clarifying the main points to be covered in the body of the presentation?

Critiquing Audience Adaptation

When evaluating the content of the speech, the listener's attention should be directed at a variety of concerns. First, you need to make a decision about the extent to which the speaker adapted the speech to the audience's interests, knowledge, and attitudes. What exactly did the speaker do to adapt to this particular audience? Do you think the speaker could have made any different choices in adapting to this audience? What choices could he or she have made differently?

Critiquing Main Points and Pattern of Organization

As you focus on the content of a speech, the speaker's main points should be clear. Can you paraphrase each main point? If not, the speaker may not have worded each point in a manner that is clearly discernible to the audience. In addition, the organization of the speech should be obvious to listeners and appropriate to the topic. For example, if a topical pattern of organization is selected, does each main point seem central to the purpose the speaker attempted to fulfill? Can you think of alternative main points that might have been more important or interesting to cover? Finally, the speaker should use transitions between the main points of the speech and also provide internal summaries to help audience members remember important arguments or pieces of information.

Critiquing Supporting Evidence

Beyond identifying main points, a more specific form of content assessment is to evaluate the supporting evidence a speaker incorporates into a speech. Evidence can be evaluated along four criteria: accuracy, objectivity, relevance, and sufficiency. First, does the evidence cited by the speaker seem accurate, or are you aware of different or competing information that contradicts what the speaker has said? For example, those who believe that human activity is causing climate change point to the high level of consensus among climate scientists that we are living in an era of climate change. People who oppose this view point to a small number of scientists who cast doubt on the certainty of climate change. Whose evidence appears stronger or more convincing, and why? Second, is the evidence taken from objective sources? For example, a spokesperson from Exxon-Mobil may argue that electric engines will never be able to replace gas engines in automobiles. Is this testimony free of bias, or does the Exxon-Mobil Corporation have something to gain by persuading the public to accept this viewpoint? Third, the evidence a speaker cites in a speech should be relevant to the claims he or she is trying to advance. You should be able to clearly understand the reason why a particular piece of evidence is included in the speech. For example, a person giving a speech that opposes capital punishment could point to historical statistics showing that the death penalty does not reduce the rate of murder in states that employ it. This evidence is cited because it calls into question the moral justification for taking a person's life for a capital crime even though it does not create a safer society. Finally, does the speaker cite evidence that sufficiently supports the point being made in the speech? For example, a speaker may wish to advance the argument that violent crime is increasing in Detroit, Michigan. However, if the only evidence she offers is personal testimony from three city residents, you can question the sufficiency of the evidence offered to support the point. To support this particular point, the speaker could have turned to evidence from the F.B.I. or some other government organization that compiles accurate records of crimes reported in major U.S. cities.

Critiquing Logic, Reasoning, and Emotional Appeals

The final dimension of content that should be evaluated by the critical listener is the speaker's use of logic, reasoning, and emotional appeals. As you listen to the speech does the speaker present ideas in a logical manner? Does the progression of ideas make sense to you? Can you follow the speaker's train of thought, or do you not see how the parts of their ideas fit together? What line of reasoning does the speaker appear to follow? Can you think of any alternative line of reasoning that makes more sense to you? If so, what line of reasoning would you follow if giving a speech on this topic? Finally, does the speaker use emotional appeals? If so, you should judge the appropriateness of each one. For example, does the emotional appeal effectively advance the speaker's purpose, or does the speaker unnecessarily pull at the heartstrings of audience members without adequate justification?

Critiquing Delivery

The next major dimension of speech criticism is to evaluate the speaker's delivery. Although you should not allow a speaker's delivery to distract you from the message, it is appropriate to study the methods different speakers use to present their ideas. In fact, by focusing on a speaker's delivery, you can learn how to present your own speeches more effectively.

A good speaker establishes eye contact with audience members. This means that the speaker looks into the eyes of audience members, not over their heads. There are also dimensions of voice quality that you can focus on as a listener. Does the speaker vary the tone or pitch of his or her voice, or is the speech presented in a monotone manner? More importantly, does the speaker use a lively and expressive voice to bring ideas to life for the audience? A speaker should also use appropriate language and grammar in a speech. For example, does the speaker use technical terms that are not defined for audience members, or does the speaker word ideas in an unnecessarily complex manner? Conversely, does the speaker use language that is too simple for audience members in a college classroom? Appropriate language use also refers to avoidance of "filler" expressions such as "um," "like," or "you know." Finally, a speech should be free of grammatical errors. Although conventions of grammar can be violated in informal conversations among friends, grammatical rules must be followed carefully in public speaking situations.

One of the goals of a public speaking class is to give students experience in extemporaneous speaking. This means that your speeches should be delivered in a conversational manner without excessive reliance on notes. When you listen to a speech, does it seem as if the speaker is talking conversationally with you, or is the speaker reading from notecards?

The final aspect of delivery that is important to critique is how the speaker uses his or her body. For example, does the speaker use hand gestures to reinforce or accent ideas for audience members? Are the gestures spontaneous and natural, or did they appear stiff or awkward? Does the speaker stand in one location throughout the speech, or does he or she move periodically from one side of the room to the other? Finally, does the speaker commit any physical distractions such as swaying, fidgeting, or pacing back and forth in front of the room?

Critiquing Visual Aids

If visual aids are used in the speech, you can evaluate their effectiveness. Can the audience members clearly see the pictures, images, model, slides, or words? Does the visual aid add to the information presented in the speech, or could the speaker have eliminated the visual aid? Visual aids should also be prepared carefully, look professional, and reflect effort on the part of the speaker. As you examine the visual aid, does it seem that he or she prepared it with care, or does it appear to have been designed carelessly?

Critiquing the Conclusion

The final part of a speech that can be evaluated by listeners is a speaker's conclusion. An effective conclusion reminds the audience of the main points of the speech. In addition, the speaker should specify what the audience can do with the information that is presented or what the audience should think or do in response to the speech. The last component of the speech should end strongly, and the speaker's closing words should be planned carefully. Does the speaker end the speech in a strong or thoughtful manner or does the speaker end with an awkward or unprofessional phrase? For example, a speaker may end a speech with inappropriate comments such as, "Well that's all I have to say," or "I'm sure glad that's over," or "Any questions?" In short, the closing words should be planned as carefully as the opening, or any other point in the body of the presentation.

Becoming an effective speech critic takes practice; however, it is worth the effort. Your ability to remember and learn from the speeches you listen to is linked to your ability to critique oral messages. In addition, you can become a more effective speaker yourself by carefully examining how other people speak in public. Focus carefully on the speeches presented in your class as well to speeches you hear in other settings. Perhaps most importantly, as you develop your speech criticism skills, you become a more critical consumer of the messages you hear.

SUMMARY

In this course, you will spend significantly more time listening than speaking. This is an opportunity for you to learn to become an effective listener as well as an impressive speaker. Here are some helpful ideas to make you a better listener:

- Remember that listening is a skill that can be developed. An initial step involves understanding the processing of messages through an internal system. More specifically, listening involves hearing, attending, interpreting, understanding, and resolving.

- Try to dispel the listening myths: listening is easy, listening is a matter of intelligence, listening does not require planning, and reading and listening involve similar skills.

- Recognize the benefits of being a good listener. Good listeners are more likely to have more satisfying personal and professional relationships. They are more likely to be active in community decision-making and to be critical consumers of media messages. Finally, good listeners are more likely to be successful at their jobs.

- Be aware that there are barriers to effective listening: pseudo-listening or faking attention, prejudging the speaker based on stereotypes, and prejudging the message because it is too complex, too boring, or opposes your point of view.

- Try to listen critically by evaluating your classmates' speeches. A speech critique is a positive and constructive effort to help your classmates improve their speeches. Does the introduction gain attention? Is the purpose clear? Is the speech adapted to audience interests, knowledge, and attitudes? Is the speech well organized? Are the main points clear? Are the main points supported well? Is the speech well researched? Is the organizational pattern logical? Is the delivery conversational? Does the speaker use his or her voice and body effectively? Are visual aids appropriate and helpful? Does the conclusion adequately summarize the main points and establish closure? Keep these questions in mind when you offer constructive feedback to your classmates.

REFERENCES

Bodie, G.D. (2011). The active-empathic listening scale (AELS): Conceptualization and evidence of validity within the interpersonal domain. *Communication Quarterly, 59*, 277–295.

Bodie, G.D. (in press). Listening as positive communication. In T. Socha & M. Pitts (Eds.), *The Positive Side of Interpersonal Communication*. New York, NY: Peter Lang.

Brooks, W.D. & Heath, R.W. (1993). *Speech Communications* (7th ed.). Dubuque, IA: Wm. C. Brown Publishers.

Cooper, L.O., & Buchanan, T. (2010). Listening competency on campus: A psychometric analysis of student listening. *International Journal of Listening, 24*, 141–163.

Edwards, A., Edwards, C., Wahl, S.T., & Myers, S.A. (2013). *The Communication Age: Connecting and Engaging*. Thousand Oaks, CA: Sage.

Ferrari, B.T. (2012). *Power Listening: Mastering the Most Critical Business Skill of All* [Kindle Edition]. New York, NY: Portfolio.

Flynn, J., Valikoski, T.R., & Grau, T. (2008). Listening in the business context: Reviewing the state of research. *International Journal of Listening, 22*, 141–151.

Gibson, J., & Walker, F. (2011). *The Art of Active Listening: How to Double Your Communication Skills in 30 Days* [Kindle Edition]. Seattle, WA: Amazon Digital Services, Inc.

Goss, B. (1982). Listening as information processing. *Communication Quarterly, 30*, 304–307.

Hardman, A. (2012). *Active Listening 101: How to Turn Down Your Volume to Turn Up Your Communication Skills* [Kindle Edition]. Seattle, WA: Amazon Digital Services, Inc.

Jones, S.M. (2011). Supportive listening. *International Journal of Listening, 25,* 85–103.

Kearney, P., & Plax, T.G. (2012). *Public Speaking in a Diverse Society* (4th ed.). Stamford, CT: Cengage Learning

Liraz, M. (2013). *How to Improve Your Listening Skills: Effective Strategies for Enhancing Your Active Listening Skills* [Kindle Edition]. Seattle, WA: Amazon Digital Services, Inc.

Lucas, S.E. (2011). *The Art of Public Speaking* (11th ed.). New York, NY: McGraw Hill.

Mintz, A.J. & Vasile, H.K. (2000). *Speak with Confidence: A Practical Guide* (8th ed.). London, UK: Longman.

Nichols, M.P. (2009). *The Lost Art of Listening: How Learning to Listen Can Improve Relationships* [Kindle Edition]. Seattle, WA: Amazon Digital Services, Inc.

Osborn, M., Osborn, S., & Osborn, R. (2011). *Public Speaking: Finding Your Voice* (9th ed.). Boston, MA: Pearson Publishing.

Sanabria, K. (2004). *Academic Listening Encounters: Life in Society.* Cambridge, UK: Cambridge University Press.

Tubbs, S. (2012). *Human Communication: Principles and Contexts* (13th ed.). New York, NY: McGraw Hill.

Van de Vord, R. (2010). Distance students and online research: Promoting information literacy through media literacy. *The Internet and Higher Education, 13,* 170–175.

Westra, M. (1996). *Active Communication.* Pacific Grove, CA: Brooks/Cole Publishers.

Wolvin, A.D., & Coakley, C.G. (1991). A Survey of the Status of Listening Training in some Fortune 500 Corporations. *Communication Education, 40,* 152–162.

CHAPTER 10

Persuasive Speaking

Bryant had a difficult task to accomplish. As president of the Financial Management Association, he had been asked by the Dean to give a speech to residence hall students on the use of credit cards. Recently, several parents had complained about dozens of credit card vendors who had been visiting campus to encourage students to apply for credit cards, many of them with limits as high as $5,000. Making matters worse, although the initial interests rates were low, within six months the rates increased to as high as 14 percent. The parents were outraged that their children were approved for three or four cards even though they had no source of income. They felt these credit card companies were taking advantage of vulnerable young adults who were sinking themselves into debt. Large interest payments and late fees were building up, and they were worried about their children's long-term credit ratings.

In researching his topic, Bryant discovered there were differing opinions regarding students' access to and use of credit cards. He wanted to make sound and ethical choices in his selection of facts and evidence. He also needed to put aside his biases since he had just maxed out his third credit card. Bryant interviewed fifteen students about their use of credit cards, and he asked about their attitudes about vendors coming to campus and approving students for a line of credit even though they had no source of income other than their parents' support. Some of the students he interviewed regretted signing up for multiple cards. They felt trapped by the debt they accumulated. Others said they would not have been able to buy books and other supplies they needed during the school year without access to credit. How should he craft his speech given these opposing views?

Bryant decided to research some factual and statistical information regarding the number of college students using credit cards nationwide, requirements for approval, average level of debt accumulated, and how many students had their credit ratings damaged when they missed or stopped making payments. He also contacted four different parents of students who had run up excessive debt on their cards. Finally, he spoke to three credit card vendors who were on campus promoting their banks' cards.

Once he had collected all of his information, Bryant decided the best way to tackle this topic was to advocate for the responsible use of credit cards by college students, including understanding interest rates and paying off balances as soon as possible, preferably by the end of each month. He also argued that if students did not have a source of income other than their parents, they should talk to their parents before filling out an application for credit. In preparing his speech, he decided that a problem-solution pattern was most appropriate for developing his ideas.

INTRODUCTION

Persuasion is the process of influencing or changing people's attitudes, beliefs, or actions (Miller, 2012). People who can speak persuasively are more satisfied in their personal relationships, more successful in promoting interests in their communities, and more likely to achieve their career goals.

Understanding the principles of persuasion is also important from the standpoint of receiving and evaluating persuasive messages. By age twenty-one, the average American has heard or seen about one million advertisements on the radio, television, or Internet (Vitelli, 2013). How do you decide what to buy based on these advertisements? During campaign seasons we are bombarded with political ads and speeches? Have you always made wise decisions based on what you heard or saw?

In this chapter we look at the principles and process of persuasive speaking. We start by looking at the ethics of persuasion. We then turn to examining the psychology of persuasion. Next, three different types of persuasive speeches are considered—those that make claims concerning facts, values, and policies. Finally, we look at how speakers build credibility, use evidence, engage in reasoning, and appeal to emotions.

THE ETHICS OF PERSUASION

When a speaker attempts to influence or change the attitudes, beliefs, or actions of a person or group of people, the ethical implications of that influence or change need to be considered. For example, are you presenting your message to meet the interests of your audience, or are you promoting your self-interests? Have you considered the potential harm that could come to your audience if they accept your ideas or arguments?

Let's say you are a financial advisor who gives presentations to people who are about to retire in five years. You became aware of an investment opportunity several weeks ago when you met with the president of an electric car manufacturing company. At the end of the meeting he gave you a check for $5,000 to encourage you to promote his company with your clients. He then promised to give you a 10 percent cut of any investments you channeled to his company after the initial $5,000 was recovered. The company seemed legitimate, and you were excited about the extra income. Over the course of the next year, you persuaded nearly two hundred people to invest a total of $750,000 in the company. Suddenly, the company filed for bankruptcy. Within a few days a local news anchor reported that the president of the company had been embezzling funds. All of the investors you spoke to in the last year lost their money.

When speaking persuasively, your goals must be ethically sound, and you need to use ethical means to present your ideas. You need to be honest, refraining from deliberately false or deceptive messages. Also, do not engage in more subtle forms of dishonesty such as taking a statement out of context or telling an audience a few details of a story, leaving out events that alter the meaning. And speakers should never resort to name-calling or other forms of abusive language.

THE PSYCHOLOGY OF PERSUASION

When speakers give persuasive speeches, they are engaging the audience in a psychological process. You recognize that there is a range of opinions on your topic: some audience members support your idea, some are neutral, and others disagree. Also, the range of support or opposition for your idea may range from weak to strong. How are you going to change the minds of audience members, strengthening the support for your message and reducing the level of opposition?

The process of changing someone's attitudes, values, or beliefs, or sparking people to take action, is both complex and challenging. The complexity and challenges faced by a speaker increase when dealing with a controversial subject. Regarding controversial subjects, your listeners are likely to be strongly committed to their ideas. In such instances, speakers need to be realistic about what they can accomplish, especially in a relatively short speech. An audience strongly opposed to immigration reform is not going to accept your arguments that undocumented immigrants should be given a path to citizenship. However, for those audience members who are not strongly committed to a topic, a speaker can realistically hope to influence the views of some. Then, for those who are strongly opposed to a speaker's ideas, it may be possible to get some to re-examine their views or to read more about the topic.

When listening to a persuasive speech, listeners engage in give-and-take with the speaker. Assessments are made of the speaker's credibility, supporting materials, arguments, reasoning, and delivery. Recognizing this, speakers should put themselves in the places of different audience members who hold a range of opinions about their topic. What objections might certain audience members have to your ideas, and how can you respond to such objections in your speech?

Recognizing that you will rarely be able to persuade all of your listeners, what can you do to have the greatest impact? Speakers can focus on reaching their **target audience.** The target audience consists of: (a) uncommitted listeners, (b) listeners who are leaning toward your point of view, and (c) those who disagree but are open to persuasion. What sorts of messages and arguments would fit the values and concerns of these three groups? For example, let's say you will give a speech on the value of becoming an organ donor. What types of messages and arguments would move an uncommitted listener to commit to the idea of becoming an organ donor? How can you move a person who is leaning toward becoming an organ donor to actually signing an organ donor card? For those who disagree, what questions or arguments can you raise that would cause them to reconsider their opposition?

Persuasive people are more successful in their relationships, communities, and careers.

When a speaker focuses parts of his or her message on the target audience, the others are not ignored. A speaker may say, for example, that he or she respects the rights of people to hold opposing views. And, remember that a speaker should never insult those who disagree.

PERSUASIVE SPEECHES ON FACT CLAIMS

Fact claims assert that something is true or false. A speaker making a fact claim holds a partisan view toward a topic and seeks to persuade the audience to accept that view. For example, consider the following fact claims:

> Energy drinks cause more health problems than coffee.
>
> Violent video games cause children to commit violent crimes.
>
> Unemployment will be lower next year.
>
> The civil war in Syria will end next year.
>
> Sexual orientation is genetically determined.

Each of these claims is debatable, since speakers may find evidence that supports or opposes each claim. Speakers may base their fact claims on things they have experienced or read. Speeches are then developed using statistics, examples, and expert testimony, and by constructing arguments using sound reasoning.

Most speeches on fact claims are organized topically. If you wanted to convince your classmates that unemployment will be lower next year, each of your main points would present a reason why your listeners should agree with you.

Specific Purpose: To persuade my audience that the unemployment rate in the U.S. will be lower at the end of 2014.

Central Idea: There are three reasons to believe that the unemployment rate in the U.S. will be lower at the end of 2014.

Main Points:
I. The Congressional Budget Office predicts the Affordable Care Act will reduce unemployment (Sargent, 2014).

II. The Federal Reserve predicts a significant increase in economic growth that will spark private sector hiring in 2014 (Torres & Gage, 2013).

III. The Department of Labor reports that millions of Americans are seeking full-time employment in 2014 (Bureau of Labor Statistics, 2014).

PERSUASIVE SPEECHES ON VALUE CLAIMS

Value claims involve matters of fact, however, they also attach a judgment to a topic. For example, a speaker argues that a subject or topic is good or bad, moral or immoral, right or wrong, fair or unfair. Supporting a value claim requires a speaker to define his or her standards for making a value judgment, and then judge the subject of the speech against those standards. For example, consider the following value claims:

> It is not morally justifiable to place prisoners in solitary confinement for extended periods of time.

> It is ethically acceptable to use stem cells from an aborted fetus for medical therapies.

> It is wrong for the U.S. government to use waterboarding as an enhanced interrogation technique.

> It is unethical for Walmart to drive down the price of labor in developing countries.

> It is unethical for coal plants to dump contaminated water into local rivers and streams.

Although a speaker can make any one of these claims, another speaker could make an opposing claim. The strength or potential persuasiveness of the claim is based on the information, support, arguments, and reasoning offered in support of the claim.

Most speeches on value claims are organized topically. In your first point you must establish the standard for your value judgment. In your second point you apply those standards to the subject of your speech. If you want to convince your classmates that it is not morally justifiable to place prisoners in solitary confinement for an extended period of time, the following outline could be used:

Specific Purpose: To persuade my audience that it is not morally justifiable to keep prisoners in solitary confinement for extended periods of time.

Central Idea: Extended periods of solitary confinement for prisoners are not morally justifiable because they violate prisoners' constitutional rights and cause physical and mental illness.

Main Points:
I. Morally justifiable punishments meet three standards.

    A. The punishment should not violate prisoners' constitutional rights.

    B. The punishment should not cause significant physical harm.

    C. The punishment should not cause mental illness.

II. Extended periods of solitary confinement are not morally justifiable because each of these standards are violated.

    A. An extended period of solitary confinement denies prisoners' rights to due process and subjects them to cruel and unusual punishment.

    B. An extended period of solitary confinement causes significant physical harm in the form of headaches, heart palpitations, insomnia, and chronic tiredness.

    C. An extended period of solitary confinement causes significant mental illness in the form of anxiety, fear of impending nervous breakdowns, obsessive ruminations, chronic depression, and suicidal ideation (Center for Constitutional Rights, 2014).

PERSUASIVE SPEECHES ON POLICY CLAIMS

A **policy claim** involves facts and values; however, it also involves a call for action by the members of your audience. In order to persuade listeners to accept your call for action, you have to show that there is a need for change because a significant problem exists with things as they are. Once you have established that a problem exists, you present your plan to solve it. Finally, you need to show that your plan will work in solving the problem without creating other more serious problems. For example, consider the following policy claims:

Same sex marriages should be sanctioned in all fifty states.

The U.S. should not force democracy upon other nations.

Parents should be able to spank their children.

The war on drugs should be abandoned.

The U.S. should pursue immigration reform.

Everyone should vote in the next student election.

Speeches on policy claims can be organized in one of four ways: (a) problem-solution, (b) problem-cause-solution, (c) comparative advantages, and (d) Monroe's motivated sequence. Let's consider each of these.

Persuasive speeches engage audiences in a psychological process.

Problem-Solution

One of the most common ways to make a policy claim is to use a problem-solution pattern of organization. When following this pattern you show that a new policy is needed because a significant problem exists for your audience members. Then you explain your plan for solving the problem and show its practicality. Let's say you wanted to persuade your listeners that the problem of hunger in America is best confronted by the continuation of the Supplemental Nutrition Assistance Program (SNAP), and by local community suppers run by volunteers.

Specific Purpose: To persuade my audience that hunger in America is best confronted through continuation of the Supplemental Nutrition Assistance Program (SNAP), and by local community suppers run by volunteers.

Central Idea: Hunger in America is a significant problem that requires action by the government and by citizens.

Main Points: I.   Hunger in America is a significant problem.

        A.   What it means to be food insecure.

        B.   Forty-nine million Americans, one in six of us, live in food-insecure households (Feeding America, 2014).

    II.   Solving the hunger problem in America requires a combination of government and citizen action.

        A.   The problem of hunger in America is so significant, the federal government's SNAP program needs to be continued (Feeding America, 2014).

            1.   The program distributes SNAP cards efficiently to those who need assistance.

2. No more efficient system has been proposed to replace it.

B. Community suppers run by volunteers reduce hunger in America and pose two significant benefits.

1. Community suppers run by volunteers provide food to people who are hungry, giving them a necessary supplement to their SNAP benefits.

2. Community suppers connect volunteers to their neighbors who are hungry, providing them with social support and reducing their isolation (Papa, Singhal, & Papa, 2006).

Problem-Cause-Solution

In this type of persuasive speech there are three points. In the first point the speaker identifies a problem. In the second, the speaker discusses the causes of the problem. Finally, the speaker presents a solution to the problem. Let's say you wanted to persuade your listeners that the federal debt is a serious problem that is caused by two actions by the federal government, and the solution calls for two action steps by the federal government.

Specific Purpose: To persuade my audience that we must take action to reduce the federal debt.

Central Idea: The federal debt is a serious problem that can be confronted by increasing revenue and reducing spending.

Main Points: I. The federal debt is a serious national problem.

   A. The federal debt is $17.5 trillion (U.S. Debt Clock.org, 2014).

   B. If the debt is not reduced, we will not be able to fund our military, build our infrastructure, and continue social programs.

II. There are two main causes of this problem.

   A. The federal government takes in too little revenue.

   B. The federal government spends too much money.

III. We can solve these problems by raising revenues and spending less.

   A. Returning to the Clinton-era tax rates would raise $1.6 trillion dollars over ten years (Newman, 2012).

      1. Only the wealthiest of Americans will experience a tax increase.

      2. During the Clinton era, Americans experienced significant economic prosperity.

   B. The U.S. could reduce its military spending by $2 trillion over ten years (Green Shadow Cabinet, 2013).

      1. A savings of $2 trillion in ten years significantly reduces the federal debt.

      2. This reduction in spending would still give the U.S. the most powerful military in the world by far.

Comparative Advantages

Persuasive speakers sometimes face audiences in which everyone agrees a problem exists, but there is an ongoing debate over which solution will best respond to that problem. In such situations, speakers can compare the advantages and disadvantages of different solutions. When using the comparative advantages organizational pattern, each main point explains why the speaker's solution is better than solutions others have proposed. For example, let's say you want to persuade your listeners that they should abandon electric or natural gas heating systems because of the advantages of geothermal energy systems.

Specific Purpose:	To persuade my audience of the advantages of converting to geothermal heating and cooling systems for their homes.
Central Idea:	Unlike electric or natural gas heating and cooling systems, a geothermal system is a renewable, nonpolluting, economical energy source, saving the consumer thousands of dollars on energy bills over the life of the system.
Main Points:	I. Unlike electric or natural gas heating and cooling systems, geothermal systems rely on a renewable source of energy not requiring the continued extraction of coal, oil, or natural gas.
	II. Unlike electric or natural gas heating and cooling systems, geothermal systems do not cause pollution by burning fossil fuels.
	III. Unlike electric or natural gas heating and cooling systems, geothermal systems are economical, saving consumers thousands of dollars on their energy bills over the life of the system (Kukreja, 2014).

Monroe's Motivated Sequence

Alan Monroe, a professor of speech at Purdue University, developed the motivated sequence in the 1930s. This pattern of organization works well for policy speeches where the speaker seeks immediate action. There are five steps to this process.

1. *Attention.* You gain the attention of the audience by beginning with a compelling story, a startling statement, a humorous anecdote, an interesting quotation, or relating to the audience.

2. *Need.* Describe a significant problem that deserves attention, using convincing supporting materials. Here you are attempting to open your listeners' minds to consider your solution.

3. *Satisfaction.* Offer a solution to the problem, showing how it will work. Enough details should be provided so your listeners know how they can solve the problem themselves.

4. *Visualization.* Using vivid imagery, help your listeners visualize solving their problem by following your recommendations, and explain how they will benefit personally.

5. *Action.* Once your audience can visualize following your recommendations, call for specific action. Tell them exactly what you want them to do.

In the following example, see how the speaker follows Monroe's Motivational Sequence. The action this speaker calls for is daily cardiovascular activity.

Attention:	Imagine running up a flight of stairs as you hurry to school or work. As you reach the top step, you feel light-headed; you are out of breath. You pause before taking your next step, remembering your doctor's advice about exercising regularly to improve your cardiovascular health. Sound familiar?

Need: Only 18 percent of Americans meet the weekly recommendation for cardiovascular activity—at least 150 minutes a week of moderately intense physical activity. "Exercise is the closest thing we have to a magic bullet against heart disease and stroke" (Skerrett, 2010).

Satisfaction: Six months ago, I was that person, gasping for breath at the top of the stairs. Then, I found time at the beginning of every day to walk briskly—outside when it's nice, inside when it's not. Now when I run up the stairs, I don't feel light-headed, I'm not out of breath. My blood pressure is lower. I've taken the steps; I've absorbed the magic bullet to live a longer, healthier life.

Visualization: Put yourself in my place. What can you do? See yourself getting up thirty to forty minutes earlier each day, putting on workout clothes, and taking a brisk walk outside, breathing in the fresh air. Or, when it's raining or snowing, walking briskly in place while watching your favorite early morning show, smelling the fresh pot of coffee brewing. That's all it takes.

Action: All you need is twenty-five minutes a day. Take those brisk steps, inside or out. Nothing could be simpler. Make a commitment to your health. Make a commitment to living a longer and healthier life, having the energy and time to spend with family and friends.

BUILDING CREDIBILITY

A speaker's credibility is always important. In persuasion there is an additional element to consider, however. Persuasive speakers are attempting to get their audiences to change their minds or actions based on the speakers' words. Why should listeners do so? To consider a change in thinking or behavior, listeners have to be convinced that the speaker has high credibility.

Providing Personal Proof of Credibility

Speakers provide personal proof of their credibility when they show their **competence** to address a topic and when they display their **character.** Competence refers to how an audience evaluates a speaker's intelligence, expertise, and knowledge of the topic. Character refers to how an audience evaluates a speaker's trustworthiness, honesty, sincerity, and concern for their needs as opposed to the speaker's self-interests.

If an audience favorably evaluates a speaker's competence and character, they are much more likely to accept what he or she says and then consider a change in thinking or behavior. When an audience has prior knowledge of a speaker, that speaker's competence and character may have been established through previous interactions or speeches. A speaker who is not well known by an audience might have his or her competence and character built by the person introducing the speaker. During the speech, competence is demonstrated when speakers show how thoroughly they have prepared for a presentation, how well they understand the complexity surrounding the topic, or how substantive are their experiences connected to the topic. Character is displayed when speakers show their sincerity through the words they choose, their nonverbal communication, and the conviction with which they present their ideas. Speakers should also demonstrate through their words and actions exactly how they have the interests of the audience in mind rather than their own self-interests.

The Evolution of Speaker Credibility

A speaker's credibility may change over time. **Initial credibility** refers to the credibility a speaker has before speaking. Judgments of initial credibility may be based on what listeners have heard about the speaker, their prior experiences with the speaker, how the speaker looks or is dressed, or the comments made by a person introducing a speaker.

Derived credibility refers to the credibility judgments that are made as audience members listen to the speech. Everything a speaker says and does during the presentation influences the extent to which their initial credibility is strengthened or weakened. A speaker's competence and character are under scrutiny as audience members listen.

Terminal credibility refers to the credibility judgments made by audience members at the conclusion of a speech (McCroskey, 2006). Sometimes audience members arrive at this judgment as soon as a speaker concludes. Other times audience members need to allow the speaker's words and actions to sink in before a final judgment is made. The higher the terminal credibility, the more likely audience members are to be persuaded by the speaker's message.

Enhancing Credibility During the Speech

Everything speakers say and do during their speeches affects their credibility. There are specific choices speakers can make, however, that may enhance credibility during the speech. Here we consider three: (a) explaining your competence, (b) establishing common ground with audience members, and (c) delivering a professional speech with conviction.

You explain your competence when you describe your expertise on the speech topic. Have you spent a great deal of time reading about this topic or speaking to experts? Have you had specific experiences with this topic that give you unique knowledge or insight? A brief statement during the introduction of the speech, describing how thoroughly you have investigated a topic or what your personal experiences are with a topic, can enhance your credibility with the audience. Your comments help them to realize they are listening to a person who has unique insights based on accumulated knowledge and/or experience.

A second way of enhancing speaker credibility is by establishing common ground with your audience. Have you had experiences that are connected to those of the audience? Then say so. Do you believe your point of view might be connected to those of your audience members? Again, tell them. For example, after several weeks in a public speaking class, a speaker realizes all of her classmates have smartphones. In a speech about GPS systems and traffic, she could say:

> We all know the frustration of driving on a highway, wanting to reach a favorite vacation spot, or arriving home, only to be stopped suddenly in traffic, our arrival delayed by hours. Today, I want to talk about an app available on many GPS systems to anticipate and avoid traffic jams.

More simply, a speaker could say, "Many of us know what it's like to overindulge in fattening but delicious foods during the holidays. I've learned a few tips that allow me to satisfy my desire for my favorite foods without packing on the pounds." Such a statement may have many of your audience members on the edges of their seats. Of course, you only enhance your credibility if you deliver, offering tips that genuinely work!

The third way of enhancing credibility is to deliver a professional presentation with conviction. Prepare your presentation sufficiently so you are fluent when addressing the audience. Also, show your interest in the topic by being lively and animated. Why should an audience consider changing their thinking and behavior if you do not show that this topic energizes and interests you? Your belief in what you are saying is shown through your conviction, the way you select your words, and how you use your voice, gestures, and body.

USING EVIDENCE

In Chapter 8 we looked at the different types of supporting materials (examples, statistics, testimony) that can be used in speeches. For persuasive speeches, we have several recommendations for using such evidence.

Use Specific Evidence

Specific evidence, whether in the form of examples, statistics, or testimony, makes a point that an audience is more likely to remember and be persuaded by. For example, in the speech on hunger in America, the speaker did not say, "Countless Americans go hungry every day." How is the audience to interpret the word *countless?* Rather, he said, "Forty-nine million Americans, one in six of us, live in food-insecure households." Here, the speaker makes his point much more effectively, enhancing his credibility by showing knowledge of specific facts.

Use Novel Evidence

If you only present the audience with evidence that is known to the general public, why should they consider you a knowledgeable, expert source that has conducted significant research on the topic? If your audience members have already been exposed to the evidence you present, how could it change their thinking or behavior? That is why credible speakers make sure they thoroughly research their topics, trying to find recent, novel information. If you have conducted hours of research on your topic, and the evidence you come across surprises you, your audience members might be surprised as well.

Use Evidence from Credible Sources

If you select biased sources that have clear self-interests, an audience is not going to be persuaded, unless perhaps they have the same bias or self-interests. For example, on March 8, 2014, Malaysia Airlines Flight 370 presumably crashed into the Indian Ocean. Whose conclusions about the airline's safety are we likely to accept, a Malaysia Airlines spokesperson or experts from the International Civil Aviation Organization? In order to persuade your listeners, select evidence from objective sources that do not have a stake in promoting a vested self-interest.

Use Evidence to Make a Clear Point for Your Audience

Examples, statistics, and testimony do not always stand alone in making a point for your audience. Speakers should consider how to drive home the point that the evidence suggests. For example, a student speaker from a Cleveland, Ohio area university wanted to drive home the point of how many people are injured and die each year in the U.S. as a result of distracted driving. He could say:

> The U.S. Department of Transportation estimates that 3,328 Americans were killed in 2012 in distraction-affected crashes, a number that approaches the population of the entire first-year class at our university. That same year, an estimated 421,000 people were injured in motor vehicle crashes involving a distracted driver, a number exceeding the entire population of Cleveland (U.S. Department of Transportation, 2014).

Listeners of this speech who are first-year students may visualize all the other first-year students they have met. Any other undergraduate student listening to this speech would realize how significant this statistic is because they attend a large public university that admits thousands of students every year. When the annual injuries caused by distracted driving in one year exceed the population of Ohio's second largest city, the speaker's point is made clear.

USING REASONING

Speakers use reasoning when they draw conclusions based on the evidence they have included in their speeches. Make sure your reasoning is sound, or your listeners will not be persuaded by the conclusions you draw. Let's consider four types of reasoning a speaker may use, along with the common fallacies or errors speakers make in their reasoning.

Inductive Reasoning

Inductive reasoning is reasoning from specific instances to draw a general conclusion. For example, you might give several descriptions of protective parents you have seen and draw the general conclusion that all parents are protective of their children. Of course, no matter how many examples you give, exceptions will always exist.

One guideline for using inductive reasoning is to avoid generalizing too quickly. You do not want to jump to a general conclusion based on a limited number of examples or observations. You also need to consider the extent to which your examples are representative of the experiences of all people, your listeners included.

One effective way of using this form of reasoning is to support your specific instances with statistics and expert testimony. Let's return to our earlier example of distracted driving. You could recount several specific experiences that you, your family, and your friends have had with distracted driving. These experiences have alerted you to the overall magnitude of this problem, and they personalize the topic for your audience, showing how you and your loved ones have been affected. Then, you could reinforce your reasoning based on specific instances, with national statistics regarding the number of injuries and deaths caused by distracted driving in the U.S. each year.

Deductive Reasoning

Deductive reasoning involves establishing a general principle or conclusion, then moving to specific examples or observations to support it. When speakers use this form of reasoning, they must consider whether or not listeners will accept their general principle or conclusion with the supporting evidence they provide. One or more of the minor premises may also need evidentiary support. Consider the following reasoning regarding the health impacts of excessive consumption of meat:

1. Excessive consumption of meat, high in saturated fat, is unhealthy.

2. Rib eye steaks are high in saturated fat content.

3. Excessive consumption of rib eye steaks is unhealthy.

In order to support her deductive reasoning, a speaker provides evidence to support the first general principle as well as the second minor premise:

> According to a 2011 study published in *Public Health Nutrition,* diets high in saturated fats have been implicated in the growing epidemics of obesity and chronic diet-related diseases (Daniel, Cross, Koebnick, & Sinha, 2011). A six-ounce serving of rib eye steak contains fifteen grams of saturated fat, the highest saturated fat content for any cut of steak (Calorie Counter: Food Nutrition Data for Healthy Eating Choices, 2014). Therefore, excessive consumption of rib eye steaks is unhealthy.

With specific evidence to support the first general principle and the second minor premise, listeners are much more likely to accept the conclusion presented in the third point.

Causal Reasoning

When we experience something, we often want to know the cause. What caused the driver to drive off the bridge? Why has the stock market increased the last five days? Why did it snow so much this year? We also speculate about effects. If we don't devote attention to our crumbling bridges and roads, what will happen? If I can't reduce my blood sugar levels, what will happen to me in ten years? What will happen if global temperatures continue to rise? When we pose and address such questions, we are attempting to describe the relationship between causes and effects.

We all use causal reasoning in our everyday lives, and it is appropriate to use this form of reasoning in persuasive speeches. There are two fallacies, however, that must be avoided. The first comes from the Latin phrase, *post hoc, ergo propter hoc,* meaning "after this, therefore because of this." Why should the fact that one event follows the other mean that the first is the cause of the second? Let's say a student who never took the bus to school suddenly starts doing so; then his math test scores increased. He told this to several classmates, arguing that the bus rides magically caused his math grades to improve, but they did not trust his reasoning. Just because the increase in test scores followed the bus rides does not mean that one caused the other.

A second problem to avoid is assuming an event has only one cause when it may have two or more causes. What causes the stock market to go up or down? Why does it snow more or less in your hometown from one year to the next? When your favorite team has the same starting players in two consecutive years, why do they win the championship one year, yet miss the playoffs the next? What causes consumer confidence to vary from year to year? Events such as these are attributable to many causes, so speakers should refrain from attributing single causes to complex events.

Analogical Reasoning

When speakers reason by way of analogy, two similar things are compared, and the argument is made that what is true for one must be true for the other. The strength or likelihood that the analogy is true is based on how similar the two things being compared actually are. If the similarities are strong, the analogy might be valid, or at least listeners will be more likely to consider it. If listeners are not as convinced of the similarities, however, they will view the analogy skeptically or dismiss it altogether.

In building the analogy, therefore, speakers must establish the fact that the two items, cases, issues, or processes are significantly similar to one another. When speakers reason from analogy in persuasive speeches, they are usually making policy claims. Essentially, the speaker argues that a policy should work in one environment because it has worked in another similar environment. Consider the claim that a single-payer, government-run health care system will work in the U.S. because it works in Canada. Are the U.S. and Canada sufficiently similar in terms of demographics, economics, health care delivery systems, and public support for a single-payer system? Answers to this question will determine whether or not the analogy will work. The more parallel the two subjects are, the more likely the audience is to accept a speaker's analogical reasoning.

Fallacies

A fallacy is an error in reasoning in which a speaker tries to justify a conclusion, but he or she does so in a way that is not justified or, in some instances, is unethical. Here we consider five fallacies: (a) the red herring, (b) ad hominem, (c) either-or, (d) band wagon, and (e) slippery slope.

THE RED HERRING

When a speaker throws out a **red herring** to the audience, he or she introduces an irrelevant idea to divert attention from the real issue under discussion. A political leader, for example, has come under attack for an extramarital affair. The politician responds:

> My opponents have nothing to focus on but my personal affairs, when the issue facing the American people today is jobs, jobs, jobs!

What does the American public's concern for jobs have to do with this politician's extramarital affairs? One has nothing to do with the other, and there may be many Americans who are legitimately interested in this politician's fidelity to his partner because it reflects on his character. The mention of jobs is a red herring intended to divert discussion away from an issue the politician would rather avoid.

AD HOMINEM

An **ad hominem** attack focuses on the person rather than the issues that are part of a legitimate dispute. For example, "Why should we listen to the Senator talk about tax reform when he has done nothing but lie since his first day in office? I've heard more truth from snakes."

Ad hominem attacks usually focus on a person's character or integrity rather than address legitimate issues that can be debated in a civil manner. If it is appropriate to criticize a person's character because it interferes with his or her ability to do a job, the criticism can occur without derision and name-calling.

EITHER-OR

This **either-or** fallacy occurs when a speaker makes it seem that the only choice is between two alternatives, although other options exist. For example, when President George W. Bush said following 9-11, "You're either with us, or you're with the enemy," he oversimplified a very complicated situation. Many people may have opposed the Bush administration's policies *and* been against the terrorists who planned and executed the 9-11 attacks. Many people were opposed to the invasion of Iraq as a response to 9-11, but they were in support of other military action in other areas of the world.

When we oversimplify, we sometimes force people to make choices between alternatives that are not in anyone's best interests. Complicated issues often require careful contemplation and complex problem-solving, uncovering solutions that take considerable time to develop.

BANDWAGON

The **bandwagon** fallacy assumes that because something is popular, it is good and desirable—the undisputed choice. Just because a large number of people arrive at a similar judgment, does not mean that it is correct. For example, new evidence may surface that changes people's minds. Or, after listening to different arguments over time, people certain of one point of view may eventually support another. Until 1920, a majority of Americans thought women did not deserve the right to vote. In the early 1960s, the vast majority of Americans thought cigarette smoking was not harmful to health. There are few who would support these positions today.

SLIPPERY SLOPE

This fallacy takes the position that once a certain course of action is taken, we will slide down a path where there is no turning back. Like falling dominoes, one problem leads to another until we are no longer living in a world like the one we once knew and loved. If an opponent of Social Security reform says, "If we reduce the rate of the cost of living adjustment (COLA) for seniors, we accelerate the day when the elderly will be living in the streets, begging for food," this is a slippery slope argument. Alternatively, when an opponent of raising taxes on the wealthiest Americans says, "If we raise taxes on the wealthy by 1 percent, we will ignite class warfare and run blindly to the inevitable conclusion, socialism," we are being pushed down a slippery slope.

APPEALING TO EMOTIONS

One of the most powerful ways of persuading an audience is to appeal to their emotions. When speakers appeal to emotions such as compassion, love, fear, anger, pride, reverence, or hatred, listeners are often moved strongly to consider a change in thinking, attitudes, or behavior toward an issue. Let's look at three ways of appealing to emotions during a speech: using affective language and vivid details, and speaking with sincerity and conviction.

Using Affective Language

Affective language appeals strongly to listeners' emotions. Consider the words of Severn Suzuki, a twelve-year-old from Vancouver, Canada speaking at the United Nations. She powerfully confronts her listeners, demanding that they work to stop damaging the environment.

Coming up here today I have no hidden agenda, I am fighting for my future. Losing my future is not like losing an election or a few points on the stock market.

I am here to speak for all generations to come. I am here to speak on behalf of the starving children around the world whose cries go unheard. I am here to speak for the countless animals dying across this planet because they have nowhere left to go.

I am afraid to go out in the sun now because of the holes in our ozone. I am afraid to breathe the air because I don't know what chemicals are in it. I used to go fishing in Vancouver, my home, with my dad, until just a few years ago we found a fish full of cancer. And now we hear of animals and plants going extinct—every day vanishing forever.

In my life I have dreamt of seeing the great herds of wild animals, jungles and rainforests full of birds and butterflies, but now I wonder if they will even exist for my children to see. Did you have to worry of these things when you were my age? All this has happening before our eyes, and yet we act as if we have all the time we want and all the solutions. I'm only a child and I don't have all the solutions but I want you to realize that neither do you. You don't know how to fix the holes in our ozone layer, you don't know how to bring the salmon back up a dead stream, you don't know how to bring back an animal now extinct and

Emotional appeals can move listeners to change an attitude about an issue.

you can't bring back the forest that once grew where there is now a desert. If you don't know how to fix it, please stop breaking it!

I am only a child yet I know we are all in this together and should act as one single world towards one single goal.

In my anger I am not blind, and in my fear I am not afraid of telling the world how I feel (Suzuki, 1992).

Vivid Details

The use of vivid details connects your audience to your topic emotionally. When speakers present clear examples and compelling stories, they share their emotions and draw out the emotions of their listeners. When President Obama addressed the nation after the tragic shooting in Newtown, Connecticut that left twenty-six people dead, including twenty children, he talked specifically about what he and Michelle as well as people around the country will do on a December evening in response to the tragedy. He also powerfully conveys the compassion all Americans feel toward the victims and their families.

This evening, Michelle and I will do what I know every parent in America will do, which is hug our children a little tighter, and we'll tell them that we love them, and we'll remind each other how deeply we love one another. But there are families in Connecticut who cannot do that tonight, and they need all of us right now. In the hard days to come, that community needs us to be at our best as Americans, and I will do everything in my power as president to help, because while nothing can fill the space of a lost child or loved one, all of us can extend a hand to those in need, to remind them that we are there for them, that we are praying for them, that the love they felt for those they lost endures not just in their memories, but also in ours.

May God bless the memory of the victims and, in the words of scripture, heal the brokenhearted and bind up their wounds (Obama, 2012).

For those of us who heard the President speak on December 15, 2012, we will never forget his words or the tears in his eyes. Many Americans across the country were moved to act in support of legislation to ban semiautomatic weapons and to keep all firearms out of the hands of the mentally ill. The story of the twenty Newtown children and their heroic teachers and administrators gives this speech an emotional impact that connects with listeners in very personal terms.

Speaking with Sincerity and Conviction

Emotional language and vivid details have the capacity to move an audience. The most important part of an emotional appeal, however, is for speakers to genuinely feel the emotions they are trying to convey through their words. If you do not feel the emotions you are trying to express, your audience will easily detect your lack of conviction, particularly through your nonverbal communication. Conversely, when speakers sincerely feel emotions, the emotions are conveyed through the words they use, their voices, their gestures, their eyes, and their facial expressions.

Ethical Use of Emotional Appeals

Emotional appeals can be used for unethical ends, inspiring an audience to hate or engage in bigotry. Such use of emotional appeals is clearly unjustified. However, emotional appeals can be used to support many noble causes. When speakers want to motivate people to act, it is wise to appeal to their hearts as well as their minds.

When using emotional appeals, keep in mind ethical guidelines. First, a speaker's goals must be ethically sound. What you promote must be for the public good and be moral, fair, and just. Second, you must be honest. Nothing loses the respect of an audience more than a dishonest speaker. Third, speakers should never arouse emotions by engaging in name-calling or by using abusive language. Speakers can strongly oppose ideas or people without using language that denigrates or derides in an abusive way.

Severn's words are full of affective language that moves our emotions. She displays her anger over the actions of adults who are destroying our planet. She shows her compassion for starving children, future generations, and animals that are going extinct every day. She speaks of her fears, both what has happened and what may happen in the future. In using affective language powerfully, she demands that action be taken.

SUMMARY

In this chapter we focused on persuasive speaking. The areas covered include (a) the ethics of persuasion, (b) the psychology of persuasion, (c) persuasive speeches on fact, value, and policy claims, (d) building credibility, (e) using evidence, (f) using reasoning, and (g) appealing to emotions.

Persuasive speakers must make ethical choices when preparing and presenting their speeches. When speakers attempt to change the attitudes, values, beliefs, or action of their listeners, they should consider the potential harms that may come from those changes. Ethical persuasive speakers give speeches that are in the best interests of their listeners rather than in their own self-interests.

In considering the psychology of persuasion, we recognized that changing attitudes, values, beliefs, or actions is a complex and challenging process. Speakers should be realistic about what they can accomplish given that they face audience members who both support and oppose their ideas. One suggestion was to focus on a target audience, those listeners who are uncommitted, leaning toward your ideas, or who are opposed but open to considering your ideas.

Persuasive speeches may be made on fact claims, value claims, or policy claims. Speeches on fact claims assert something is true or false. Speeches on value claims assert a topic is good or bad, moral or immoral, right or wrong, or fair or unfair. Speeches on policy claims call for action because a serious problem exists. Policy claim speeches can be organized four ways: (a) problem-solution, (b) problem-cause-solution, (c) comparative advantages, or (d) Monroe's Motivated Sequence.

In persuasive speaking it is important for speakers to build credibility with their audience. First, credibility is built through demonstrating your competence and character. Second, credibility evolves during a presentation. Speakers begin with initial credibility, speak to produce derived credibility, and end with a level of terminal credibility. Credibility is enhanced during speaking by explaining your competence to address the topic, establishing common ground with your audience, and delivering your speech with conviction.

When speaking persuasively, speakers use evidence to support their ideas and arguments. Audience members are more likely to evaluate evidence positively if it is specific and novel, and if it comes from a credible source. Speakers also need to use evidence to make a clear point for the audience.

In order to get listeners to agree with your ideas and arguments, engage in sound reasoning. We discussed four types of reasoning: inductive, deductive, causal, and analogical. We also looked at five common fallacies or errors in reasoning: red herring, ad hominem, either-or, bandwagon, and slippery slope.

Finally, we examined the ways that speakers appeal to the emotions of their listeners. Effective emotional appeals require using affective language, vivid details, and speaking with sincerity and conviction. We also considered the importance of ethics in using emotional appeals. Persuasive speakers must pursue goals that are ethically sound, be honest, and refrain from name-calling or abusive language.

REFERENCES

Bureau of Labor Statistics. (2014, April 4). Economic News Release. U.S. Department of Labor. Retrieved April 16, 2014, from http://www.bls.gov/news.release/empsit.nr0.htm

Calorie Counter: Food Nutrition Data for Healthy Eating Choices. (2014). Count your calories for a healthier lifestyle. Retrieved April 18, 2014, from http://www.caloriecount.about.com

Center for Constitutional Rights (2014, April 16). Torture: The Use of Solitary Confinement in U.S. Prisons. Retrieved April 16, 2014, from http://ccrjustice.org/solitary-factsheet

Daniel, C. R., Cross, A. J., Koebnick, C., & Sinha, R. (2011). Trends in meat consumption in the U.S. *Public Health Nutrition, 14,* 575–583.

Feeding America (2014). Hunger and Poverty Statistics. Retrieved April 16, 2014, from http://feedingamerica.org/hunger-in-america/hunger-facts/hunger-and-poverty-statistics.aspx

Green Shadow Cabinet. (2013, November 13). 10 Ways to Cut the Military Budget by 25 to 50%. Retrieved April 16, 2014, from http://greenshadowcabinet.us/statements/10-ways-cut-military-budget-25-50

Kukreja, R. (2014). Advantages of Geothermal Energy. *Conserve Energy Future.* Retrieved April 18, 2014, from www.conserve-energy-future.com/Advantages_GeothermalEnergy.php

McCroskey, J. C. (2006). *An Introduction to Rhetorical Communication* (9th ed.). Boston, MA: Allyn & Bacon.

Miller, G. R. (2012). On being persuaded: Some basic distinctions. In J. P. Dillard & L. Shen (Eds.), *The Sage Handbook of Persuasion: Developments of Theory and Practice* (2nd ed.). (pp. 70–82). Thousand Oaks, CA: Sage Publications, Inc.

Newman, R. (2012, November 14). Here's How Obama Can Get $1.6 Trillion in New Tax Revenue. *U.S. News & World Report.* Retrieved April 16, 2014, from http://www.usnews.com/news/blogs/rick-newman/2012/11/14/heres-how-obama-can-get-16-trillion-in-new-tax-revenue

Obama, B. (2012, December 15). President Obama's Emotional Speech on Connecticut School Shooting. Retrieved April 18, 2014, from http://haveuheard.net/2012/12/president-obamas-emotional-speech-connecticut-school-shooting-video/

Papa, M. J., Singhal, A., & Papa, W. H. *Organizing for social change.* New Delhi, India: Sage Publications.

Sargent, G. (2014, February 5). CBO Director: Obamacare will Reduce Unemployment. *The Washington Post.* Retrieved online April 16, 2014, from http://www.washingtonpost.com/blogs/plum-line/wp/2014/02/05/cbo-director-obamacare-will-reduce-unemployment/

Skerrett, P. J. (2010, October 6). Americans lag on exercise. *Harvard Health Publications: Harvard Medical School.* Retrieved April 18, 2014, from http://www.health.harvard.edu/blog/americans-lag-on-exercise-20101006590

Suzuki, S. (1992). The girl who silenced the world in 5 minutes. Retrieved April 18, 2014, from http://www.youtube.com/watch?v=TQmz6Rbpnu0

Torres, C. & Gage, C. S. (2013, December 18). Fed Officials Lower Projection for Unemployment Rate in 2014. *Bloomberg News.* Retrieved online April 16, 2014, from http://www.bloomberg.com/news/2013-12-18/fed-officials-lower-projections-for-unemployment-rate-next-year.html

U.S. Debt Clock.org. (2014, April 16). U.S. Debt Clock: Real Time. Retrieved April 16, 2014, from http://www.usdebtclock.org/

U.S. Department of Transportation. (2014). What is Distracted Driving? Retrieved April 18, 2014, from www.distraction.gov/content/get-the-facts/facts-and-statistics.html

Vitelli, R. (2013, July 22). Televisions, commercials, and your child. *Psychology Today.* Retrieved April 17, 2014, from http://www.psychologytoday.com/blog/media-spotlight/201307/television-commercials-and-your-child

CHAPTER 11

Verbal and Nonverbal Communication

" There I was, dressed in a t-shirt, shorts, and flip flops, and carrying a six-pack of Bud Light to a Sunday afternoon cook-out at Joe Taylor's house, my immediate supervisor at Drake Manufacturing. When I walked into the backyard, I was horrified to see men in dress shirts, and some were even wearing jackets. The women were also dressed up. I felt like I stepped into the wrong party or received the wrong invitation. Without saying a word, I quickly and discreetly started to walk back to my car when a voice yelled out, "Sam, where are you going?" Reluctantly I turned around, resigned to being noticed. Luckily it was Zena, my coworker, calling out to me. I motioned to Zena to meet me by the bushes so we could talk privately. She nodded knowingly and scurried over to join me. Huddled behind the

We use words to represent ideas, observations, feelings, and thoughts.

evergreens, I whispered in Zena's ear, "The invitation said casual dress, I look like an idiot, what's going on?" Zena looked at me and mouthed the words, "BUSINESS casual." "Oh," was the only word I could muster. "

INTRODUCTION

Although all species communicate, only humans use language. Words (spoken and written) are the building blocks of language, which is one of the "symbol systems we use to communicate" (p. 202). We use words to represent ideas, observations, feelings, and thoughts. Words have a profound influence on how we relate to others (McClone & Giles, 2011). Perhaps you have been in a situation similar to the one Sam detailed above. A missing word here and there can be quite consequential. In Sam's case, he admitted that he skimmed the evite and obviously didn't see the word *business,* as in *business casual.* As you read this chapter, you will find that words and behaviors are a remarkable message delivery system for both verbal and nonverbal communication. However, like Sam, you must be vigilant in your effort to avoid misunderstandings and miscommunications.

In this chapter, you will read about the characteristics of verbal communication, the influence of culture, context, and gender, and the impact of confirming and disconfirming communication. The second half of the chapter is devoted to nonverbal communication and the various vocal and nonvocal codes and functions served. Influencing factors such as age, culture, and gender will also be explored. First, let's talk about the various features of verbal communication.

CHARACTERISTICS OF VERBAL COMMUNICATION

Language Is Governed by Rules

Every language is governed by rules. Generally, the rules are socially constructed and affirmed by a community. **Syntactic rules** dictate the order and arrangement of words. Although the following two sentences employ the same words, they evoke different meanings due to their arrangement:

> Christmas is a national holiday.

> Is Christmas a national holiday?

At an early age, a human exhibits the capacity to combine symbols (i.e., words) into meaningful sentences that are completely original. This remarkable feat is accomplished without much cognitive effort or instruction, leading some theorists to conclude that this ability is innate (McClone & Giles, 2011). The proper pronunciation of words is also informed by syntactic rules. Former President George W. Bush was famous for his unconventional use of the English language and some of his gaffes were referred to as "Bushisms." For example, he regularly mispronounced the word *nuclear;* instead he pronounced it as *NU KU LER.*

Semantic rules govern the meaning of words and features how words can change over time. For example, the phrase "turning the tables" refers to a time in the early development of this country when people actually turned their tables over to use the surface for different tasks such as preparing a meal, slaughtering an animal, eating dinner, or doing surgery. **Constitutive rules** define how messages are interpreted and establish permissible boundaries and parameters. For example, you know that when you and your girlfriend tease each other it is a sign of love and not meant to be an indication of a dysfunctional relationship. **Regulative rules** govern appropriate responses and behaviors in interaction, and they serve as the rules of engagement. For example, if your friend tells you that she "needs to talk," you should be prepared to listen and refrain from detailing your story about your weekend exploits.

Language Is Symbolic

A symbol is something that stands for or represents something else, either by association, resemblance, or convention. Words are symbolic as there is no direct association between the symbol and what it signifies. There are two categories that define the symbolic nature of words. **Denotative** meanings refer to the conventional and accepted definition of a word that is codified in a dictionary. The dictionary is a vibrant and dynamic repository of previously accepted and new words and is ever evolving. The Oxford Dictionary updates their word holdings on a quarterly basis (see OxfordDictionaries.com). Many new entries reflect popular culture, the culinary arts, new technology, current events, and cultural and social movements. New words entries for December 2014 include *hot mess, jel, key board warrior, respawn, vape, al desko,* and *man crush.* If you would like to coin a new word, visit the Oxford Dictionary at http://global.oup.com/uk/oedsubform/.

Connotative meanings are more personal and informed by experience. Think of the words used at home and with those people in your personal network. Outside these circles, the meanings of these words might not translate very well. Interestingly, many connotative words are so widely used that they quickly become part of the public lexicon and take on denotative meaning. Think of the suffix "gate" reflective of the 1972 Watergate break-in. Today, any scandal with any traction has the suffix "gate" attached to it. Recently we have seen *deflategate, textgate, selfiegate, bridgegate,* and *weinergate,* among others.

Just as words are added to the dictionary, there are efforts to remove some words from common usage as well. What started out at as a party game forty years ago has turned into a yearly tradition at Lake Superior State University. Through open nominations gathered on the university's website, overused and useless words and phrases are identified for placement on the list of Banished Words (see www.lssu.edu/banished/). The 2015 list of banished words includes *bae, polar vortex, CRA-CRA, foodie,* and *enhanced interrogation.* Are there any words you would like to see banished?

Language Is Arbitrary

Because language is symbolic, words have only an arbitrary correspondence to what they represent. Words have no inherent or intrinsic meaning that is universally understood. A table could have been called a *mugpie,* but we decided that the word *table* would suffice to name the flat oblong or circular surface used to support objects. Words and their meanings evolve and change regularly. For example, the word *awful* once meant "full of awe," and *neck* referred to "a parcel of land." Words vary in meaning across and between cultures, ages, and social class. The only exception to the arbitrary rule is onomatopoeic words which are formed by imitating the sound associated with its meaning. Words such as *buzz, meow, splash, click,* and *plop* are onomatopoeic.

Language Is Abstract

Simply put, we are limited by our language. At times we have trouble communicating (with words) what we really mean or cannot articulate all that we want to say. Many love songs and poems speak of the inadequacy of our words to express feelings. There are two strategies that, when practiced properly, can alleviate some of the abstractness of language. The first is **concreteness,** which is a necessary component of descriptive and clear communication. For example, the statement, "You really disrespect me when I'm talking," is ambiguous and unclear. A descriptive and concrete statement would be, "When you interrupt me when I am in the middle of telling a story, it makes me feel that you do not value what I have to say." **Owning feelings** is the second strategy used to enhance clarity, and it involves taking responsibility for your own thoughts and feelings through language choices. Speak for yourself and don't hide behind others, as in the following statement, "Everyone thinks you have changed—all your friends feel the same way." Recast the statement in a less abstract way: "I have noticed a change in you. I am not sure how to interpret unreturned text messages, last-minute cancellations, and your reluctance to commit to going away on spring break with me."

The abstract use and nature of words can work in our favor, however. Politicians use abstract language because specific and concrete words might offend someone or may clarify and reveal their views on a subject. **Euphemisms** can be helpful in some circumstances because they are vague and mild expressions that symbolize something unpleasant and harsh. For example, the term "friendly fire" refers to accidentally killing a member of one's own "friendly" military troop. The phrase "collateral damage" suggests unintentional or accidental harm that can occur to innocent bystanders in the pursuit of attacking an intended target. Although euphemisms can take the sting out of words, they can also diminish meaning and contribute to the abstract nature of language.

Language Is Ambiguous

Ambiguous language indicates that there is more than one meaning associated with a word. For example, the word "set" has over 400 meanings (see oxforddictionaries.com/us). A woman was upset because her boyfriend would never say, "I love you." Instead he would use the words "Luv ya." She tried to explain to him that his profession of love was inadequate and revealed a degree of reservation. He simply did not understand how the absence of a few vowels could cause such uncertainty. Both of their interpretations of the expression of love are valid, but they are also different. Words have different meanings for different people and are culturally and contextually bound. Both **jargon** and **slang** refer to a specialized language employed by group members. However, *jargon* is a technical language whereas *slang* is informal language. Through the use of inclusive and exclusive language, group membership is defined.

Language Is Contextually and Culturally Bound

Words are used and interpreted in different ways, and they reflect cultural and social class perspectives. For example, economically advantaged and disadvantaged people have different perceptions of words. For a middle-class person, the meaning of the word "broke" requires that they dip into savings to pay rent. To someone who has been unemployed for six months, the word "broke" means that they will be homeless by the end of the week, a starkly different reality. In the aftermath of Hurricane Katrina, when people were searching for food and water, African Americans were reported as "looting" food whereas white people were described as "foraging for" food. These and other racially charged word choices prompted Raina Kelley (2009), writing for *Newsweek,* to claim, "if you use language to make another person feel inferior based on color of his skin, you're being a racist. And no, it doesn't matter if you are black or white" (p. 54).

Dialects are defined as regional speech patterns that reflect ethnic group or social class membership (Finegan, 2007). Basil Bernstein (1973), a noted linguist, claimed that there are two types of codes that reflect social class: restricted and elaborate. **Restricted codes** are simple, efficient, and often monosyllabic terms that we use in talking with friends and family. Shared meanings facilitate the use of restricted codes, which are shortcuts in communication. For example, while watching TV you say to your friend, "Before you sit back down, get me another one of those, you know, the good ones." Your friend deciphers your request, goes to the refrigerator, and then hands you an ice-cold Heineken. Your friend knew what you were referring to because you share the same context and code.

Elaborate codes are more complex and are comprised of carefully chosen words. In unpredictable situations, such as a job interview or meeting strangers, we do not take for granted shared meanings for words. In new and unfamiliar situations, we elaborate on the words we use. An elaborate code is context free, as there is no association between the words and a particular context.

When we use elaborate codes, we create a context with language that is universal rather than particular to a group or context.

Elaborate and restricted codes are both useful and necessary and, when properly deployed, quite effective. The ability to match the code to the context is termed **code switching.** Bernstein's (1973) research suggests that people from lower-class backgrounds do not have the ability to code switch and primarily use a restricted code for all communication. Although in some circumstances, individuals use restricted codes by choice as a strategic means of displaying group identification and loyalty. Regardless of the motivation, the ability to code switch is an indication of behavioral flexibility.

Language Is Influenced by Gender

There is a great deal of evidence to support the conclusion that men and women are more alike than different in their language use. However, there are several notable gender distinctions that merit discussion (Dindia, 2006). For example:

- **amount of talk**   Evidence suggests that men are more talkative than women, particularly in two-person interactions (Leaper & Ayres, 2007).

- **forcefulness of expletive**   There is no statistically significant difference between the amount of expletives used by men and women (Johnson & Lewis, 2010).

- **questions**   Women ask more questions than men, and the questions are less direct and assertive (Mulac, 2006).

- **tag questions**   Women ask for more confirmation from others than men do. Tag questions take the form of, "I did a good job, didn't I?" (Mulac, 2006).

- **use of upspeak**   Women are more likely to use "upspeak" which involves raising your voice at the end of a sentence which effectively turns a statement into a question. It sounds childish and unsophisticated.

- **use of qualifiers**   Women use more qualifiers more than men. Qualifiers include *perhaps, I guess, I could be wrong but…,* and *this may sound crazy but…* (Mulac, 2006).

- **interruptions**   Men interrupt more than women do (Wood, 2014).

- **positive feedback** · Women give more positive back-channel responses including vocal nonverbal responses such as *uh-huh* and *hmm* and nonverbal responses including head nods and positive facial expressions (Hall, 2006; Wood, 2011).

- Men tend to engage in instrumental communication and women engage in expressive communication (Mulac, 2006).

CONFIRMING AND DISCONFIRMING MESSAGES

As much as words are arbitrary, ambiguous, and abstract, we cannot deny their powerful and consequential nature. With words we can create an interpersonal climate that can legitimize and reinforce or deny and discourage. Language, like other forms of self-expression, communicates who we are and what we value. Martin Buber (1957), a German philosopher, believed that a barometer of a society's humanity is the degree to which its members confirm one another. Influenced by Buber's ideas, Evelyn Sieberg and Ken Cissna (1981) conceptualized communication as **confirming** if it functions to recognize, acknowledge, and endorse another's existence. Conversely, **disconfirming** communication signals a disregard or denial, and it suggests that the other is without value and is insignificant. Sieberg and Cissna argue that whenever we communicate with people we confirm and/or disconfirm them not only through words but through nonverbal communication as well. A nod, a smile, a roll of the eyes, a shake of the head, they all communicate something about your thoughts and feelings toward others.

Confirming messages signal that you value others and accept their definitions of themselves.

Confirming messages communicate

- recognition *(I see you, you exist)*
- acknowledgement *(I hear you, we are relating)*
- endorsement *(I accept you, your experiences are valid)*

For example:

> Sally: I'm disappointed that I only scored a 60 on my interpersonal communication test.
>
> Kiera: I'm sorry to see you so frustrated, Sally. I know that test was important to you. You are a good student and this test just didn't show it.

Kiera confirmed Sally's disappointment about her performance on her test. She acknowledged that this test did not reveal Sally's true talents and assured her that she is justified in feeling badly about her test score.

Disconfirming messages communicate disregard and dismissal of others.

Disconfirming messages communicate

- indifference *(you are invisible, you do not exist)*
- imperviousness *(lack of accurate awareness, we are not relating)*
- disqualification *(disparagement and deny your experiences are invalid)*

For example:

> Olive: I detest it when my boyfriend gives me the silent treatment. I'd rather he do anything but ignore me. I could take it if he would scream or shout or tell me to go to hell—at least if he is yelling at me I know he knows I'm there. When he gives me the silent treatment, I feel invisible, like I do not even exist.
>
> Wayne: I have gotten a lot of kickback since I told my girlfriend that I didn't ever want to have children. When I told her, she said, "Oh, you'll change your mind, you'll see." I told her I had thought about it a lot and really don't even like kids, and she said, "You don't know what you want—you're too young to really know what is important."

Both statements are disconfirming and deny Olive's and Wayne's views and existence through indifference, imperviousness, and disqualification. Do not confuse confirming messages with absolute agreement and positive regard. You can disagree and still be confirming in your communication. It is appropriate to vigorously engage in spirited conversation without resorting to disconfirming communication.

Confirming communication is consequential and can produce a host of positive relational outcomes. Sybil Carrere and John Gottman (1999), renowned marriage specialists, concluded that long-lasting relationships are characterized by supportive and confirming messages. Neglecting to confirm one's partner in everyday conversation is a strong predictor of divorce and relationship breakups. Children who regularly receive confirming messages from their parents experience enhanced development and stability (Schrodt, Ledbetter, & Ohrt, 2007). Confirming teacher behaviors increases students' affective and cognitive learning (Ellis, 2004). The consequences of disconfirming communication are equally profound. Language that denies, disqualifies, and disregards others is at the heart of racism, sexism, heterosexism, regionalism, ageism, and any other -isms that serve to limit others' experience and invalidate their existence.

Using language effectively and improving your communication skills requires self-monitoring, an awareness of your goals, and the desire and motivation to modify your communication practices. You can improve your communication skills if you want to. Remember good communicators are not born, they are made! Let's now turn our attention to nonverbal communication.

NONVERBAL COMMUNICATION

The study of nonverbal communication and behavior can be traced to Charles Darwin. After years of observational study, Darwin concluded that animals and humans share many ways of physically expressing emotions. The underlying conclusion of this finding is that certain facial expressions are innate. His views were met with widespread criticism and debate, as Darwin was suggesting the unity of humans with animals, an evolutionary conclusion. Although Darwin was vindicated, and today his views are elemental, there is still discussion concerning the innateness of some nonverbal behaviors (Ekman, 2007).

In this section of the chapter you will learn about the value and importance and the various codes and functions of nonverbal communication. Influencing factors such as age, culture, and gender will be explored. As you continue to read, think about the role that nonverbal communication plays in your everyday life, and identify situations that went awry because you misunderstood the meaning of another's nonverbal message. Remember Sam's predicament? He knew immediately that something was wrong as soon as he saw how others at the picnic were dressed. Recall an occasion when nonverbal communication was the only way to express an emotion or share an intimate thought. Before we begin, let's consider the definition of nonverbal communication.

Definition of Nonverbal Communication

Nonverbal communication is defined as those behaviors and characteristics that convey meaning without the use of words. This broad definition includes nonlinguistic vocalized sounds such as laughing, sighing, physical appearance, touch, smell, and personal adornments. The use of time and space also communicates who you are and what you value. Nonverbal communication is anchored in the present, whereas verbal communication is more flexible. We can speak of the past and refer to the future and communicate about hypothetical nonexistent matters. We cannot transcend time, space, and reality without the use of words, a profound difference between verbal and nonverbal communication (Hockett, 1960).

For nonverbal communication to be successful, communicators must share a coding system enabling them to understand which behaviors are meaningful and which are not. To comprehend which behaviors are meant to communicate and which are not requires that we clarify the role of intentionality and conscious awareness. Some behaviors might be unconsciously enacted but intentional. For example, you intended to drive to school today, park your car, and then walk to class, but you might not have been consciously aware of your actions because this process is largely automatic and habitual. On the other hand, some behaviors are consciously enacted but not intentional. For instance, you were consciously aware that you laughed when your friend told a story but you did not intend to hurt her feelings. Rather than mocking your friend through laughter, you were remembering something funny that happened last night. While we cannot control how others interpret our behavior, we are responsible for our offensive behavior even when it is unintended and enacted without conscious awareness. Communication scholars offer further clarification of the definition, and they concluded that nonverbal communication messages are "typically sent with intent and include communication practices that are displayed without conscious awareness" (Burgoon et al., 2011, p. 240).

The Importance of Nonverbal Communication

Nonverbal behavior plays a large part in the overall communication process. The primacy of nonverbal communication, our first language, and its fundamental value in interpersonal relationships is well supported. Nonverbal communication is powerful and can be used to regulate and manage conversations, express emotions, deceive, influence what we believe, show like and dislike, illustrate power, form impressions, influence others, conceal information, and develop, maintain, and dissolve relationships. Nonverbal communication is the primary means by which we communicate emotion, and it is central to social interaction (Moore, et al., 2014).

Characteristics of Nonverbal Communication

NONVERBAL COMMUNICATION IS MULTI-CHANNELED

There are multiple channels to share and express our thoughts. Communication can be verbal and nonverbal and vocal and nonvocal and a combination of both, creating a complex array of possible channels and means of communicating. As you read, keep in mind that although each channel is identified separately, each works in tandem in an interdependent seamless fashion when we communicate. Vocal and nonvocal communication expressed via nonverbal communication channels is the focus of this part of the chapter.

Channels of Communication

	Nonvocal Communication	Vocal Communication
Nonverbal Communication	Nonverbal behavior (i.e., kinesics, personal adornments proxemics, haptics, chronemics)	Paralinguistic sounds (e.g., *haha*, laughs, sighs, clearing throat)
Verbal Communication	Written words	Spoken words

Source: Stewart & D'Angelo (1980, p. 22)

NONVERBAL COMMUNICATION IS INEVITABLE

It is not possible to *not* engage in behavior nor is it possible to control others' perception of your behavior. Even if you intentionally and consciously choose not to communicate, these very actions nonetheless communicate that you are intentionally and consciously choosing not to communicate! This sentiment has been expressed quite succinctly in *You Cannot Not Communicate* (Watzlawick, Bevan, & Jackson, 1967). Regardless of your intentions, all behavior communicates something about us.

NONVERBAL COMMUNICATION IS AMBIGUOUS

Edward Sapir (1949) coined the expression, "Nonverbal communication is an elaborate code written nowhere, known to none, and understood by all" (p. 556). Sapir's statement underscores the difficulty in interpreting nonverbal messages. Have you ever misread a friend's facial expression? Reacted to a tone in your significant other's voice? Chances are you have misinterpreted nonverbal behaviors and you undoubtedly will again in the future. Nonverbal codes are elusive, abstract, and sometimes difficult to define.

Ambiguous nonverbal communication is central to a current social issue. Campus sexual assaults are in the national spotlight, and university officials are scrambling with ways to ensure students' safety and stem the tide of this behavior. Geoffrey Stone (2015), writing for the *Huffington Post,* makes the case that the

Nonverbal communication is the primary means by which we communicate emotion.

problem is compounded by the lack of clarity surrounding the meaning of the word "consent." He questions whether consent is based on the victim or the perpetrator's understanding of the word. In contrast to the previous campaign against sexual assault that promoted the *No Means No* mantra, the new *Yes Means Yes* campaign features affirmative consent. California is the first state to legislate affirmative consent, and now "on California campuses, consent is no longer a matter of not struggling or not saying no. If the student initiating the sexual encounter doesn't receive an enthusiastic 'yes,' either verbally or physically, then there is no consent" (New, 2014, n.p.).

The ambiguous nature of nonverbal communication can be particularly consequential in courtship and sexual encounters. There is a compelling need for clarity, consensus, and mutual understanding in all communication encounters, especially those in which ambiguity is likely to play a significant role. Perception-checking is a useful means of combatting ambiguity and will help you avoid misunderstandings.

NONVERBAL COMMUNICATION IS INFLUENCED BY AGE

When verbal and nonverbal messages conflict, adults are inclined to believe the nonverbal message, and children believe the verbal component of the message. The evolution of nonverbal communication decoding abilities is quite paradoxical. Although the nonverbal code is our first language, as children hone their verbal skills they become literalists, prioritizing verbal over nonverbal interpretations. As children mature, they develop a sophisticated understanding of the interface of verbal and nonverbal communication and are able to accurately decipher verbal and nonverbal meanings (Feldman & Tyler, 2006). However, the nonverbal interpretive skills gained through maturation and experience can sadly atrophy with age, especially in the presence of cognitive and perceptual deficits (Burgoon et al., 2011).

When you were younger, you might have read the stories about the exploits of Amelia Bedelia, the storybook character who takes everything literally. When her baseball coach instructs her to steal second base, Amelia runs to second base, picks up the base, and runs home, literally stealing the base. We enjoy Amelia's antics because we understand how ironic her behavior is: her literal interpretation of the message causes her to misinterpret its meaning. Children with developed decoding abilities can appreciate this rather sophisticated word play.

NONVERBAL COMMUNICATION IS INFLUENCED BY GENDER

If we believe that "gender is performative" as researchers suggest (see Burgoon et al., 2011, p. 247), then there are likely nonverbal differences in the way that men and women communicate. For example, women smile more than men, speak at a higher pitch, sit in submissive ways, and offer more kinesics (e.g., head nods) and paralinguistic affirmations (e.g., "hmmm") than men (Hall, 2006). Men, often by virtue of size, command more space and talk more than women in mixed sex dyads, contrary to conventional wisdom. Men also interrupt women more often. Women are more conversationally responsive and accommodating (Burgoon, Guerrero, & Floyd, 2010; Burgoon et al., 2011). Although men and women display different nonverbal characteristics, they also share many commonalities in their communication (Dindia, 2006). The next time you are at a social gathering, observe the nonverbal communication patterns of both genders to see if there are marked differences or similarities between men and women in your social circles.

NONVERBAL COMMUNICATION IS INFLUENCED BY CULTURE

Nonverbal behavior is strongly influenced by culture, and members are enculturated largely through socialization practices (Matsumoto, 2006). Nonverbal behavior varies widely from culture to culture and is evidenced in differences in touching, eye contact, gestures, emotional expressions, interpretation of time, use of space, and volume, rate, and pitch of speech (Burgoon et al., 2010). The interpretation of time is particularly dependent on culture. North Americans are very aware of time and often convert a question of distance to a metric of time, which reveals what is important in their culture. For example, when you ask how far it is to the mall, an American would likely respond, "About a ten-minute walk from campus."

Travelers from North America, a **noncontact culture,** are counseled to apply a liberal definition of time, space, and displays of affection when visiting Latin American countries. People from **contact cultures** such as Central and South America are very warm and welcoming, and their nonverbal behaviors reveal a preference for a high-sensory experience (Samovar, Porter, & McDaniel, 2009). Although nonverbal communication is influenced by culture, there are many commonalities across cultures as well. Paul Ekman (2007) conducted numerous studies around the world and concluded that several fundamental emotions such as happiness, fear, disgust, anger, sadness, and surprise are enacted very similarly across cultures. To test these assumptions, turn off the volume on CNN International and see if you can, without benefit of interpretation by the newscaster, identify the emotions being expressed in the news story.

Nonverbal Communication Codes

In this section we will examine nine codes that capture the ways that we communicate nonverbally. As you read, keep in mind that although we will discuss each code separately, in reality, verbal and nonverbal codes are interdependent and operate in a seamless fashion when we communicate.

KINESICS

Kinesics is the study of body movement, gestures, and posture. Unlike Darwin, who thought that nonverbal emotional displays were innate, Raymond Birdwhistell (1970) believed that kinesic behavior is learned. Kinesics were previously referred to as body language and received ample attention in the popular press, particularly in the 1970s. This nonverbal code was so broad, however, that Ekman and Friesen (1969) developed five classifications of kinesic behavior that are detailed below.

Kinesics is the study of body movement, gestures, and posture.

Emblems. Emblems are intentional cues that are symbolic. Although they have a verbal counterpart, emblems can replace words and stand alone without a verbal message. Several examples are listed below. To see how pervasive and useful emblems can be, identify and physically display the emblem associated with each phrase listed below.

Peace sign	Zip your lips.
OK.	Wait—hold it.
Yes/no.	Get lost; go away.
What time is it?	Be calm.
Sit down beside me.	Stop.
Be silent, hush.	I'm hot.
I can't hear you.	I'm cold.
I promise.	I agree.
I don't know.	I need a ride.
Be silent, hush.	What stinks?

Illustrators. Illustrators are gestures that accompany verbal messages and represent, enhance, and emphasize the verbal content. Illustrators are more universal than emblems because they literally "illustrate" and "complement" the verbal message. Snapping your fingers as you command, "We have to hurry, and I mean now," or running your hands through your hair while you say, "I'm so stressed," illustrates the verbal message. Illustrators lend themselves to exaggeration, especially when we are excited and wish to emphasize the magnitude of our feelings about something. While gesturing with your hands to show that something is big, you might simultaneously shout, "The guy I tackled was so big, his thighs were the size of my waist!"

Adaptors.   Adaptors refer to nervous habits, and they include behaviors designed to satisfy physical and emotional needs and are usually enacted without conscious awareness. Examples of self-adaptors include grooming behaviors such playing with your beard, biting your nails, and primping. Object adaptors involve playing with objects such as pencils, pens, paperclips, and other inanimate objects. Have you ever been at a bar and discovered that you have scratched the entire label off the beer bottle? Baseball players, a notoriously superstitious group, engage in multiple self- and object-adaptor behaviors. Former major league baseball player and coach Mike Hargrove was nicknamed the "Human Rain Delay" for his excessive adaptor rituals while at the plate. He drove pitchers crazy with his routine which entailed: (1) adjusting his helmet, (2) adjusting his batting glove, (3) pulling each sleeve up about an inch, (4) wiping each hand on his uniform pants, (5) carefully placing his left foot in the batter's box, and finally (6) carefully placing his right foot in the batter's box. He engaged in this ritualistic behavior between every pitch (see www.baseball-almanac.com/players/player.php?p=hargrmi01).

Affect Displays.   Affect displays are nonverbal behaviors that reflect emotions. While we are not always aware that we are revealing information about our emotional state, others perceive them, nonetheless. One of Darwin's early findings revealed that both humans and animals communicate emotions nonverbally. Indeed, the face indicates the emotion being expressed while the body tells you how intense the emotion is (Mehrabian, 2007). We wring our hands when we are nervous, jump up and down when happy, growl when mad, and cry when sad. We slump down in our seats when we are tired or depressed and speak in a dejected fashion when disappointed. Think of how little children react when they don't get their way; they respond with their entire bodies. They may lie on the floor and kick and scream with complete abandon. Of course not everyone communicates emotion so freely—we all know people who reveal very little information about their emotions.

Kinesic behaviors differ from culture to culture.

Regulators.   Regulators are behaviors that control the flow of communication. Often when students are asked questions in class, they lower their heads to avoid being called upon by the instructor. The use of nodding and hand gestures can indicate whose turn it is to speak. You can tell a speaker to continue or hurry up by rolling your hand in a circular fashion. You can open your mouth to signal you want to talk or raise your hand to request a turn. You might hold up your index finger to signal that you are not quite finished speaking. Each of these nonverbal behaviors serves to regulate the flow of conversation.

Kinesic behaviors do not have universal meaning, and a gesture in the United States might communicate something entirely different in another part of the world. For example, the A-OK sign in the United States signals, "Everything is good and I'm fine." However, the same hand gesture in Europe is considered obscene (Matsumoto, 2006). In the Greek language the word "yes" sounds like "no" and the word "no" sounds like "yes." As is evident, cultural sensitivity is essential for appropriate and effective interactions.

FACIAL EXPRESSIONS

The face communicates more information than any other nonverbal communication channel (Knapp, Hall, & Horgan, 2014). Our face is central to who we are and is the key determinant in identity verification. Think about it for a moment, your face is featured on your driver's license, passport, and facial recognition software can authenticate your identity using 3D imagery. Perhaps this explains the resistance some people have to face transplants.

The face is capable of expressing the following emotions: fear, anger, surprise, disgust, sadness, and happiness (Ekman & Friesen, 1969). Happiness and surprise are communicated in the lower half of the face and eyes, while anger is revealed in the lower half of the face and forehead, fear and sadness are evident in the eyes, and disgust is revealed in the lower half of the face (Ekman, Friesen, & Ellsworth, 1972). Not surprisingly, women are reported to be more expressive, smile more, and make more eye contact than men (Hall, 2006). There are even gender specific terms such as "resting bitch face" to describe women's facial expressions. The use of, and facility with, encoding and decoding facial expressions and reading subtle nonverbal cues may contribute to why women are generally better at this form of communication (Hall, 2006).

EYE BEHAVIORS

Eye behavior, formally known as **oculesics,** can communicate more than any other part of the face. For example, our pupils dilate when we like someone, we roll our eyes to communicate disbelief or disagreement, we intently examine something of great interest, we avert our eyes in reaction to something distasteful, and we signal turn-taking and regulate communication through intermittent and sustained eye focus. Eye contact is a sign of respect and attention in some cultures but is a sign of disrespect in others (Samovar, Porter, & McDaniel, 2009). We commonly use phrases and expressions that capture the meaning and emotion behind specific eye behaviors such as "the evil eye," "stink eye," and "giving someone the eye." Dominance is displayed through conducting a stare down, and attraction and interest are manifest in both gazing and gawking behaviors (Andersen et al., 2006). It seems that Shakespeare's words, *the eyes are the window to our soul,* continue to resonate today.

The face conveys fear, anger, surprise, disgust, sadness, and happiness.

HAPTICS

Haptics is the study of touch. At times, touch can convey more information than words. Touch is the first of our five senses to develop, and links between touch and healthy development in babies, children, and adults is plentiful. We communicate liking, love, friendship, warmth, and social support through touch (Mehrabian, 2007). Interesting research revealed that couples who agreed to increase the frequency of kissing for a six-week period experienced reduced stress, increased relationship satisfaction, and reduced cholesterol compared to those who did not increase their kissing behavior (Floyd, Boren, Hannawa, Hesse, McEwan, & Veksler, 2009).

Touch can be used to reveal and exert power too. Individuals with higher status or power are often the first to initiate touch. Your boss might put his/her hand on your shoulder, but you would not likely reciprocate or initiate the same physical contact. Perhaps due to their expressive tendencies, women touch more than men (Hall, 2006). However, touch is best interpreted in context. Former Green Bay Packer quarterback Brett Favre was known as an infamous butt-slapper and had great fun catching other players by surprise with his playful antics. On the field this behavior was quite acceptable and considered a sign of team spirit and camaraderie. Off the field, this same butt-slapping would be met with great offense.

In the absence of pain receptors, a condition known as congenital analgesia, we risk injury and even death because we would be insensitive to harmful elements in the environment. As much as we cherish our senses of sight, taste, smell, and hearing, without the sense of touch we would be unknowingly susceptible to heat, cold, broken bones, and other injuries that could be life threatening.

PARALANGUAGE

Paralanguage, also known as **vocalics,** is defined as the vocal cues that accompany speech and includes tone of voice (resonance), volume (loud or quiet), pitch (high or low), inflection (variation in pitch), rate (speed), and tempo (rhythm). Think of the communication value of audible murmurs, gasps, laughter, and sighs. Vocal qualities are a critical means of communicating and creating meaning with others (Burgoon, et al., 2011). Paralanguage adds clarity, emotion, and life to speech and serves three functions:

Paralanguage gives meaning to sentences.   Using the same content, slight variations in inflection and tone can create a question or a statement.

"We're going to dinner tonight?"
A raised tone of voice at the end of the sentence indicates a question.

"We're going to dinner tonight!"
A lowered tone of voice at the end of the sentence indicates a declarative sentence.

Paralanguage reveals attitudes.   Tone of voice reveals one's attitude regardless of the content of the message. For example, the statement, "I just love the gift you gave me," could be vocalized as a sincere or sarcastic sentiment through subtle changes in the emphasis placed on certain words and tone of voice (Hinkle, 2001). As we know, when the nonverbal and verbal messages are contradictory, adults privilege the nonverbal code whereas children respond to the verbal one.

Paralanguage influences impression formation.   Listeners are capable of assigning sex, age, and social class from vocal indicators (Knapp, et al., 2014). Furthermore, paralinguistic cues contribute to perceptions of attractiveness (Moore et al., 2014), and impressions are formed based on the following vocal characteristics:

- Breathy voice: women are perceived as sexy and spacey; men are viewed as effeminate and young (Heinberg, 1964; Knapp, et al., 2014).

- Nasal voice: too much resonance in the nasal passages which creates an impression of a dull, whiny, complaining individual (Heinberg, 1964).

- Orotund voice: big full orator's voice, associated with the clergy, politicians, and authority figures (Heinberg, 1964). James Earl Jones (voice of Mufasa in *The Lion King* and Darth Vader from *Star Wars*) is famous for his full-bodied voice.

- Monotone voice: no variation of pitch or vocal cues, boring and dull (Malandro, Barker, & Barker, 1989). Ben Stein, political commentator and writer, consistently speaks without inflection and is celebrated for his monotone delivery.

Dialects (the use of particular words) and **accents** (the sound of words) are verbally and vocally revealed, and they engender both positive and negative assessments from others. In the United States, for example, people with northern accents are viewed as competent and in-charge, and people with southern accents are perceived as nice and sociable (Kinzler & DeJesus, 2013). The London newspaper, *The Independent,* reported on February 16, 2015, that the British accent is the most attractive in the world. American accents came in second, and Irish was voted as the third most attractive accent. The primacy of nonverbal codes, particularly vocalics, illustrates the importance of *how* something is said as much as *what* is said.

PROXEMICS

Proxemics is the study of how we communicate with space and is divided into two classifications: **personal space** and **territoriality.** Personal space refers to the invisible and intangible bubble we create and carry with us from one encounter to the next. Territoriality is the use of both fixed and nonfixed space.

First let's examine personal space. Anthropologist Edward T. Hall (1966) defined four levels of personal distance that range from intimate to public distance that are influenced by the nature of the relationship, the context, goals, and the topic of conversation. The key is to match the optimal distance with these features (see the following table). A conversation about the "state of the relationship," an intimate topic, would not likely occur at a distance reserved for public communication. Likewise, a discussion with your boss about quarterly earnings would not typically occur at a distance reserved for intimate conversations, unless the information is top secret and whispering is necessary. In both circumstances the inconsistency between the message and the spatial zone is evident.

Hall's Spatial Zones

Distance	Appropriate to Use for...
Intimate distance 0–18 inches	Intimate conversations and activities
Personal distance 18 inches–4 feet	Close but not intimate conversations
Social distance 4–12 feet	Professional conversations
Public distance over 12 feet	Formal public communication

Personal space preferences differ by culture, gender, age, status, and desire for interaction. A number of studies focus on intercultural norms regarding the use of space (Samovar et al., 2012). For example, Arabic people stand much closer to each other than Americans (Hall, 1966) which should not be surprising since the United States is an "individualistic noncontact culture." In North American cultures, men, often by virtue of their size, command more space, yet as men they also experience more restrictions in their use of that space. Unless they are participating in a sporting activity, social norms dictate more distance between men, whether sitting, walking, or standing with one another. Paradoxically, women are afforded less space but have more freedom with the use of their limited space and can choose to sit side by side with other women without fear of recrimination or questions about their sexual orientation (Knapp et al., 2014). In romantic relationships, couples typically desire less distance and prefer physical contact. Interaction is facilitated by shared space and the physical arrangement of furniture (Guerrero & Floyd, 2006). Interestingly, as we age, we tend to appreciate a greater degree of physical distance between others and ourselves (Moore et al., 2014).

Personal space differs according to culture, gender, age, status, and desire for interaction.

Whereas personal space is invisible, **territoriality,** the second classification of proxemics, refers to how we communicate through the use of fixed and semi-fixed space. Humans, much like animals, are territorial beings. We mark our territory and claim ownership by placing objects and personal belongings, known as **territorial markers,** on chairs and tables to signal to others that this space is occupied. Sometimes we do not actually own the territory that we claim (e.g., your seat in class), but because you have occupied the same seat all semester you feel as though it is your seat—at least for the duration of the course. In other circumstances, we do own the space and we employ territorial markers such as fences, bushes, and foliage to define our property.

Territoriality is a useful means of communicating power. Those with status and power command more private and desirable space, and they are protected from outside interference and access by office location as well as office personnel who serve as gatekeepers. Supervisors may trespass into a subordinate's workspace; however, reciprocal behavior is less likely. Powerful people sit at the head of the table, control the conversation, and are the first to approach others in conversation, thereby signaling a desired distance for the interaction (Burgoon et al., 2011).

For now, think about the last time your personal space was invaded. Chances are, your reaction was consistent with the research findings, which suggest that we respond by a reduction in eye contact, less direct body orientation, and even flight. How would you react if you came to class and found someone sitting in "your" seat? Perhaps you had the same reaction that the three bears had to Goldilocks's intrusion into their home. The bears undoubtedly felt that their territory had been invaded when they exclaimed: "Someone's been eating my porridge! Someone's been sitting in my chair! Someone's been lying in my bed!" Although Goldilocks was breaking and entering as far back as 1837, some themes endure because they capture an elemental aspect of our humanness. Expectancy Violations Theory suggests that we compare what we imagine will occur with what really occurs, and then modify our behaviors accordingly (Burgoon, 1993).

Humans are territorial beings.

CHRONEMICS

Chronemics, sometimes referred to as **temporal communication,** is the study of time. How we perceive, structure, and use time communicates who we are and what we value. There are cultural, relational, and organizational implications associated with the use of time. Time is perceived differently across cultures. Americans, for example, view time as a commodity, something to be spent and saved, something tangible and highly valued. Our language reveals how time is commodified when we say, "time is money," or "budget my time," and speak of "billable hours."

Although Hall (1976) defined three conceptions of time, only two have immediate bearing on how we organize our everyday lives. **Formal time** is the way society structures time, and it is measured in seconds, minutes, hours, days, weeks, months, years, decades, and so on. There is collective agreement on the metrics of time. Society operates on a similar understanding of formal time. We know that banks are probably not going to open for business at 4:00 AM, however a 24/7 convenience store is a viable option. We would not show up at the dentist's office without an appointment, and we can be reasonably assured that Christmas will be celebrated on December 25th. Formal time is typically not negotiable.

Informal time is negotiable and refers to the unspecified rules and norms that reflect how cultures understand and use time. Hall (2012) identified two classifications of informal time, termed **monochromic** and **polychromic** time. North American and Northern European cultures practice monochromic time that features punctuality, adherence to schedules, and attention to independent task completion. Mediterranean, African, and South American cultures emphasize polychromic time because they value flexibility and have a relaxed interpretation of schedules and punctuality. Of course within each larger culture there are subcultures that also experience different conceptions of time. For example, although both New York City and Baton Rouge are located in North America, people living in these regions view time differently (Moore et al., 2014). The last classification is **technical time,** which is based on scientific measurement (i.e., atomic time) and regarded as a very specialized definition and not widely employed in everyday life.

How we perceive, structure, and use time shows what we value.

We are fast becoming a binge culture, primarily because binging appeals to a desire for immediate consumption and alleviates the need to wait. For example, binge-watchers set their own television viewing patterns, independent of TV network and motion picture studio schedules. This viewing trend reveals the increased effort to control both time and consumption. Are there other aspects of your life that you are no longer willing to wait for? How have you tried to control your time?

We also communicate power through the use of time (Moore et al., 2014). We wait for some people that we consider powerful and important, and we keep others waiting without regard for their time (Richmond & McCroskey, 1995). It is quite common to wait to see a physician or supervisor; however, if your supervisor needs to see you, you are likely to comply immediately. The differential response signals a power imbalance and the principle of supply and demand. If someone has something you want or need, whether it is medical assistance, companionship, or continued employment, you will commit the time to fulfill the need. There are relational implications associated with time as well. A commitment of time reflects interpersonal priorities and it signals that you desire to be with a person. Perhaps this is why it is disturbing when a friend or romantic partner is consistently late when you make plans. A lack of punctuality is revealing and suggests that you are not a priority to them. Chronemics plays a critical role in how we navigate cultural, personal, and professional relationships.

OLFACTICS

Think about phrases such as, "I smell rain," "This situation stinks," "I smell trouble," and "The nose knows." These statements are emblematic of the association between olfactory senses and perception, and they reveal the influential nature of our sense of smell. Olfactics is the study of smells and scents and how they are perceived. Rachel Herz, a professor at Brown University and the foremost expert on the psychology of scents, reports that smell is a central component of mental health, happiness, and mate selection. Although the study of olfactics is relatively new (Knapp, et al., 2014), Herz (2008) believes that smell is "the most emotionally evocative sense" and a powerful form of communication. Think about how the smell of fresh-cut grass, warm chocolate chip cookies, ocean salt, or freshly brewed coffee can prompt a memory, alter your mood, and transport you to another time and place. This process, termed **olfactic association** or **olfactory memory,** is physiological and is usually spontaneous and automatic (Knapp, et al., 2014). Take a moment to reflect on your favorite smell, and identify its origin as well as the memory it evokes. What effect does this scent have on your emotions?

From an evolutionary perspective, research suggests that each individual has a singular identifiable "odorprint" similar to a fingerprint that distinguishes each of us (Herz, 2008). Pheromones, chemicals emitted through sweat glands, make up one's scent and are theorized to influence sexual attraction, especially for women. Olfactory scents trigger attraction differentially for men and women, although contradictory findings have been reported. Have you ever "breathed in" a loved one's scent by physically smelling that person or an article of their clothing? It may sound silly, but if you are willing to try, you will see how this exercise can spark a memory or elicit an emotion.

Native and artificial scent has long been thought to drive sexual attraction, and many industries have capitalized on this with perfume, cologne, scented soap, and deodorant. These products can enhance, eliminate, or camouflage scents. Consistent with other nonverbal codes, olfactics is influenced by culture. People from different cultures do not smell the same. Norms dictating hygiene practices and diet are responsible for many of the cultural differences in personal scents and smells (Herz, 2008).

PHYSICAL APPEARANCE

Physical appearance includes body features, height, weight, hair, and body art. First impressions are strongly influenced by physical appearance, and assessments of attractiveness are quickly registered. The core components of attractiveness include symmetrical facial features, youthful appearance, sexual development, healthy weight, adequate height (especially for men), good hygiene, and a friendly, warm, and expressive demeanor (Andersen, Guerrero, & Jones, 2006; Cunningham, Barbee, & Philhower, 2002; Floyd, 2006; Kurban & Weeden, 2005; Sprecher & Regan, 2002). Most of these physical characteristics are inborn; however, some can be altered through surgical procedures and medical interventions. Cosmetic surgery is a billion-dollar industry, and grooming products and cosmetic lines are substantial commercial enterprises.

Attractiveness is consequential, and there are significant advantages including high self-esteem, active dating life, better jobs, nicer treatment from others, and more leniency in criminal defense hearings (Moore, et al., 2014). You will probably not be surprised to learn that height in men (Guerrero & Hecht, 2008) and thinness in women (Davies-Popelka, 2011) are highly prized physical attributes in Western white cultures. Teachers see attractive students as capable; due to these expectations, attractive students receive more attention and they do perform better in school, supporting the concept of self-fulfilling prophesy (Ritts, Patterson, & Tubbs, 1992). Perceptions of attractiveness are not fixed judgments. Research supports the tendency for us to alter our perceptions of attractiveness after we get to know and like or dislike a person (Abdala, Knapp, & Theune, 2002).

Remarkably, hair can provoke personal, political, social, and cultural reactions more than any other physical attribute. Hair can signify one's religion, culture, race, and group membership. During the 1960s and 1970s, young men grew their hair long to protest the establishment and to show solidarity with their generation. Hair can also be emblematic of religious commitments and beliefs. Some Orthodox Jewish men and boys grow sidelocks or sidecurls called Payot, and elders refrain from trimming their beards. When an Amish man marries, he grows a beard as a sign of adulthood. There is meaning associated with Arab and Muslim men's facial hair. Ashraf Khalil, a journalist for the *BBC News Magazine,* deciphered the significance of various Middle Eastern grooming practices and reported, "In Egypt, Muslim Brotherhood members generally tend to go with the full but well-groomed beard and moustache. However Salafists— the ultraconservative fundamentalist Muslims— like to let their beards grow long and wild, often leaving their upper lip clean-shaven as a nod to how the Prophet Mohammed wore his own beard 1,400 years ago" (n.p.).

During the 1990s, New Jersey women were mercilessly maligned for their big hair and were even facetiously accused of putting a hole in the ozone layer due to excessive use of hair spray. Southern women have been subjected to similar stereotypes. Although unnaturally colored hair is still forbidden for Starbucks baristas, the company recently relaxed the ban on piercings and tattoos (Gonzalez, 2014). Tattoos are no longer grim reminders of concentration camp markings but are now considered body art and a form of self-expression. Regardless of how we personalize our physical appearance, our choices communicate who we are and what is important to us. Look at yourself in the mirror—what are you communicating?

SUMMARY

In this chapter, you learned about the role of verbal and nonverbal communication in a variety of contexts. You read about the characteristics of language, the influence of culture, context, gender, and confirming and disconfirming communication. The second half of the chapter was devoted to nonverbal communication and various codes, including kinesics, facial expressions, eye behavior, haptics, paralanguage, proxemics, chronemics, olfactics, and physical appearance. Influencing factors such as age, culture, and gender were explored and differences were noted. To use language effectively and improve your communication skills requires self-monitoring, an awareness of your goals, and the desire and motivation to modify your communication practices. Think about your verbal and nonverbal communication as you embark on skill development and navigate meaningful relationships with others.

REFERENCES

Albada, K. F., Knapp, M. L., & Theune, K. E. (2002). Interaction appearance theory: Changing perceptions of physical attractiveness through social interaction. *Communication Theory, 12,* 8–40.

Andersen, P. A., Guerrero, L. K., & Jones, S. K. (2006). Nonverbal behavior in intimate interactions and intimate relationships. In V. Manusov & M. L. Patterson (Eds.), *The SAGE handbook of nonverbal communication* (pp. 259–277). Thousand Oaks, CA: Sage.

Bernstein, B. (1973). *Class, codes and control, Volume 2—Applied studies towards a sociology of language.* London: Routledge & Kegan Paul.

Birdwhistell, R. L. (1970). *Kinesics and context: Essays on body motion communication.* Philadelphia, PA: University of Pennsylvania Press.

Buber, M. (1957). Distance and Relation. *Psychiatry, 20,* 97–104.

Burgoon, J. K. (1993). Interpersonal expectations, expectancy violations, and emotional communication. *Journal of Language and Social Psychology, 12,* 3–48.

Burgoon, J. K., Guerrero, L. K., & Floyd, K. (2010). *Nonverbal communication.* Boston, MA: Allyn & Bacon.

Burgoon, J. K., Guerrero, L. K., & Manusov, V. (2011). Nonverbal signals. Interpersonal skills. In M. L. Knapp & J. A. Daly (Eds.), *The SAGE handbook of interpersonal communication* (pp. 239–280). Thousand Oaks, CA: Sage.

Carrere, S., & Gottman, J. M., (1999). Predicting divorce among newlyweds from the first three minutes of a marital conflict discussion. *Family Process, 38,* 293–301.

Cissna, K. & Sieburg, E. (1981). Patterns of interactional confirmation and disconfirmation. In C. Wilder-Mott & J. H. Weakland (Eds.), *Rigor and imagination: Essays from the legacy of Gregory Bateson* (pp. 253–282). New York, NY: Praeger,

Cunningham, M. R., Barbee, A. P., & Philhower, C. L. (2002). Dimensions of facial physical attractiveness: The intersection of biology and culture. In G. Rhodes & L. A. Zebrowitz (Eds.), *Facial attractiveness: Evolutionary, cognitive, and social perspectives* (pp. 193–238). Westport, CT: Ablex.

Davies-Popelka, W. (2011). Mirror, mirror on the wall: Weight, identity, and self-talk. In D. O. Braithwaite & J. T. Wood (Eds.), *Casing interpersonal communication* (pp. 25–32). Dubuque, IA: Kendall Hunt.

Dindia, K. (2006). Men are from North Dakota, women are from South Dakota. In K. Dindia & D. J. Canary (Eds.), *Sex differences and similarities in communication* (2nd ed., pp. 3–18). Mahwah, NJ: Erlbaum.

Ekman, P. (2007). *Emotions revealed: Recognizing face and feelings to improve communication and emotional life.* New York, NY: Macmillan.

Ekman. P., & Friesen, W. V. (1969). The repertoire of nonverbal behavior: Categories, origins, usage, and coding. *Semiotica, 1,* 49–98.

Ekman, P., Friesen, W. V., & Ellsworth, P. (1972). *Emotion in the human face.* Elmsford, NY: Pergamon Press.

Ellis, K. (2004). The impact of perceived teacher confirmation on receiver apprehension, motivation and learning. *Communication Education, 53,* 1–20. doi:10.1080/0363452032000135742

Feldman, R. S., & Tyler, J. M. (2006). Factoring in age: Nonverbal communication across the life span. In V. Manusov & M. L. Patterson (Eds.), *The SAGE handbook of nonverbal communication* (pp. 181–199). Thousand Oaks, CA: Sage.

Finegan, E. (2007). *Language: Its Structure and Use* (5th ed.). Boston, MA: Thomson Wadsworth.

Floyd, K. (2006). An evolutionary approach to understanding nonverbal communication. In V. Manusov & M. L. Patterson (Eds.), *The SAGE handbook of nonverbal communication* (pp. 139–157). Thousand Oaks, CA: Sage.

Floyd, K., Boren, J. P., Hannawa, A. F., Hesse, C., McEwan, B., & Veksler, A. E. (2009). Kissing in marital and cohabiting relationships: Effects on blood lipids, stress, and relationship satisfaction. *Western Journal of Communication, 73,* 113–133. doi:10.1080/10570310902856071

Gonzalez, A. (2014, October 16) Starbucks boosts pay, OKs tattoos, offers 'Starbucks for Life' prize. *The Seattle Times.* Retrieved from http://seattletimes.com/html/businesstechnology/2024799030_starbuckspayxml.html

Guerrero, L. K., & Floyd, K. (2006). *Nonverbal communication in close relationships.* Mahwah, NJ: Erlbaum.

Guerrero, L. K., & Hecht, M. L. (2008). *The nonverbal communication reader: Classic and contemporary readings* (3rd ed.). Long Grove, IL: Waveland.

Hall, E. T. (1966). *The hidden dimension.* Garden City, NY: Doubleday.

Hall, E. T. (1976). *Beyond culture.* Garden City, NY: Doubleday.

Hall, E. T. (2012). Monochromic and polychromic time. In L. Samovar, R. Porter, & E. R. McDaniel, (Eds.) *Intercultural communication: A reader* (13th ed.), (pp. 313–319). Boston, MA: Wadsworth, Cengage.

Hall, J. A. (2006). Women and men's nonverbal communication. In V. Manusov & M. L. Patterson (Eds.), *The SAGE handbook of nonverbal communication* (pp. 201–218). Thousand Oaks: CA: Sage.

Heinberg, P. (1964). *Voice training for speaking and reading aloud.* New York, NY: Ronald Press.

Herz, R. (2008). *The scent of desire: Discovering our enigmatic sense of smell.* New York, NY: Harpercollins.

Hinkle, L. L. (2001). Perceptions of supervisor non-verbal immediacy, vocalics, and subordinate liking. *Communication Research Reports, 18,* 128–136. doi.10.1080/08824090109384790

Hockett, C. F. (1960). The origin of speech. *Scientific America, 203,* 89–96.

Johnston, I. (2015, February 16). The British accent is the world's most attractive, according to poll. *The Independent.* Retrieved from http://www.independent.co.uk/news/uk/home-news/the-british-accent-is-the-worlds-most-attractive-according-to-poll-10032596.html

Kelley, R. (2009, March 9). No apologies. *Newsweek.* p. 54.

Khalil, A. (2013, February 1). Decoding facial hair in the Arab world. *BBC News Magazine.* Retrieved from http://www.bbc.com/news/magazine-20877090

Kinzler, K., & DeJesus, J. M. (2013). Northern = smart and Southern = nice: The development of accent attitudes in the United States. *Quarterly Journal of Experimental Psychology, 66,* 1146–1158.

Knapp, M. L., Hall, J. A., & Horgan, T. G. (2014). *Nonverbal communication in human interaction* (8th ed.). Boston, MA: Cengage.

Leaper, C., & Ayres, M. (2007). A meta-analytic review of moderators of gender differences in adults' talkativeness, affiliative, and assertive speech. *Personality and Social Psychology Review, 11,* 328–363.

Malandro, L. A., Barker, L. L., & Barker, D. A. (1989). *Nonverbal Communication* (2nd ed.). Reading, MA: Addison-Wesley.

Matsumoto, D. (2006). Culture and nonverbal behavior. In V. Manusov & M. L. Patterson (Eds.), *The SAGE handbook of nonverbal communication* (pp. 219–235). Thousand Oaks, CA: Sage.

McClone, M. S., & Giles, H. (2011). Language and interpersonal communication. In M. L. Knapp & J. A. Daly (Eds.), *The SAGE handbook of interpersonal communication* (pp. 201–237). Thousand Oaks, CA: Sage.

Mehrabian, A. (2007). *Nonverbal communication.* Piscataway, NJ: Transaction Publishers.

Moore, N. J., Hickson, M., & Stacks, D. W. (2014). *Nonverbal communication* (6th ed.). New York, NY: Oxford University Press.

New, J. (2014, October 17). More college campuses swap 'No means no' for 'Yes means yes.' *PBS Newshour. The Rundown.* Retrieved from http://www.pbs.org/newshour/rundown/means-enough-college-campuses/

Richmond, V. P., & McCroskey, J. C. (1995). *Nonverbal behaviors in interpersonal relations.* Needham Heights, MA: Allyn & Bacon.

Ritts, V., Patterson, M. L., & Tubbs, M. E. (1992). Expectations, impressions, and judgments of physically attractive students: A review. *Review of Educational Research, 62,* 413–426.

Samovar, L., Porter, R., & McDaniel, E. R. (2009). *Communication between cultures* (12th ed.). Belmont, CA: Thomson.

Samovar, L., Porter, R., & McDaniel, E. R. (2012). *Intercultural communication: A reader* (13th ed). Boston, MA: Wadsworth, Cengage.

Sapir, E. (1949). The unconscious patterning of behavior in society. In E. Mandelbaum (Ed.), *Selected writings of Edward Sapir in language, culture, and personality.* Berkeley, CA: University of California Press.

Schrodt, P., Ledbetter, A. M., & Ohrt, J. K. (2007). Parental confirmation and affection as mediators of family communication patterns and children's mental well-being. *The Journal of Family Communication, 7,* 23–46. doi:10.1080/15267430709336667

Sprecher, S., & Regan, P. C. (2002). Liking some things (in some people) more than others: Partner preferences in romantic relationships and friendships. *Journal of Social and Personal Relationships, 19,* 463–481. doi:10.1177/0265407502019004048

Stewart, J., & D'Angelo, G. (1980). *Together: Communicating interpersonally* (2nd ed.). Reading, MA: Addison-Wesley.

Stone, G. R. (2015, February 7). Campus sexual assaults. *The Huffington Post.* Retrieved from http://www.huffingtonpost.com/geoffrey-r-stone/campus-sexual-assault_b_6586428

Watzlawick, P., Bevan, J., & Jackson, D. (1967). *Pragmatics of human communication: A study of interpersonal patterns, pathologies, and paradoxes.* New York, NY: Norton.

CHAPTER 12

Interpersonal Communication and Personal Relationships

The 1970s was a tumultuous time in the United States. College students experienced an awareness of social inequalities and were vocal supporters of the civil rights movement, the peace movement, the women's movement, and the war on poverty. Then the escalation of the Vietnam War was a particularly polarizing force, culminating in student protests on college campuses across the nation.

Although this was a difficult time, student activism played a key role in bringing about several positive changes at colleges and universities. Today, student membership on college committees and governing boards is commonplace, and university decision-making is informed by student concerns. Out of great hardship and strife grew the recognition that training in interpersonal communication, conflict resolution, and mediation was essential to meaningful dialogue, collaborative problem-solving, and collective understanding. Today these courses are a mainstay in college curriculums across the country.

INTRODUCTION

Now that you know some of the historical impetus for the study of interpersonal communication, let's learn about both the theory and practice of it. Several useful communication skills, concepts, and principles essential to effective communication will be discussed. Building your interpersonal tools is vital to your personal health and well being and to your professional success. Next, five prominent theories and perspectives on communication and relating with others are detailed. Making meaningful connections with significant people in your life is central to interpersonal satisfaction and success.

Interpersonal communication has been defined as "the process of two or three people exchanging messages in order to share meaning, create understanding, and develop relationships" (O'Hair & Wiemann, 2004, p. 6). The truth is, you have been engaged in interpersonal communication since birth. Despite your long history of communicating, are you as effective as you can be? Do you relate well with others? Are you an interpersonally competent communicator? If you are not sure of the answer to these questions, you are in good company because this issue has been on the minds of great thinkers and philosophers for centuries.

Interpersonal competence can be learned with training, effort, and practice.

We do know that interpersonal competence is a valued skill sought by all, practiced by few. The wealth of positive outcomes associated with interpersonal skills is remarkably robust and ever-growing. Noted researchers Brian Spitzberg and William Cupach (2011) report that communication competence is responsible for quality of life, professional success, and relational, physical, and emotional health and well-being. Interpersonal competence also contributes to success in college (Rubin, Graham, & Mignerey, 1990) and can enhance relationships with loved ones, friends, and colleagues (Beebe, Beebe, & Redmond, 2014).

Fortunately, interpersonal competence can be learned with training, effort, and practice. Unlike some unalterable aspects of your being, such as eye color or height, you can improve your ability to relate effectively with others. Developing an awareness and knowledge of what constitutes appropriate and effective communication is the first step. Unless you identify a specific objective, you are not likely to accomplish your goal. Think about challenges you have conquered. Before you ran a marathon, you set reasonable goals such as running one mile, then a 5K, a half marathon, and ultimately a twenty-six-mile marathon. Once you identify your goal, it is easier to accomplish the second step, self-assessment, which requires that you determine how far you are from your objective.

It is important to identify and monitor your communication proficiencies as well as your challenges. Self-monitoring involves developing an awareness of yourself, which means that you are simultaneously a participant and an observer of your own communication behavior. The third step is the most risky because it necessitates that you practice new behaviors and ways of communicating with others. The following quote clarifies the value of taking risks:

> "Before the beginning of great brilliance, there must be chaos. Before a brilliant person begins something great, they must look foolish to the crowd."

— Anonymous

Trying on new ways of being and acting is not easy; you might feel vulnerable and risk looking foolish. Asking others for feedback is the final step, requiring you to be open to others' thoughts about your communication behavior. Let's imagine you have been focusing on becoming more forthright and taking responsibility for your thoughts and feelings when communicating with others. In the past you were reluctant to *own* your communication and often hid behind comments such as, "Other people think you are a troublemaker," or "Your friends think you have been distancing yourself from the group." Now you are more likely to make statements such as, "I am upset by your behavior." Your friends might not notice your efforts to practice new communication skills, so let them know you are on a quest to enhance your interpersonal competence. Be sure to enlist the assistance of friends and family, as they can help you achieve your goal by providing you with instructive feedback. You can certainly improve your interpersonal communication competence but not without a clear understanding of the skills you wish to improve, the motivation to change, and a willingness to risk untried ways of communicating.

Identify your specific objectives in developing interpersonal skills.

CHARACTERISTICS OF COMPETENT COMMUNICATORS

> "The single biggest problem in communication is the illusion that it has taken place."

— George Bernard Shaw

Interpersonal communication competence is defined as the ability to accomplish "interpersonal goals during an encounter while maintaining the face and line of fellow interactants within the constraints of the situation" (Wiemann, 1977, p. 198). To affect interpersonal change, you need to develop the knowledge, skill, and motivation to improve your communication abilities (Spitzberg & Cupach, 2011). Although exhaustive lists of communication skills have been identified, let's start by examining five skills that communication researchers agree are core characteristics of interpersonal competence (Bochner & Kelly, 1974; Wiemann, 1977).

Empathy

Empathy is a key characteristic of competent communicators (Bochner & Kelly, 1974; Wiemann, 1977). Empathy means you see the world through another's eyes and are sensitive to his or her feelings. You may think that *empathy* sounds like *sympathy,* and you are not entirely wrong. Sympathy involves feeling sorry for another whereas empathy is the ability to feel with another person (Adler & Proctor, 2014). Empathy requires that you validate and be clued-in to others' thoughts and needs. Your communication tells your partner that you see and understand him or her. An expression of concern can be verbal and nonverbal and take the form of a knowing look, a hug, or a brief touch. Comments such as, "I see the challenges you've faced in your life, and now I understand you much better," and "I'm here for you," are statements that illustrate your awareness and empathy for others.

Unfortunately, the absence of empathy is bountiful, especially in an age in which people can offer anonymous and visceral attacks online. Stephanie Rosenbloom, writing for the *New York Times,* recently reported the Pew Research Center's findings that almost 70 percent of adults report observing cruelty toward others on social networking sites. It seems in the digital arena, empathy can sometimes be in short supply.

If you are tempted to think empathy is one of those "soft skills" that isn't very important in today's marketplace, think again. Reporter Hannah Morgan, writing for *U.S. News & World Report,* noted that the U.S. Department of Labor claims that 97 percent of occupations today require soft skills. The value of right-brain thinking (where soft skills reside) is detailed in a book by David Pink (2005), in which he identifies the many ways empathy is central not only to personal success but to professional success as well. The ability to understand others and engage in perspective shifts can foster leadership skills, competitive advantages in marketing, and comprehension and insight into employee, customer, and stakeholder concerns.

Empathy is seeing the world through another's eyes.

Defensive vs. Supportive Communication

In a hallmark article published in 1961, Jack Gibb detailed how effective communication involves reducing defensiveness. To illustrate this concept, he developed categories of defensive and supportive communication that when used, can create a defensive or supportive communication climate. As shown in the table below, Gibb identified six defensive and six supportive behaviors.

Characteristics of Supportive and Defensive Communication

Defensive Climates	Supportive Climates
Evaluation	Description
Control	Problem Orientation
Strategy	Spontaneity
Neutrality	Empathy
Superiority	Equality
Certainty	Provisionalism

Effective communication involves reducing defensiveness.

EVALUATION VS. DESCRIPTION

The difference between evaluation and description is *judgment*. Consider the following evaluative and descriptive statements: "I could not help but hear how you stumbled into the house like a freight train last night, well past 3:00 AM" versus "I looked at the clock when you got home last night and it was 3:30 AM." While neither statement bodes well for the recipient of the message, the first statement, which is evaluative, will likely evoke a defensive response whereas the descriptive statement simply states obvious and observable behavior.

CONTROL VS. PROBLEM ORIENTATION

Control orientation and problem orientation rest on the difference between imposing your views on another and arriving at a mutually agreed-upon decision or solution. The statement, "I know you can't do much because of your broken leg, but we are still going on the ski trip as planned," is a command and doesn't communicate respect. Instead, signal a desire to work together with a statement like, "We need to figure out what to do about the ski trip, in view of your broken leg."

STRATEGY VS. SPONTANEITY

Intent is what separates strategic versus spontaneous communication. It is insulting to be "played," and the following statement sounds very strategic, "Remember when you said that you would do anything for me? Well…?" A more spontaneous comment with essentially the same message might be, "Hey, I'm in a jam and I need some help." Both statements are requests for assistance, but the first one sounds cagey and sly whereas the second is straightforward and honest.

NEUTRALITY VS. EMPATHY

Neutrality signals a lack of concern for others whereas empathy involves placing yourself in another's situation. A neutral statement is disconfirming and unsupportive and will likely provoke defensiveness and hurt feelings. If I say to you, "Maybe I'll see you on your birthday; that is, if not too much is going on at the frat house that night," versus "Let's do something special on your birthday—it's such an important day." The first statement communicates indifference and the second one exudes care, responsiveness, and warmth.

SUPERIORITY VS. EQUALITY

Messages that reveal feelings of superiority are insulting and can arouse defensiveness. Conversely, support and respect for others can be conveyed as well. The statement, "You will never meet anybody online with the profile you are using; it says absolutely nothing about you," is condescending in tone compared to, "It is so hard to design the right profile. After failing a few times, I based my profile on suggestions I found online. Do you want to see the post?" The certainty in the first statement indicates a "know-it-all" attitude and is in stark contrast to the second statement, which also offers advice but signals respect for the other.

CERTAINTY VS. PROVISIONALISM

Statements sprinkled with the words "should," "always," and "never" belie a certainty that tends to marginalize the recipient of the message. Provisionalism, on the other hand, is characterized by messages that allow for contrary information and opinions. Statements such as, "You always act that way around guys you like. You are so obvious," will likely arouse feelings of embarrassment and defensiveness. A provisional statement would be, "Have you thought about how to compose yourself when you are around someone you like a lot?"

Choose to cultivate a supportive—not defensive—climate when talking.

The defensive and supportive messages detailed above provoke starkly different responses. Do you wish to cultivate a defensive or supportive climate when talking with loved ones, friends, and work associates? The choice is yours.

Self-Disclosure

Sharing information that reveals what you are feeling, thinking, and wishing for is the essence of self-disclosure. Self-disclosure is an essential component of interpersonal relationships and is necessary for personal well-being as well as emotional and physical health. However, not everyone knows how to do it effectively (Petronio, 2002). If not conducted appropriately, self-disclosure can be risky, inappropriate, untimely, and lead to hurt and rejection. You have undoubtedly been in circumstances in which a stranger has volunteered too much information to you. You probably felt uncomfortable and wondered about this person's social skills. Managing your personal disclosures and being mindful of the circumstances and target of shared information are important interpersonal competence skills (Petronio, 2002).

Self-disclosure is neccessary for well-being but can also result in rejection.

In the past, most self-disclosures were shared in face-to-face conversations. Today, however, social media offers a variety of portals for sharing details about yourself and learning about others (Mazer, Murphy, & Simonds, 2007). Social networking sites, particularly Facebook, have altered the content, frequency, and opportunity to share and receive self-disclosures (Stewart, Dainton, & Goodboy, 2014). We can troll sites and passively gather information and form impressions of others based on information readily available online. In fact, Walther (2015) proposed that as in face-to-face interactions, people do come to know one another, share information, and develop relationships online. As the following story illustrates, self-disclosures are both personal and powerful.

Morgan's Story

Self-disclosing is a difficult thing for me to do. It's a hard choice to make about when and where you will self-disclose information and, of course, to whom you disclose. In my situation, as soon as I met Pat, I really liked him a lot. He made me feel so special. I disclosed too much information too quickly and to the wrong person, and I got hurt in the end. Unfortunately, I shared a secret about my past—stuff I do not usually tell anyone. The day after I told him my secret, he texted me and said that he needed to break off our relationship because he really needed to spend more time on his studies. I was crushed. Needless to say, I will be more careful about whom I disclose to in the future.

Behavioral Flexibility

> "The only constant in life is change.
>
> — Heraclitus

As the Greek Philosopher Heraclitus so astutely noted, change is ever present, which means that adaptability is necessary. The ability to "act in new ways when necessary" (Bochner & Kelly, 1974, p. 291) is the essence of behavioral flexibility. Competent communicators have a large repertoire of options available to them and are capable of selecting any number of appropriate responses to a situation (West & Turner, 2016). Accepting that there is no single way to communicate in every situation, behaviorally flexible communicators have many tools at their disposal, and they can meet the demands of various communication predicaments. In fact, researchers suggest, "the size and diversity of a communicator's repertoire may distinguish more effective from less effective communicators. Indeed, the greater the number of alternative communication strategies at your disposal, the greater your chances of accomplishing your goal" (Knapp et al., 2014, p. 435).

In February 2014, Thomas Friedman, author and columnist for the *New York Times,* interviewed Laszlo Bock, Google's agent responsible for hiring. Bock detailed what Google looks for in a potential new hire and concluded that "…the No. 1 thing we look for is general cognitive ability, and it's not I.Q. It's learning ability. It's the ability to process on the fly. It's the ability to pull together disparate bits of information" (p. SR11). What Bock is describing is behavioral and cognitive flexibility. Thinking on one's feet, being nimble, absorbing all the available information at one's disposal, and then acting, is a useful interpersonal skill. Behavioral flexibility is a central component of interpersonal competence.

Competent communicators have the flexibility to respond appropriately in various situations.

Interaction Management

Interaction management is a central component to interpersonal competence and is "concerned with the 'procedural' aspects that structure and maintain an interaction. These include initiation and termination of the encounter, the allocation of speaking turns, and control of topics discussed" (Wiemann, 1977, p. 199). Learning to skillfully control the ebb and flow of conversation and adapt to situations requires additional interpersonal skills, including listening and mindfulness.

While talking with someone you just met, you may not be sure how to interpret his or her interpersonal cues. For example, you may wonder if your partner is simply pausing or is he or she done speaking? Is it time to yield the floor, or should I tell another story? Paying attention to verbal and nonverbal cues is an excellent way to determine the answers to these questions. We often signal to partners that we are finished talking through silence or by lowering the tone of our voices at the end of a statement (DeVito, 2013). If you find that others enjoy your stories, as evidenced by their laughter and their encouragements for you to continue, the requests are likely genuine. Keep in mind that conversation is a dialogue, not a monologue. Yielding the floor to others and turn-taking in equal measure is an appropriate and useful communication strategy.

As we know from experience, it is very easy to bungle a conversation through miscommunication. Misreading subtle nonverbal cues, misinterpreting another's intentions, and failing to consider context are all likely contributors to ineffective interaction management. Even the smallest conversational hiccup such as an interruption or extended pause can result in perceptions of incompetence (Knapp et al., 2014; Weimann, 1977). When this occurs, regroup and attempt to repair the conversational failure through honest and sincere statements that signal a desire to remedy the problem. Be mindful that communication via social media platforms is rife with unintended consequences. In the absence of nonverbal signals and due to the asynchronicity of the medium, it is difficult to assess meaning, intention, and other subtle forms of communication. In addition to the potential for miscommunication, research suggests that those with limited face-to-face social skills (i.e., individuals who are highly communication apprehensive) are more likely to communicate online (Mazer & Ledbetter, 2012). These results signal a consistent need for the development of interpersonal competence.

In summary, a competent communicator is one who is empathetic, uses supportive communication, practices appropriate self-disclosure, is behaviorally flexible, and can successfully manage interactions with others.

PERSONAL RELATIONSHIP THEORIES

Self image and relationships are constituted and given meaning in our interactions with others. As Duncan reminds us, "we do not relate and then talk, but we relate in talk" (1967, p. 249).

David's Story

Maria and I have been together for four years. We met in high school and found that there was instant chemistry. We both liked the same kind of music, movies, books, and hobbies; we simply had too much in common not to start dating. We had petty arguments over political issues or whether a book we had to read in class was any good (I hated *The Great Gatsby,* Maria loved it), but speaking in totality, we never really had any serious disagreements. This changed recently when we began to start talking about our future.

Moving in together was the big topic. It's not that I didn't want to move out of my parents' house, I just didn't want to have to deal with the financial burden until we were done with school. Maria started talking about what life would be like for us five years down the road, then ten, then twenty. She talked about a joint bank account, what kind of house we would live in, how many kids we would have and what their names would be. I don't oppose marriage, kids, and the whole domestic construct, however I am only twenty years old and a college sophomore. When I tell Maria that planning out our entire lives together makes me so nervous it feels like there's an elephant sitting on my chest, she thinks I'm not in love with her anymore. It makes me sad because this is our first real serious argument.

As the preceding conversation between David and Maria suggests, relationships are complex and require strategic navigation. Perhaps you have been in similar situations and can relate to either Maria's or David's predicament. As you have come to realize, relationships are sometimes fraught with unexpected and confusing turns. How will David and Maria manage their relationship now that their differences have been revealed? How and why people develop relationships with one another is both fascinating and mysterious. Why is it that some relationships "stick" and others fall away?

Relationships are complex and require srategic navigation.

As you read about the five personal relationship perspectives detailed in the following section, keep David and Maria in mind and think about which theory best explains the complications they are experiencing. While a theoretical understanding of relationships will help answer some of these questions, there is still a great deal that we simply do not know about the human condition and even less about matters of the heart.

Social Penetration Theory

The Social Penetration Theory focuses on how relationships develop and mature. Psychologists Irwin Altman and Dalmas Taylor developed the theory in 1973 because they believed that relationships could only begin and deepen through self-disclosure. Their theory claims that from the start, people establish relationships by disclosing information about themselves through small talk at the beginning and more intimate self-disclosures as the relationship grows. Familiarity and intimacy occur when communication moves from trivial non-intimate interactions to deeper personal levels. There is quite a difference in sharing that you are yawning today because you hardly slept last night and the revelation that you are yawning becuse you had a sleepless night after discovering that your romantic partner of nine months cheated on you. The first explanation might be shared with an acquaintance; the latter disclosure would be appropriate to share with your best friend.

An onion is an apt visual metaphor of the Social Penetration Theory. Altman and Taylor described the process of self-disclosure as peeling back the layers of an onion. Personal characteristics such as your height, weight, gender, and eye color are obvious to others; however, the qualities that make up your private self (opinions, beliefs, attitude, and values) reside at the core of your being and are not evident to others.

Amber's Story

As the bonds of our relationship grew stronger, there was one conversation that I knew we had to have. It kept eating away at me. What will he say? What will he think? Will he be able to look at me in the same way? Will he think that I am crazy? Will he breakup with me? These questions ran rampant through my mind. One day when we were talking seriously about our relationship, he asked me if we could make a promise never to keep anything from each other. I knew right then that I had to tell him that I once suffered from severe anorexia. I anxiously reassured him that I had it under control but that it is always

The process of self-disclosure is like peeling back the layers of an onion.

something I will need to be vigilant about. As I said these words I felt a tremendous relief. He just gazed at me with this look of understanding and love, very similar to one that you might see in those cheesy romantic movies. I didn't care, though, because I truly felt closer to him than I ever had before. He said the same thing. Telling him was the best decision I ever made.

As is evident in Amber's story, the intimate disclosure she shared with her boyfriend propelled the relationship to a new level, one perhaps not attainable until Amber shared her innermost self. Self-disclosure is the vehicle by which people progress through the various stages of intimacy. According to Altman and Taylor, those stages include:

1. **Orientation Stage.**   This is the initial interaction stage in which communication is routinized and fairly scripted and is typified by statements such as "Hi, how are you?" and "Nice to meet you." Small talk is exchanged but a limited amount of personal information is shared.

2. **Exploratory Affective Stage.**   Communicators begin to reveal more about themselves and their opinions on a larger assortment of topics. Personal information is still kept private. This is the beginning of a casual friendship, perhaps with a person at work or school.

3. **Affective Stage.**   This is the close friend or romantic partner stage in which communicators begin to disclose very personal information about themselves. Partners might express their love for one another and develop an intimate and private language that includes sophisticated nonverbal codes.

4. **Stable Stage.**   Partners are completely open with one another and share their personal core values and beliefs and reveal their full identities. Altman and Taylor (1973) did not believe many people reached this stage.

5. **Depenetration.**   Altman and Taylor observed that the depenetration process was simply the penetration process in reverse. Essentially, partners stop self-disclosing to one another, which serves to end the relationship.

Relationship Stage Model

Consistent with the Social Penetration Theory, the **stage model** of relationship development also features changes in communication as a means of marking relationship development and deterioration. Mark Knapp, a communication researcher, developed the model and offered the staircase as a metaphor to visualize progressive movement in and out of the relationship. In total there are ten steps or stages—five devoted to the process of coming together and five stages reflective of relationships coming apart. Changes in verbal and nonverbal communication are the primary means by which people move from one stage to the next. The five coming together stages are initiating, experimenting, intensifying, integrating and bonding. The coming apart stages are differentiating, circumscribing, stagnating, avoiding, and terminating. Partners can exit any stage at any point in time. Each stage is characterized by specific verbal and nonverbal communication behaviors and patterns (Knapp, 1978; Knapp, Vangelisti, & Caughlin, 2014).

COMING TOGETHER STAGES

The first stage, **initiating,** as the name suggests, is the initial point of contact. You might notice someone in class that looks interesting, or you see a person out of the corner of your eye at a party talking and laughing with others. Something about these people captured your attention. It could be their physical appearance or demeanor, or your interest might be based on whom they are interacting with or what they are doing. It is during this stage that you decide to make contact with the other. "Hi" or "Hey, how's it going?" have been identified as the most preferable opening lines by both men and women (Kleinke, Meeker, & Staneski, 1986). This is a critical moment because it is your only opportunity to make a first impression. This interaction is usually brief, and the decision to proceed to the next sage is made in a matter of seconds.

Individuals move together or apart through verbal and nonverbal communication.

The next stage, **experimenting,** involves information exchange and may take the form of small talk, termed **phatic communication.** Examples of small talk are questions such as "What's your major?" or "Which residence hall do you live in?" or "Do you know Jeremy, the guy on the second floor who plays hockey in the hallway day and night?" This stage is characterized by casual conversation and a search for commonalities. If the other person assists you in finding those commonalities, this signals their interest in continuing the conversation. At this stage, relationships are pleasant and inconsequential, as most associations do not pass beyond this stage.

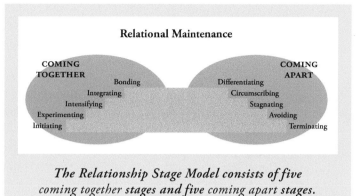

The third stage is **intensifying,** a phase of the relationship marked by personalized and intimate verbal and nonverbal communication. Partners might have cute pet names for one another, and sophisticated nonverbal messages are used to signal, for example, that *it is time to leave the party* or *please save me from this conversation with the guy who talks too much.* Words such as *me, mine,* and *I* are replaced with *us, ours,* and *we.* Couples present themselves as a unit, and their lives are increasingly enmeshed. Favors are asked and are freely given. Self-disclosures increase in frequency and depth as secrets and the self are revealed.

The fourth stage, **integrating,** occurs when lifestyles, routines, schedules, and social circles merge and differences are minimized. You might find yourself dressing up more because your partner prefers a more formal look. The twosome is treated as a singular unit and others question when you are apart. Physical intimacy is a mainstay and couples likely identify themselves as a unit on social media platforms. Secrets and empathy are shared, and couples are fully enmeshed in one another's lives. Once a night owl, you might find yourself acquiescing to your partner's love of the early morning hours. Soon enough, you are heading to bed at 9:30 PM. Except for physical intimacy, friendships at this stage are also characterized in much the same way.

The **bonding** stage involves a public declaration and sometimes a public ritual announcing that the couple shares an enduring relationship. The bond can be legal as in the exchange of marital vows or symbolic as in a commitment to an exclusive romantic relationship. The bonding stage represents a critical point in a relationship. Friendship bonds are forged in the form of symbolic gestures such as serving as best man/maid of honor in a best friend's wedding—a coveted and meaningful role in most cultures. In romantic relationships, "the relationship" is often the subject of conversation as rules are solidified and expectations are made clear. For example, unless otherwise negotiated or culturally sanctioned, marriage usually signals an end to one's dating life. Once bonding has occurred it is much more difficult to end the relationship as lives, possessions, families, and emotions are enmeshed and not easily restored to their previous state.

At the bonding stage, couples often engage in maintenance behaviors to stabilize the relationship. **Relationship maintenance** behaviors can include spending time with each other's family and friends, openness to talking about the relationship, offering assurances of one's commitment to the relationship, and engaging in positive, optimistic, and cheerful communication with one another (Canary & Stafford, 1994).

COMING APART STAGES

Jenna's Story

Within the first semester of my freshman year I had gotten an on-campus job, met many new people, and began to find out who I was and what I wanted to do with my life. I also found out that I was no longer clicking with my high-school boyfriend, Rob. I started to realize that the things we had in common in high school were becoming obsolete. School was not important to him but it was for me. I noticed that I stopped telling him things, and we no longer had the same friends. He spent much of his time working out at the gym, and I spent my time studying or hanging out with my new friends. The fact that we both knew the end was inevitable made the breakup easier.

Specific communication patterns indicate weakening relationship bonds in the coming apart stage.

As Jenna's story illustrates, couples grow apart, often as a result of different life goals and experiences. Emotional and physical distance contributes to a decrease in self-disclosure, time spent together, and favors asked and granted. Unlike Altman and Taylor's Social Penetration Theory, Knapp's **coming apart** stages are not simply the reverse of the coming together stages; rather, they are marked by specific communication patterns indicative of the weakening of the relationship bonds.

Differentiating, the sixth stage, features communication that signals a plea for independence and autonomy. Fighting and conflict are more prevalent, and discussions focus more on differences than commonalties. The words *me, mine,* and *I* creep back into usage, indicative of a desire for individualism. Topics of conflict are shepherded off to a growing "Do Not Discuss" list. Instead of searching for an activity the two of you can share, you might find yourself saying to your partner, "Since you don't like that kind of movie anyway, I am going with Chris." Jenna's story illustrates this stage as her interests branched off from her boyfriend's, and the two of them had very little in common.

The **circumscribing** stage reflects less self-disclosure and fewer meaningful exchanges between partners. The "Do Not Discuss" list grows even larger, limiting conversational topics and making talking more difficult and uncomfortable. Meanwhile, you and your partner continue to present yourselves as a couple in public and become well-schooled in *appearing* to be a happy couple.

The **stagnating** stage implies that the relationship is at a standstill. Verbal and nonverbal communication is tense and awkward. Individuals in this stage often think that conversation is not really worthwhile because they already know how it will turn out. Essentially, you have quit the relationship but you have not yet physically removed yourself or discussed the matter with your partner.

Avoiding, as the name suggests, is putting distance between yourself and your partner. The distance can be physical, emotional, or both. Partners limit their conversations, but if they must talk, communication is instrumental and restricted to essential information exchanges such as, "Did you remember to cancel the concert tickets?" and "Before you leave, be sure to pay the cell phone bill." It is clear that partners wish to end the relationship. Communication is direct and may even include statements such as, "From now on, only contact me if it is absolutely necessary."

The **terminating** stage signals the end of the relationship. Research suggests that meta-communication about the impending relationship dissolution is common (Dailey, Rossetto, McCracken, Jin, & Green, 2012). For example, summary messages that wrap up loose ends may include statements such as, "We had a great relationship," "I was my best self with you," and "I hope we always stay in touch." Friends and family are alerted that the two of you are no longer together, and a breakup story is sometimes jointly constructed and shared. Couples may have a cordial breakup, brought on by the gradual decay of the relationship or the breakup may be a dramatic, emotional, and turbulent severing of ties in which hurtful and unkind words are voiced.

Stage models are efficient and linear, and they offer a predictable depiction of relationship development and deterioration. Both the Social Penetration Theory and the Stage Model of Relationship Development, despite the metaphors of the onion and the staircase, recognize that not all relationships follow this sequential pattern of development and deterioration (Altman, Vinsel, & Brown, 1981; Knapp et.al., 2014). For example, stages are sometimes skipped, as is the case of *friends with benefits*. Physical

People who have stronger relationship ties use more media to maintain their relationships.

intimacy without commitment is the hallmark of these relationships (Hughes, Morrison, & Asada, 2005). *Hooking up* would also be an instance in which the methodical movement from stage to stage is absent. Perhaps it is time to reevaluate the normative undercurrents of both the Social Penetration Theory and Knapp's stage model. Crafted over forty years ago, stage models do not account for the increasing tendency of college students to engage in intimacy prior to self-disclosure (Bogle, 2008). Nor do the stage models account for the influence of technology. For example, the **Theory of Media Multiplexity** states that people who have stronger relationship ties use more media (i.e., Facebook, text, instant messaging, email) to maintain their relationships, and more media use serves to strengthen relational ties (Ledbetter, 2015).

Movement between stages is common. A relationship transgression might prompt you to revert back to a previous, safer, and less intense stage. For example, if trust has been lost, subsequent self-disclosures might not be forthcoming and favors may not be readily granted. Other relationships experience a pattern of frequent breakups and make-ups—on-again, off-again—which is characterized by chaotic movement between and within the stages (Dailey et al., 2012). The stage model also does not explain the consequences of partners being at different stages in the relationship. For example, you may be at the bonding stage but your partner is still in the integrating stage, just as David and Maria were at different relationship stages. Although the stage model is most often applied in romantic relationships, it does have utility in any developing union between two people, particularly friendships; however, the model has not been applied to LGBTQ relationships (Mongeau & Henningsen, 2015).

Social Exchange Theory

While stage models explain how people develop relationships, Social Exchange Theories account for why people stay or leave relationships. The metaphor of the scales held by Lady Justice represents the essence of Social Exchange Theory. Known as the economic model of relationship development, John Thibault and Harold Kelley developed this theory in 1959. This theory is very methodical and looks at associations from a rewards and costs perspective to determine the attractiveness of a relationship. The Social Exchange Theory is rooted in several beliefs which include: (1) people are motivated to maximize rewards and minimize costs, (2) people are calculating and mindful, and (3) people have different interpretations of rewards and costs.

A simple mathematical equation captures the components of the Social Exchange Theory.

$$\text{Rewards} - \text{Costs} = \text{Relationship Outcome}$$

Rewards are defined as those aspects individuals find pleasurable, enjoyable, gratifying, and satisfying. Your partner makes you feel good about yourself, offers friendship and love, or can provide you with a raise, promotion, and/or sex. This person is friendly, good-humored, and fun to be with. Costs are anything that you consider a drain on your personal resources such as time, energy, money, or an emotional and physical commitment that you find too taxing to provide.

According to Social Exchange Theory, if a relationship offers more rewards than costs, the relationship will continue. On the other hand, if the costs exceed the rewards, then the relationship will likely be terminated. To some, subjecting relationship analysis to a metaphorical balance sheet is devoid of feeling and too calculating. Others might point out that they know people who stay in unsatisfying relationships that yield more costs than rewards. For example, your friend Michael knows his girlfriend is cheating on him, a definite cost to most people, yet he continues his commitment to the relationship. Your sister Lucy constantly complains about her job and the horrible working conditions and hours, yet she remains on the job. Social Exchange Theory offers two additional concepts that help explain Michael's and Lucy's seemingly poor decisions (Kelley & Thibault, 1978).

Social Exchange Theory is an economic model of relationship devlopment, balancing costs and rewards.

The first concept, **Comparison Level (CL),** is the personal standard by which you measure the desirability of a relationship. It is the baseline norm that is a conglomerate of all your previous relationships and a lifetime of influencing agents (e.g., parents, family, friends). The CL represents your expectations of all future relationships. A high CL indicates that you have had good fortune in your previous relationships and therefore have rather high expectations of future relationships.

The second factor, termed the **Comparison Level for Alternatives (CLalt),** determines the relative attractiveness of a relationship when it is compared to alternative relationships. This assessment will determine whether you will maintain or abandon the current relationship. For example, Chandra has an unhealthy relationship with Terrence. They fight all the time and she suspects he has a substance abuse problem. She is not happy and knows she deserves better (CL), but unfortunately she does not believe that there are alternative relationships available to her (CLalt), so she will stay in the relationship. The reason Michael stays in an unsatisfying relationship (CL) with a cheating girlfriend is because he does not believe he has any alternatives (CLalt). Michael suffers from communication apprehension, and the thought of initiating a brand new relationship is simply too frightening for him to consider. Lucy also has few alternatives and realizes that although her current job is unpleasant (CL), there are no other jobs that pay $12.00 per hour (CLalt), and she desperately needs the money for her college tuition. Both Michael and Lucy knowingly choose relationships that are unsatisfactory because the alternatives are below their comparison level.

As noted earlier in the chapter, stage models have been criticized for their linear treatment of relationships. Similar charges have been waged against the Social Exchange Theory. In addition, critics claim that relationships do not lend themselves to a balance sheet in which costs and rewards play such a central role in determining whether the relationship thrives or is terminated. On the other hand, the Social Exchange Theory, with its emphasis on the evaluation of alternatives, offers an excellent explanation for why individuals remain in relationships that appear costly.

Uncertainty Reduction Theory

Professors Charles Berger and Richard Calabrese, two communication specialists, proposed the Uncertainty Reduction Theory in 1975 after noting that initial interactions between individuals followed predictable patterns of information seeking. They believe that uncertainty reduction is the primary concern of individuals meeting for the first time. Uncertainty is cast as an unnecessary evil that limits the ability to control and predict behavior (Feeley, 2015). The main assumptions of Uncertainty Reduction Theory include: (1) uncertainty is uncomfortable and (2) to alleviate that discomfort, people communicate (Berger, 1987).

Like living thermostats, we collect information to reduce uncertainty in relationships.

The metaphor of a living thermostat that seeks information from its environment in order to adjust its operation is an apt descriptor of this theory. Uncertainty represents a departure from the machine's ideal state, and the thermostat must gather information to return to homeostasis. Uncertainty reduction is particularly important in relationship development, as the information gathered through observation and interaction can be used to predict a person's current and future behavior. Uncertainty reduction occurs primarily through asking questions and self-disclosure. Social media research supports this contention, revealing that when romantic partners feel uncertainty they use more Facebook monitoring as a means of stabilizing their relationship (Stewart, Dainton, & Goodboy, 2014).

Charles Berger identified three strategies for gathering information in order to decrease uncertainty:

1. **Passive Strategy.** Information about the other is gathered through both physical observation and electronic surveillance. No contact is made with the other.

2. **Active Strategy.** Information is gathered by questioning others about the person of interest. Again, electronic surveillance is usually an anonymous and useful means of gathering information about the target of your interest.

3. **Interactive Strategy.** Contact is finally made and information is gathered by communicating with the person directly, and interaction takes the form of question-asking and self-disclosure.

We are not motivated to reduce uncertainty about everyone; indeed, we are quite selective in our interests (Berger, 1987). Generally we are motivated to reduce uncertainty in three circumstances:

1. **Anticipation of Future Interaction.** If you will see this person again, you are more motivated to understand their current and future actions. For example, the person who lives in the dorm room across the hall is someone you will undoubtedly see again, so it is worth your time and effort to seek information about this person.

2. **Incentive Value.** If someone such as a possible romantic partner, boss, teacher, or new friend has the power to provide or withhold rewards, you will be motivated to seek information about these individuals.

3. **Deviance.** It is not unusual to want to reduce uncertainty about people who are odd, novel, or unusual, especially if they are deviating from normative behavior.

Although Uncertainty Reduction Theory has greatly influenced communication studies, it's not without its critics. Some scholars say that uncertainty reduction is not always the factor motivating communication; some people interact out of a genuine desire to connect positively with others. Austin Babrow questioned the basic premise of Uncertainty Reduction Theory and proposed that uncertainty is not necessarily bad and information-seeking is not the only response to uncertainty. For example, imagine that you visited your doctor because you were not feeling well, and through various tests it was determined that you are afflicted with a serious health condition. Uncertainty Reduction Theory states that you would be motivated to know everything possible about this condition to gain a degree of control and to reduce uncertainty. Babrow's **Problematic Integration Theory,** on the other hand, would direct you to examine the probability of an outcome and the evaluation of that outcome—is it positive or negative? Returning to our previous example, if the condition you are suffering from is likely to result in dire consequences for you (high probability of negative outcome), then you may not seek uncertainty reduction. Uncertainty reduction will result in more clarity about your predicament; however, operating from a problematic integration perspective will allow you to both cope with the situation and maintain hope about the outcome (Babrow & Striley, 2015).

In addition to experiencing uncertainty about others' behavior, it is also common to feel uncertainty about yourself and your relationship, especially established relationships. Knobloch and Solomon (1999) addresses the notion of uncertainty about the state of the relationship. For example, you might wonder if you are really ready for an exclusive intimate relationship at this time in your life. It is common to question whether the relationship will last or how much commitment is required to keep the relationship going. These concerns are at the heart of managing and reducing uncertainty and of making sense of our relational world.

Although Uncertainty Reduction Theory has greatly influenced our understanding of how we interface with our social world and respond to uncertainties, it does not explain all of our communication motivations. For example, sometimes it is enjoyable and exciting to entertain a degree of uncertainty. It is great fun not to know what your partner will do next, and a certain amount of uncertainty can be very exciting. Most of us would choose uncertainty over the boredom that can accompany total certainty. Arun's story illustrates this point.

> ### Arun's Story
>
> I think I have figured out what went wrong with Reva. For months now, I've been wondering if the problem was that she simply disclosed too much information. At the beginning I loved hearing Reva's inner feelings and secrets, and it made me feel really close to her. Later I realized that I did not want to know absolutely everything about her. I feel really guilty about this, but the more information Reva shared with me, the less I began to care and share, and strangely, the less I liked her.

Relational Dialectics Theory

"Relationships are messy" sums up Relational Dialectics Theory (RDT), which was, in part, a reaction to the stage and economic models of relationship development. Leslie Baxter (1990), a communication theorist, articulated the Relational Dialectics Theory and continues to refine the theory today (Baxter & Norwood, 2015).

As the dialectical perspective gained traction and support from other communication researchers, a different way of thinking about relationships emerged—one that characterizes communication in relationships as:

1. fluid and ever-changing

2. unfinalized

3. interplay between opposing forces

Dialectical theory directs us to view relationships from a perspective that recognizes that change is constant, inevitable, and evident in all relationships. Movement occurs as a pull toward one force is more compelling than the pull toward the opposing force. Each movement produces changes in the relationship. The visual metaphor of yin-yang is used to illustrate opposite or contrary operating forces inherent in relationships. Rather than progressing from one stage to the next, as some other relationship development theories suggest, RDT reflects the "...pushes and pulls inherent in relating" (Baxter & Norwood, 2015, p. 289).

Relational Dialectics Theory reflects the pushes and pulls of opposite forces.

Although there are many different pushes and pulls, termed *dialectical contradictions,* Baxter and Braithwaite (2010) identified three primary tensions that are most characteristic in interpersonal relationships: **connection-autonomy** (we vs. me), **openness-closedness** (tell vs. not tell), and **predictability-novelty** (certainty vs. uncertainty). *Autonomy* refers to independence, and *connection* is characterized as a pull toward interdependence. *Closedness* denotes privacy and nondisclosure, and *openness* references revealing information and disclosiveness. *Predictability* implies certainty, and *novelty* is signified by uncertainty. Relationship partners try to manage the competing tensions that pull people in contrary and opposing directions. Baxter and Braithwaite (2010) report that the autonomy-connection dialectic is the most primary relational contradiction.

Gunnar's Story

Sal and I have been dating since our first year in college. We met in our Public Speaking course and even sat next to each other. Well, that was three years ago and we have been a couple ever since. We spend as much time together as possible. I love her very much and she is a great person, but sometimes I need a little freedom. My friends mock me because when I am hanging out with them, it never fails that Sal will text me to see what I am doing and wants to know when she and I will get together. It is kind of surprising to me, but when I am apart from Sal, I realize how much I need her and want to be with her. I know I sound crazy, but it's how I feel.

Gunnar's story speaks to the interplay between autonomy and connection and illustrates how two people can be in different relationship places, experience different relationship needs, and experience them for different periods of time. At this point you might be wondering, "How do I embrace and ultimately manage competing contradictions such as those experienced by Gunnar and Sal?" It is important to realize that dialectical contradictions are neither good nor bad; they are simply an elemental component of all relationships.

Baxter (1990) identified several ways to manage dialectical contradictions. For example, it is sometimes useful to privilege one opposing force and ignore the other. Gunnar could ignore Sal's repeated text messages or he could respond to all of them. Gunnar and Sal could have a discussion and agree on rules for texting and calling one another while apart. Reframing the source of the tension is perhaps the most useful strategy to manage the inevitable changes inherent in a relationship. Instead of choosing to ignore Sal's text messages, an undesirable strategy, Gunnar could reframe the tension and tell Sal, "I love our time together and when we are apart, it just makes me value you even more." His message to Sal transcends the texting problem and refocuses the attention on Gunnar's love for Sal; it assures Sal that Gunnar values the relationship as highly as she does.

"My profile says 'In a relationship', but his says 'It's complicated'."

Two people can be in different relationships places and have different needs.

Each relationship perspective offers a different lens through which to view how relationships form, evolve, change, flourish, dissolve, and deteriorate. Taken together, it is easy to see how people relate to one another and why some relationships in our lives move forward and others fall away. The centrality and importance of relationships in our lives compels us to improve and foster a positive communication climate in our interactions with others.

SUMMARY

In this chapter you first learned about how students played a central role in the need to have courses such as interpersonal communication in the curriculums of colleges and universities in the United States. Next you read about several communication skills reflective of interpersonal communication competence. The specific skills include empathy, supportive communication, self-disclosure, behavioral flexibility, and interaction management. Remember that competence can be developed if you are motivated to change and develop new communication behaviors. The benefits of being a competent communicator far outweigh the risk required to learn new skills. Good communicators are likely to have more satisfying personal and professional relationships, and they tend to be successful at their jobs.

Next you learned about five perspectives that describe and explain how relationships develop, change, stabilize, dissolve, and deteriorate. The stage models, including Social Penetration Theory and the Relationship Stage Model, suggest that relationships go through various stages which are characterized by differences in communication. The Social Exchange Theory, often termed the economic model of relationship development, shows how cost, rewards, and profits may be considered in continuing or ending relationships. This theory also explains why people may stay in unsatisfying relationships, especially if they do not believe they have suitable alternatives. Uncertainty Reduction Theory highlights the desire to reduce uncertainty as a necessary prerequisite to forming close relationships with others. Finally, Relationship Dialectics Theory, unlike the other four perspectives, rejects stages, profits, and losses, and embraces uncertainty and change, and it features the pushes and pulls inherent in all relationships.

Think about these skills and relationship theories as you embark on your own skill development efforts and navigate meaningful relationships with others.

REFERENCES

Adler, R. B., & Proctor, R. F. (2014). *Looking out looking in* (14th ed.). Boston, MA: Wadsworth.

Altman, I., & Taylor, D. A. (1973). *Social penetration: The development of interpersonal relationships.* New York, NY: Holt, Rinehart and Winston.

Altman, I., Vinsel, A., & Brown, B. B. (1981). Dialectical conceptions in social psychology: An application to social penetration and privacy regulation. In L. Berkowitz (Ed.), *Advances in experimental social psychology* (vol. 14, pp. 107–160). New York, NY: Academic Press.

Babrow, A. S., & Striley, K. S. (2015). Problematic integration theory and uncertainty management theory. In D. O. Braithwaite & P. Schrodt (Eds.), *Engaging theories in interpersonal communication: Multiple perspectives* (pp. 103–114). Thousand Oaks, CA: Sage.

Baxter, L. A. (1990). Dialectical contradictions in relationship development. *Journal of Social and Personal Relationships, 7,* 69–88.

Baxter, L. A. & Braithwaite, D. O. (2010). Relational dialectics theory, applied. In S. W. Smith & S. R. Wilson (Eds.), *New directions in interpersonal communication research.* (pp. 48–66). Thousand Oaks, CA: Sage.

Baxter, L. A., & Norwood, K. M. (2015). Relational Dialectics Theory: Navigating meaning from competing discourses. In D. O. Braithwaite & P. Schrodt (Eds.), *Engaging theories in interpersonal communication: Multiple perspectives* (pp. 279–291). Thousand Oaks, CA: Sage.

Beebe, S. A., Beebe, S. J., & Redmond, M. V. (2014). *Interpersonal communication.* Boston, MA: Pearson.

Berger, C. R. (1987). Communicating under uncertainty. In M. E. Roloff & C. R. Berger (Eds.), *Interpersonal processes: New directions in communication research* (pp. 39–62). Newbury Park, CA: Sage.

Berger, C. R., & Calabrese, R. J. (1975). Some Explorations in Initial Interaction and Beyond: Toward a Developmental Theory of Interpersonal Communication. *Human Communication Research, 1,* 99–112.

Bochner, A. P., & Kelly, C. W. (1974). Interpersonal competence: Rationale, philosophy, and implementation of a conceptual framework. *The Speech Teacher, 23,* 279–301. DOI:10.1080/03634527409378103

Bogle, K. A. (2008). *Hooking up: Sex, dating, and relationships on campus.* New York, NY: New York University Press.

Canary, D. J., & Stafford, L. (1994). Maintaining relationships through strategic and routine interaction. In D. Canary & L. Stafford (Eds.), *Communication and relational maintenance* (pp. 3–22). San Diego, CA: Academic Press.

Dailey, R. M., Rossetto, K. R., McCracken, A. A., Jin, B., & Green, E. W. (2012). Negotiating breakups and renewals in on-again/off-again dating relationships: Traversing the transitions. *Communication Quarterly, 60,* 165–189.

DeVito, J. A. (2013). *The interpersonal communication book.* Boston, MA: Pearson.

Duncan, D. H. (1967). The search for a social theory of communication in American sociology. In F. E. X. Dance (Ed.), *Human communication theory* (pp. 236–263). New York, NY: Holt, Rinehart and Winston.

Feeley, T. H. (2015). *Research from the inside out.* New York, NY: Routledge.

Friedman, T. L. (2014, February 22). How to Get a Job at Google. *The New York Times,* SR11.

Gibb, J. R. (1961). Defensive communication. *Journal of Communication, 11,* 141–148.

Hughes, M., Morrison, K., & Asada, K. J. (2005). What's love got to do with it? Exploring the impact of maintenance rules, love attitudes, and network support on friends with benefits relationships. *Western Journal of Communication, 69,* 49–66.

Kelley, H. H., & Thibaut, J. W. (1978). *Interpersonal Relationships.* New York, NY: John Wiley & Sons.

Kleinke, C. L., Meeker, F. B., & Staneski, R. A. (1986). Preference for opening lines: Comparing ratings by men and women. *Sex Roles, 15,* 585–600.

Knapp, M. L. (1978). *Social intercourse: From Greeting to goodbye.* Boston, MA: Allyn & Bacon.

Knapp, M. L., & Vangelisti, A. L., Caughlin, J. P. (2014). *Interpersonal Communication and human relationships.* Boston, MA: Pearson.

Knobloch, L. K., & Solomon, D. H. (1999). Measuring the sources and content of relational uncertainty. *Communication Studies, 50,* 261–278.

Ledbetter, A. M. (2015). Media Multiplexity Theory: Technology use aand interpersonal tie strength. In D. O. Braithwaite & P. Schrodt (Eds.), *Engaging theories in interpersonal communication: Multiple perspectives* (pp. 363–375). Thousand Oaks, CA: Sage.

Mazer, J. P., & Ledbetter, A. M. (2012). Online communication attitudes as predictors of problematic internet use and well-being outcomes. *Southern Communication Journal, 77,* 403–419.

Mazer, J. P., Murphy, R. E., Simonds, C. J. (2007). I'll see you on "Facebook": The effects of computer-mediated teacher self-disclosure on student motivation, active learning, and classroom climate. *Communication Education, 57,* 1–17.

Mongeau, P. A., & Henningsen, M., L., M. (2015). Stage theories of relationship development: Charting the course of interpersonal communication. In D. O. Braithwaite & P. Schrodt (Eds.), *Engaging theories in interpersonal communication: Multiple perspectives* (pp. 389–402). Thousand Oaks, CA: Sage.

Morgan, H. (2014, March 19). The soft skills all employers seek. *U.S. News and World Report,* from http://money.usnews.com/money/blogs/outside-voices-careers/2014/03/19/the-soft-skills-all-employers-seek

O'Hair, D. O., & Wiemann, M. O. (2004). *The essential guide to interpersonal communication.* Boston, MA: Bedford/St. Martin's.

Pink, D. (2005). *A whole new mind: Moving from the information age to the conceptual Age.* New York, NY: Penguin Group.

Petronio, S. (2002). *Boundaries of Privacy: Dialectics of Disclosure.* Albany, NY: State University of New York Press.

Rosenbloom, S. (2014, August 23). *Dealing with digital cruelty. The New York Times,* SR1.

Rubin, R. B., Graham, E. E., & Mignerey, J. T. (1990). A longitudinal study of college students' communication competence. *Communication Education, 39,* 1–14.

Spitzberg, B. H., & Cupach, W. R. (2011). Interpersonal skills. In M. L. Knapp & J. A. Daly (Eds.), *The SAGE handbook of interpersonal communication* (pp. 481–524). Thousand Oaks, CA: Sage.

Stewart, M. C., Dainton, M., & Goodboy, A. K. (2014). Maintaining relationships on Facebook: Associations with Uncertainty, Jealousy, and satisfaction. *Communication Reports, 27,* 13–26.

Thibault, J. W., & Kelley, H. H. (1959). *The Social Psychology of Groups.* New York, NY: John Wiley & Sons.

Walther, J. B. (2015). Social information processing theory: Impressions and relationship development online. In D. O. Braithwaite & P. Schrodt (Eds.), *Engaging theories in interpersonal communication: Multiple perspectives* (pp. 417–428). Thousand Oaks, CA: Sage.

West, R., & Turner, L. H. (2016). *Interpersonal Communication.* Boston, MA: Cengage.

Wiemann, J. M. (1977). Explication and test of a model of communicative competence. *Human Communication Research, 3,* 195–213.

Note: Special thanks is extended to The University of Akron students Morgan Alley, Jenna Payne, and David Trujillo for generously sharing their personal stories and granting permission to print them in this chapter.

CHAPTER 13

Small Group Communication

Ziya worked with her group all semester to put together a thirty-minute presentation for her group communication class. She coordinated their evolving agenda, kept a timeline, took notes on their progress, and tried to keep everyone involved, but it was not easy. Callie tried to wrestle control of the group away from Ziya although she never had a clear idea of what she wanted to do. She also interrupted frequently when others were speaking, which suppressed participation. Ryan just wanted to socialize and joke around. At the end of every meeting he said, "Can't we meet at a bar next time?" Shani was just dead weight. After the first group meeting she never worked with the group. She then showed up the day of the presentation and said, "Tell me what to do." Eric had something negative to say about every idea that was brought up. Typical comments were, "That's a dumb idea" or "We don't have the time to do that." The presentation met the minimum requirements of the assignment, but it could have been so much better. Ziya was disappointed and frustrated. She thought to herself, "Are all groups like this?"

INTRODUCTION

Many people have had experiences like Ziya's; however, not all groups struggle to accomplish their tasks. Some groups work very well together in completing their work and getting along socially. Other groups experience problems but work through their difficulties and ultimately perform well. There are also groups that are disasters. These groups might be composed of people with different work styles or the members may not be compatible socially. In this chapter we focus on small group communication, explaining why it is important to learn about small groups and defining small group communication. We then cover communication competence in groups, small group development, establishing group culture, group cohesiveness, groupthink, leadership in small groups, problem-solving and decision-making, technology, social media, group communication, and conflict in groups.

WHY SHOULD YOU LEARN ABOUT SMALL GROUPS?

Small groups are an essential part of the human experience. They allow us to build the society in which we live. Families, work groups, support teams, community associations, and study groups are just some of the many types of groups we will experience in a lifetime. As you enter the professional world, you will find that groups are where most of the work in organizations is accomplished. Although much of what has been written about groups focuses on members getting together face-to-face, in the information age people can interact over the World Wide Web as well. This can occur in families, among friends, or in organizational settings.

Most of the work in professional organizations is accomplished in groups.

Although we all have had countless experiences with groups, many people report frustrations in completing work or in sustaining social relationships in them. In fact, 75 percent of workers report that time spent in meetings could be more productive (Herring, 2006). That is why learning about small group communication is so important. You will be in groups your entire life, so why not develop the skills that will allow you to succeed in them?

Working in groups is part of nearly every activity we perform. Groups also meet some of our most important needs. William Schutz, a psychologist who studied group communication, said that groups meet our needs for **inclusion, affection,** and **control** (Schutz, 1958). Our need for inclusion speaks to our desire for being involved with others. Humans have a strong need to belong to or be included in groups. In fact, much of our identities—our beliefs about who we are—is derived from the groups most important to us (family, friends, religious congregations, interest groups, work groups, etc.). Our need for affection involves the emotions we experience in caring for others and being cared for. Humans need to love and be loved. Finally, we have a need for control, which means we have the ability to influence our environment. Working together with others in groups increases our ability to exercise such control. One person cannot build a house, construct a road, or start a new business. We need others to work with us.

WHAT IS SMALL GROUP COMMUNICATION?

When communication occurs in small groups, it is both task-oriented and goal-directed. In order to accomplish tasks and achieve goals, group members must work together interdependently. So, how do small groups function? Let's consider six features of small group communication: size, interdependence, task, norms, identity, and group talk.

The first feature is **group size,** or number of members. Small group communication is the interaction among three to fifteen people who work together to achieve a goal (Adams & Galanes, 2011). Research has shown the ideal group size to be five to seven members (Cragan & Wright, 1999). Smaller groups might find it difficult to accomplish complex tasks. Groups larger than fifteen can result in loafing by members who seek to avoid work because others can take up the slack without much additional effort. The exact number of members is less important, however, than each member knowing who belongs to the group and interactions occuring among all members. Members should also recognize the roles that each person plays (Bales, 1976).

The second feature is **interdependence,** meaning members cannot achieve their goals without working together. The efforts of all members are needed if the group is to be successful. When members coordinate their efforts to accomplish a task and contribute their ideas, they are able to complete a task that no one person could complete alone. In our opening example, four group members displayed problems with interdependency. Rather than working cooperatively toward a common goal (giving an excellent presentation), Callie struggled with Ziya over control of the group, Ryan just wanted to socialize, Shani was a noncontributor, and Eric was overly negative.

The third feature is the **task** the group performs. Small group communication is not needed unless a task exists. For example, a family may need to make a decision about where they will go on a summer vacation. This decision requires considering the budget available and the interests of each family member (swimming, boating, site seeing, hiking, etc.). For a good decision to be made, everyone needs to contribute his or her ideas. Compromise may also be helpful to ensure that as many individual needs and interests as possible are met.

The fourth feature is **norms,** the guidelines or rules that regulate behavior. Norms may be *explicit,* meaning that they are clearly stated. For example, the members of a work group may agree that everyone will show up to weekly meetings on time and stay for the entire meeting. Norms may also be *implicit.* This occurs when members do not formally state a guideline or rule, but the group's history of behavior establishes the norm. If a local community association has always handled disagreements without anger being displayed, an implicit norm is created where it is tacitly understood that anger is not appropriate. When a group member violates a norm, the group may choose a form of punishment to discourage the behavior from occurring again. So, if a member of the community association becomes angry during a meeting, the other members may exit the town hall without talking to or saying goodbye to the offending member.

Small group communication is both task-oriented and goal-directed.

The fifth feature is **identity,** which defines how the group perceives itself as unique, separating it from other groups (Myers & Anderson, 2008). Two types of boundaries assist in the development of identity: psychological and physical. Psychological boundaries may involve feelings of affection, attachment, and pride. Physical boundaries may involve artifacts such as special clothing to display your group membership to others.

The sixth feature is **group talk,** the types of communication engaged in to complete group tasks. Most of the communication needed to complete tasks focuses on problem-solving and decision-making. Problem-solving involves defining and analyzing the problem confronting the group and identifying several possible solutions. Decision-making involves talking about the possible solutions and selecting the one that appears to best meet the group's objectives.

What distinguishes effective decision-making groups from ineffective groups? Randy Hirokawa and Kathryn Rost (1992) developed the idea that group interaction affects group decisions by shaping critical thinking. Hirokawa's position and others like it are known as *vigilant interaction theory.* This theory claims that the quality of group decisions depends on the group's vigilance (attentiveness) in interaction concerning four questions:

1. **Problem analysis:** Is there something about the current state of affairs that requires change?

2. **Objectives:** What do we want to achieve or accomplish regarding the problem?

3. **Choices:** What are the choices available to us?

4. **Evaluation:** What are the positive and negative aspects of those choices? (Hirokawa & Rost, 1992, p. 269)

Over the years, Hirokawa and his colleagues have accumulated extensive evidence to support the theory. One study by Hirokawa and Rost (1992) is particularly important because it involved groups from a large utility company. Many group decision-making studies are laboratory experiments, but this study shows clearly that vigilant interaction theory applies to groups in real organizations. In the utility company groups, interactions that facilitated problem analysis and evaluation of both positive and negative features of choices led to high-quality decisions. Interactions that inhibited problem analysis, development of standards to assess choices, and evaluation of positive features of choices led to low-quality decisions.

COMMUNICATION SKILLS: COMMUNICATION COMPETENCE IN GROUPS

Among the most important skills for group members is **communication competence.** The simplest way to describe communication competence is the ability to select and perform a communication behavior that is both appropriate and effective in a given situation (Rothwell, 2012). Behaving in an appropriate manner means that you do not violate a relational or situational rule. Effective behavior allows you to accomplish your goals through communication. Spitzberg and Cupach (1984) developed the model most often used to describe competence. Their model includes three components: knowledge, skill, and motivation. *Knowledge* refers to knowing what behavior is best-suited for a particular situation. *Skill* is having the ability to perform that behavior. *Motivation* refers to the desire to communicate in a competent manner.

In small groups, communication competence is a vitally important skill to possess to accomplish individual goals within the group, promote group productivity, and sustain good interpersonal relationships within the group. Without effectiveness in communicating your ideas, you cannot accomplish any of your personal goals within a group. Thus, the ability to communicate

Communication competence requires knowledge, skill, and motivation.

your ideas logically and persuasively is important, as well as your ability to establish alliances and coalitions to build support for your ideas. At a group level, effective communication is important because it allows each member to offer their best contributions to solving group problems. Accomplishing personal and group goals is only part of what competence is, however. Group members also need to communicate in ways that are relationally or situationally appropriate. Every group develops rules that determine what is appropriate communication and what is not. Sometimes these rules are explicitly stated: "There will be no personal attacks when arguing over an issue." Other times the rules will be established subtly through interaction. For example, over a period of several months in a newly formed student organization, no group member raises his or her voice when arguing with another member. This rule is internalized through repeated interaction within the group. If a member violates this rule he or she will likely receive negative verbal or nonverbal reactions from other group members, even though the rule was never explicitly stated. Behaving in appropriate ways helps to sustain good relationships within the group. Appropriate communication also contributes to the development of a group culture where members want to continue their association with one another.

SMALL GROUP DEVELOPMENT

What stages do groups go through from first getting together to becoming experienced in making decisions together? Small group communication researchers have discovered that many groups go through a certain developmental process as they become oriented toward the task and form relationships with one another. As they progress through these stages, they become better at performing tasks, they learn to work together, and they become more comfortable working with each other. Bruce Tuckman's (1965) model of development suggests that groups go through five stages: forming, norming, storming, performing, and adjourning. These stages do not necessarily occur in order. In fact, groups may get stuck in a stage, skip a stage, or revert back to an earlier stage depending on the communication that takes place (Poole & Roth, 1989). Although no two groups are identical in terms of how they develop, each group will experience some aspects of the five stages. Let's consider each stage in greater detail.

FORMING

In the **forming stage,** group members get to know one another by sharing personal information (name, interests, personal experiences, etc.). Rather than address the task, group members are more concerned with being accepted and included. Given this concern, members tend to be cautious during the forming stage because each person is concerned with the impressions they make on others. One way to increase the effectiveness of this stage is to engage in talk about what the group values and expectations are. Prior experiences with group work, both positive and negative, will influence how members approach any new group experience.

NORMING

In the **norming stage,** group members begin to establish rules and roles. Procedures for addressing the task at hand are developed. Different patterns of interaction might also be considered to see which works best for this group. Rather than the cautious interaction that takes place during the forming stage, communication during the norming stage tends to be more open and starts to focus on the task confronting the group. Group members begin to trust one another during this stage as they display their commitment to the group and signal a willingness to cooperate and collaborate.

Group members begin to trust one another in the norming stage.

STORMING

In the **storming stage,** conflict emerges as members share ideas, focus on the task, and recognize that different views exist about how to proceed. Open disagreement surfaces during this stage, and conflict takes place as each person attempts to influence what occurs during group discussion. Some members may be comfortable with the direct verbal confrontation that occurs, others will withdraw because of their discomfort with conflict. Groups that are willing to risk confrontation, and that work to manage their conflict productively, are more likely to be creative and effective in addressing the task.

PERFORMING

In the **performing stage,** the group focuses on completing the task it confronts. Problem-solving and decision-making techniques (discussed later in this chapter) are used that allow the group to accomplish its task. As members commit themselves to accomplishing their goals, they develop a sense of shared responsibility toward moving forward and not allowing obstacles to prevent completion of the task. If the group needs more information, one or more members find that information. If one decision-making technique does not work, the group considers another. Although conflict may surface during this stage, the group figures out how to manage it.

A group focuses on completing its task in the performing stage.

ADJOURNING

The **adjourning stage** may occur in different ways. If the group faces a complex task requiring several meetings, there is adjournment after each meeting. In this case it is helpful if someone in the group summarizes the progress the group has made and shares that summary in writing with everyone immediately following the meeting. If the group finishes its task, but it is an ongoing or standing group, adjournment may occur, but there is recognition that another meeting will be called when a new task surfaces that the group must confront. Finally, a group may adjourn permanently because their assignment was to complete a single task. In this case members are likely to have different reactions. Some will be happy the group has accomplished its task, while others will miss the camaraderie that surfaced during the group's meetings. This may lead some members to try to keep the group together to socialize or to work on other tasks. Of course, in the information age, members may also stay in contact through email, social media, texting, or phone calls.

ESTABLISHING GROUP CULTURE

Differences between national cultures in their methods of group decision-making can be explained in part by the degree to which a given culture is *individualistic* or *collectivistic.* As explained by Hofstede and Bond (1984, p. 419), people in individualistic cultures (e.g., U.S.) "are supposed to look after themselves and their immediate family only," while those in collectivistic cultures (e.g., South Korea) "belong to in-groups or collectivities which are supposed to look after them in exchange for loyalty." When Hofstede and Bond talk about *in-groups,* they are referring to people such as coworkers, colleagues, friends, and classmates. Out-groups include strangers or anyone who is not specifically a member of an in-group.

Gudykunst, Yoon, and Nishida (1987) argued that in-group relationships are more intimate in collectivistic cultures than in individualistic cultures. Consequently, in-group communication should be more personalized, better coordinated, and less difficult in collectivistic cultures than in individualistic cultures. Results from their study of in-group communication among students from South Korea (highly collectivistic), Japan (moderately collectivistic), and the United States (highly individualistic) supported this hypothesis. In-group communication was more personalized, better coordinated, and less difficult for the South Koreans than for the Japanese, and more personalized, better coordinated, and less difficult for the Japanese than for the Americans.

These results do not necessarily mean that we should make American society more collectivistic. Individualistic values may offer some communicative advantages. Gudykunst, Yoon, and Nishida also found that American students had somewhat better experiences than the Japanese and Koreans with out-group communication. Interaction with strangers was easier and better coordinated (though less personal) for American students. Infante and Gordon (1987) also have claimed that independent-mindedness of organization members, a condition that can be troublesome for in-group interaction, is essential to productivity in American organizations.

Collectivistic and individualistic cultures have different strengths and weaknesses in group activities.

There are two additional observations that are crucial to decision-making and culture. First, nationalistic cultures are not monolithic. Some groups in nations like Korea and Japan may display individualistic features, just as groups in the U.S. may display collectivistic features. Second, there are aspects of culture that influence decision-making beyond individualism and collectivism. For example, a group within an organization may be guided by a "customer is always right" culture. In such a culture, the needs and concerns of employees will always be subordinate to customers, and all organizational decisions will be guided by customers' views. Alternatively, a group within an organization may be guided by a "protect the bottom line" culture. In such an organization, all decisions will be framed by options that protect financial interests.

In addition to national culture, two components of group communication that influence the culture of every group are how *norms and conformity* and *group member roles* are negotiated. Let's consider these two aspects of group communication.

Norms and Conformity

Many scholars and professionals have suggested that groups do not like uncertainty. Indeed, we depend on some degree of regularity and predictability to structure our interactions with others. In group communication, many of these regularities are derived from norms. Although we have looked briefly at norms as a feature of small group communication and as a stage in group development, their importance in small group interaction warrants a more detailed explanation. As defined by Secord and Backman (1964), "A norm is a standard of behavioral expectations shared by group members against which the validity of perceptions is judged and the appropriateness of feelings and behavior is evaluated" (p. 323).

Norms—shared expectations for behavior, thought, and feeling—may be developed within the group or imported from the larger system of which the group is a part (e.g., standards prevailing in the larger organization of which a group is a part, or mutual expectations acquired through prior experience in other groups). The internal development of norms occurs as the group negotiates and tests certain rules for interaction (e.g., think back to our earlier example of not raising one's voice when arguing with another group member).

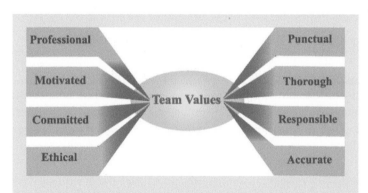

A norm is a standard of behavior shared by group members.

As discussed earlier, norms also may be explicitly stated or implicitly understood. Explicit normative standards could include policies, written rules, and verbally communicated procedures and standards. Implicit norms and other rules are not explicitly articulated, but the individual group member can observe and learn about their functions. Sometimes, new members of groups discover implicit norms only when they inadvertently violate such norms. This type of violation is illustrated in the following example.

A group of workers in the District Sales Department of a large company often met over lunch in order to discuss problems associated with increasing sales of the firm's various products. However, on one particular day, the initial topic of conversation involved a recent string of losses by the local professional football team. Later, there was some specific discussion of work-related matters but nothing directly relevant to the project itself. During a lull in the conversation, a new member, who had been with the group for less than one week, made a remark about the unusually brutal November temperatures and then said, "I sure hope it clears up some. I hate for my kids to walk home in this kind of weather."

The comment seemed perfectly harmless, but there was no reply from the other members—only downcast eyes and sullen expressions. The new member was quite embarrassed by this response. When the new member later asked some of the other members about their reaction to the comment, they testily replied that luncheons are "business meetings where personal topics like families and children are off limits." Apparently, however, discussion of the football team's win/loss record was not regarded as inconsistent with the purpose of a "business meeting." In fact, the catalyst that triggered this uncomfortable situation may well have been gender. The new member was a woman; all the rest were men. As long as she talked about football like "one of the boys," everything was fine, but the mention of children may have provoked the men's stereotype of a "women's" topic.

This example illustrates one of the ways in which groups exert pressure for conformity to norms. Methods for producing this pressure include the following:

1. Delay action toward the deviant, allowing for self-correction.

2. Joke humorously with the deviant about the violation.

3. Ridicule and deride the violation.

4. Seriously try to persuade the deviant to conform.

5. Engage in heated argument with the deviant.

6. Reject or isolate the deviant.

Bormann (1969) indicated that these methods actually reflect several stages of pressure toward conformity. If conformity does not occur after delaying action, the group might engage in humor. Should deviance still continue, the group would move to ridicule. As pressure toward conformity progresses through these steps, the amount of communicative action directed at the deviant increases until, at stage six, attempts to communicate cease.

Rules and norms are essential to group action for at least two reasons. First, they help to reduce uncertainty. When we understand the norms and rules in a situation, we can have more confidence about the appropriateness of our own actions and in our expectations of others. Second, some predictability is required for joint action and cooperation. In order to collaborate at all, we must have some shared expectations for one anothers' behaviors. But norms also have some unfortunate effects. As Baird and Weinberg (1981) noted, norms can hamper group creativity and protect inefficient and archaic practices (e.g., changes in policy can only occur if there is consensus about the change). Such practices may take the form of certain traditions or so-called sacred cows. Norms also enforce inequities within and between groups. They can be used as instruments of repression that primarily serve the interests of a privileged few (e.g., only upper-level managers may take advantage of the flexible work hours policy). Nevertheless, norms and rules are ever-present in group interaction.

Roles

Group action, whether it is effective or ineffective, is produced through member enactment of roles. George Kelly (1955) defined a role as "an ongoing pattern of behavior that follows from a person's understanding [or misunderstanding] of how others who are associated with him or her in his or her task think" (p. 97). Simply stated, the enactment of a role depends on a person's interpretation of a given situation. Other people's expectations do not necessarily dictate what a person will do to fulfill a certain role.

Wofford, Gerloff, and Cummins (1979) attempted to clarify the idea of role by distinguishing between perceived, expected, and enacted roles:

> The *perceived role* is the set of behaviors that the occupant of the position believes he or she should perform. The *expected role* is the set of behaviors that others believe he or she should perform. *Enacted role* is the actual set of performed behaviors. (p. 39)

There may be a high level of agreement between perceived, expected, and enacted roles, but the three frequently differ. Suppose that the members of a work group expect Callie to be a democratic leader, providing guidance and encouraging participation. Callie's perception of the leadership role, based on a belief in autocratic methods such as controlling decisions, dictating orders, and using punishment to gain compliance, is quite different from the members' expectations. Moreover, Callie's actual behavior—the enacted role—turns out to be a laissez-faire approach of "cool your heels on the desk and leave things alone," in which she actually relinquishes much

Group action is produced through member enactment of roles.

of the leadership responsibility. As we shall see later, disparities between expected, perceived, and enacted roles can be significant sources of conflict in groups.

Any role is enacted. It is not only defined by others' expectations for appropriate behavior, but it is also defined by the perceptions, capabilities, and choices of the person who enacts it. Even so, there do seem to be some types of roles that frequently occur in task groups. A classic description of typical task group roles that Benne and Sheats developed in 1948 is still widely accepted today. Their description includes:

Task roles

Initiator:	defines problem, contributes ideas and suggestions, proposes solutions or decisions, offers new ideas
Information seeker:	asks for clarification, promotes participation by others, solicits facts and evidence
Energizer:	prods members into action
Orienter:	keeps group on track, guides discussion
Secretary:	keeps track of group progress, remembers past actions

Maintenance roles

Encourager:	provides support, praise, acceptance for others
Harmonizer:	resolves conflict, reduces tension
Comedian:	provides humor, relaxes others
Gatekeeper:	controls communication channels, promotes evenness of participation
Follower:	accepts others' ideas, goes along with others

Self-centered roles

Blocker:	interferes with progress of group by consistently making negative responses to others
Aggressor:	attacks other members in an effort to promote his or her own status
Dominator:	monopolizes group time with long, drawn-out monologues
Deserter:	withdraws from group discussion by refusing to participate, engages in irrelevant conversations
Special-interest pleader:	brings irrelevant information into discussion, argues incessantly for his or her own point of view

As you read these descriptions, most may seem familiar from your own experience in group activities. It is very likely that you have seen some, if not all, of these roles enacted in task groups. Sometimes a particular individual will consistently enact one of these roles, but Benne and Sheats do not imply that any given member has only one role. Generally, the actions of a given member will reflect some of these roles but show little or no evidence of others, and more than one member may enact any given role.

GROUP COHESIVENESS

A cohesive group is one where members want to work with one another to accomplish goals. Cohesion refers to the attraction that group members feel for one another and the degree to which they are willing to work cooperatively to accomplish tasks. Cohesion can be built through two important behaviors. Members need to *trust* one another. This may mean that private information should be kept private and members trust one another to do so. Trust also means trustworthiness, meaning members keep their promises to perform tasks on time. The second behavior is *supportiveness*. When members provide social support or task support for one another a group climate is created where every one helps everyone else when a problem is experienced. When trust and support are high in a group, cohesiveness is high as well.

Cohesion refers to group members' willingness to work cooperatively.

GROUPTHINK

In order to be successful in completing tasks, group members must actively engage one another in discussing the problem they confront. This is not always the case, however, when group members recognize problems. Irving Janis (1972) identified a phenomenon known as "groupthink" in which extreme efforts are made to suppress conflict and stop the input of any information that contradicts an established or dominant view. Individual group members surrender their own beliefs and begin to see things only from the group perspective. The group develops a dogmatic commitment to the "moral rightness" of its position and may even believe it is being persecuted by enemies. Janis argued that the ill-fated Bay of Pigs invasion during John F. Kennedy's presidential administration was a product of groupthink. Virtually anyone outside Kennedy's cloistered group of advisors would have said that the plan to invade Cuba to oust Fidel Castro was misguided and unworkable, but suppression of competing views, avoidance of conflict, and a quest to gain consensus merely for its own sake resulted in a disastrous decision. Actions by members of the Nixon administration during the Watergate era, Jimmy Carter's ill-fated decision to attempt a military rescue of American hostages in Iran, Bill Clinton's decision to bomb a weapons plant that turned out to be a pharmaceutical manufacturing company in Sudan, and George W. Bush's decision to invade Iraq may also have been products of groupthink.

Janis also illustrated how the groupthink figures into corporate decisions to continue selling inferior or hazardous products. In a film on the development of groupthink, Janis showed how a pharmaceutical company arrived at a decision to market a drug with some extremely dangerous side-effects by downplaying the importance and validity of studies demonstrating the hazards. The management team justified its decision by highlighting the benefits of the product and suggesting that those who had qualms about the drug were "not being team players." The group even developed a vision of itself as a heroic paragon of moral virtue in standing behind the product.

Janis (1972) identified six suggestions that may be followed to avoid groupthink. First, the leader should assign the role of critical evaluator to each group member. This alerts group members that part of their role is to critically evaluate all solutions that are suggested. Second, the leader should avoid stating preferences and expectations at the outset so that he or she does not influence how the discussion proceeds. Third, each member of the group should discuss the group's deliberations with a trusted person who is not a group member, and report back to the group that person's reactions. Fourth, one or more experts should be invited to each meeting on a staggered basis. These outside experts should be encouraged to challenge the views of the group members. Fifth, at least one articulate and knowledgeable group member should be assigned the role of devil's advocate. This person needs to question assumptions and plans that surface during the group's deliberations. Finally, the leader should set aside a significant block of time to survey warning signals from rivals. The leader and the group should then construct alternative scenarios of their rivals' intentions.

LEADERSHIP IN SMALL GROUPS

Although the leadership function can be shared among group members, most groups have an identifiable leader. Group members may formally designate leaders (e.g., through voting), or people may emerge as leaders through their communication. Alternatively, an outside member (e.g., community leader or manager) may select a leader for the group. However leadership emerges or is designated, leaders will display different styles that characterize how they lead groups. Let's consider two approaches to understanding leadership styles: *early styles theory* and *transformational leadership*.

Early Style Theory

One early and classic version of stylistic theory was developed by White and Lippitt (1960). They identified three basic styles of leadership that they labeled *laissez-faire, authoritarian,* and *democratic.*

Laissez-faire leaders relinquish virtually all control of decisions and group processes to members. Such leaders may remain available for consultation or problem-solving, but they generally delegate all authority for tasks to members and avoid decisions and responsibilities. You might say, with good reason, that the idea of a "laissez-faire leader" is an oxymoron, a contradiction in terms, because this leader's style is non-leadership.

Group members usually prefer democratic leaders because their input is valued.

Authoritarian leaders exercise strong command and control over decisions and tasks. They issue and enforce orders to ensure that their plans are executed in an acceptable manner. They closely monitor and supervise the work of members. They demand respect for and compliance with their authority as leaders.

Democratic leaders are more oriented toward guiding and coaching members rather than completely controlling their activities. They share authority with members and seek member input in decision-making. They delegate responsibilities, provide recognition, and promote development for their members. Although some people have strong preferences for laissez-faire and authoritarian leaders, most group members prefer democratic leaders who value their input.

Transformational Leadership

Transformational leadership theory is classified appropriately as a theory of leadership style (Kirkbride, 2006), but this theory differs from earlier stylistic theories and models in some of its key assumptions. The first scholar to lay groundwork for the concept of transformational leadership may have been Burns (1978), who distinguished between transacting and transforming leadership (Rafferty & Griffin, 2004). Bernie Bass (1985, 1996) elaborated this idea into a coherent theory that not only generates intensive academic interest, but also enjoys widespread popularity among practitioners today (Kirkbride, 2006).

According to Burns, *transactional* leaders work on exchange principles, which means they provide rewards for accomplished goals and for compliance with leadership. *Transformational* leaders actually change members' values. More to the point, they motivate members to perform beyond expectations (Bass, 1985). Bass along with Avolio (Bass & Avolio, 1997; Avolio, 1999) developed a model of eight leadership styles that differs from earlier stylistic models in at least three respects. First, the styles are assumed to operate on a continuum of performance effectiveness (Kirkbride, 2006). Second, any leader may exhibit any or all of the styles (Bass & Avolio, 1997). Finally, while traditional leadership theories rely on concepts of rational processes, transformational theory is concerned with emotions, values, symbolic behavior, and "the role of the leader in making events meaningful for followers" (Yukl, 1999, p. 286).

The first (and least effective) style is **laissez-faire,** the non-leader leadership style, where members are without direction and often in conflict with one another. The second and third styles are **passive** and **active management-by-exception** (MBE). MBE is still basically laissez-faire, but the MBE leader does pay attention to deviations from normal conditions (i.e., errors and problems) in order to correct the deviations and return to normal conditions. Expressed in terms of systems theory, MBE aims for homeostasis and operates on negative feedback. In the passive form, the leader is roused into action only when problems become obvious. In the active form, the leader is vigilant, relying on elaborate systems to monitor and control activity. MBE is presumed to lead to marginal performance at best.

The fourth style, **contingent reward,** fits the basic definition of transactional leadership as an exchange process. The contingent reward or transactional leader understands the objectives, acquires and coordinates the resources that members need to accomplish objectives, supports their efforts, and rewards accomplishments. According to Kirkbride, "If done successfully, this style will produce performance at the required levels" (p. 26).

Moving member performance beyond "required levels" presumably requires something more than transactional leadership. The next four styles, in theory, lead progressively to performance beyond expectations, and each of the four is a form of transformational leadership. These styles are *individualized consideration, intellectual stimulation, inspirational motivation,* and *idealized influence.*

Individualized consideration involves leader recognition of individual differences, management of work in light of those differences, open communication, and member development. **Intellectual stimulation** involves the leader more actively as a facilitator, advisor, and catalyst for problem-solving by members. Some of the attributes in these two styles also appear in descriptions of democratic and team leadership.

The last two styles clearly move into the symbolic domain and involve member identification with leaders. The leader with an **inspirationally motivating** style has a vision for the future and is able to communicate that vision in a clear, compelling, and engaging way so that members adopt that vision and pursue it. Finally, in **idealized influence,** the summit of transformational leadership, the leader is virtually iconic—a person who is perceived as the personification of the best group values and regarded as a model to emulate.

As we noted earlier, Bass's version of transformational leadership has inspired many research studies, and there is evidence to support the performance continuum suggested in the theory (Kirkbride, 2006). Specifically, transformational leadership correlates more highly than transactional leadership with leadership effectiveness. In turn, transactional leadership is more effective than MBE, and MBE is more effective than laissez-faire. Yukl (1999) also stated that studies have shown a link between transformational leadership and group effectiveness.

GROUP DECISION-MAKING AND PROBLEM-SOLVING

Many groups exist primarily for decision-making and problem-solving purposes. Project teams, task forces, and committees typically serve such functions. Sometimes groups are created temporarily to deal with one special contingency. The members of such ad hoc groups work through to the solution of a particular problem, then disband and move on to other projects. The importance of group decision-making has led researchers in small group communication to study these processes almost to the exclusion of any other aspects of group communication (Littlejohn, 1992).

Group decision-making is a rule-bound process, but members often seem to be only tacitly aware of the norms, roles, and regularities that they enact in the process. Status and power factors are accepted implicitly without reflection or examination. Members often note the presence of conflict, but they do not seem to understand its nature. Certain patterns

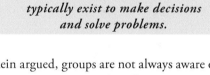

Project teams, task forces, and committees typically exist to make decisions and solve problems.

of interaction and ways of doing things are simply taken for granted. Thus, as Schein argued, groups are not always aware of their own processes for problem-solving and decision-making, even when these processes are inefficient and ineffective. Schein (1969) pointed out that groups typically make decisions in one of six ways, even though members may not recognize that their groups are operating in these ways.

1. **Lack of response.**   This method is evident in a group when ideas are introduced but then immediately dropped without discussion. In effect, ideas are vetoed by silence.

2. **Authority rule.**   In this case, the power structure in the group places final authority for decision-making with one person, usually the leader. The group may discuss an issue, share information, and suggest ideas, but the authority figure has the last word.

3. **Minority coalition.**   Schein describes this method as a process of "railroading" decisions through a group by a vocal minority, especially a minority with a powerful member. When other members remain silent in the face of strong minority support for an idea, it can create the impression that the group has reached a consensus. In fact, most members may be opposed to the idea, but no one voices an objection for fear of disrupting what appears to be a consensus.

4. **Majority rule.**   This is a familiar system of decision-making through voting. Majority rule is typical of highly formal decision-making procedures. An issue or problem is discussed, then a policy or proposal is adopted or rejected on the basis of the percentage of members who favor it.

5. **Consensus.**   When the members of a group are prepared to accept an idea, even though they may have some reservations about it, a group has a consensus. Schein points out that consensus does not necessarily mean that the group unanimously and enthusiastically endorses an idea. Consensus only implies that discussion of the problem has been open and all points of view have been considered. Although group members may not be in complete agreement, the solution or proposal falls within their ranges of acceptability.

6. **Unanimity.**   This rare but ideal mode of decision-making occurs when all of the members in a group are in full agreement on a point of view, proposal, policy, or solution.

Schein (1969) regards consensus and unanimity as preferred modes of arriving at decisions. Although the processes required to achieve consensus can be inefficient and time-consuming, the result is more effective implementation of the decision. More recent research by Renz (2006) supports and extends this view. Specifically, she discovered that a group's use of consensus decision-making allowed the members to balance three goals: making an appropriate decision, meeting members' needs, and maintaining the group's well-being. Although decisions that are made by authority, minority coalition, and majority rule may be arrived at quickly, members with other viewpoints may feel frustrated and have little incentive to support the decision. Why are some groups able to achieve consensus-based decision-making while others are not? What do you think?

Group Decision Development

In addition to Hirokawa's work on the differences between effective and ineffective group decision-making, another important line of research has addressed the stages or phases of decision development within groups. One of the most complete treatments of this topic was developed by B. Aubrey Fisher (1970) who identified four stages in group decision-making processes: *orientation, conflict, emergence,* and *reinforcement.*

The **orientation** phase begins as the members of a group meet for the first time. The members are not sure what to expect. Behavior is based on members' understanding of social norms regarding politeness and initiation of relationships. These norms are brought into the situation as the group has evolved no rules of its own.

Politeness norms become less important as members acquire some familiarity with one another, and the group moves into a **conflict** phase characterized by disputes, disagreements, and hostility. The group gradually works through conflict, entering an **emergence** stage in which increased tolerance for ambiguity in opinions is reflected. Ambiguity at this point allows for face-saving and reconciliation of conflicts. Finally, the group moves to a **reinforcement** stage in which the members develop and endorse a decision. The idea of reinforcement implies that group members engage in a mutual process of justifying and committing themselves to the decision. For example, they might say, "This is the right decision because..." or "This solution is better than the other possibilities."

Many studies of group development, including Fisher's own studies, have examined the processes of groups during a relatively limited time frame (e.g., over several meetings or even in only one meeting). The results of these studies suggest that group development occurs in an orderly, linear fashion, proceeding from one step to the next. Fisher points out, however, that a phase model may not apply to all task-oriented groups. A series of studies by Marshall Scott Poole (1981, 1983a, 1983b) reinforces the limitations of phase models like Fisher's. Poole found that the stages of decision development in small groups may follow any one of several possible sequences. For example, a group of experts who have worked together for years may be able to focus immediately on evaluating alternative decisions to implement. There is no need for orientation, and there may be little or no conflict as members consider alternative proposals by logically evaluating evidence in support of each idea. Poole concluded that a "logical" or unitary sequence of problem-solving course of action emerges from many complicated factors. In other words, groups in different situations act in different ways. Even when group decision-making fits a phase model, the specific types and cycles of interaction within any given phase differ substantially from group to group.

Technology, Social Media, and Group Communication

In the Information Age, technology such as the Internet and social media allow group members to connect with each other and complete tasks in a variety of face-to-face and computer-mediated contexts. For example, some members may be face-to-face during a meeting while others are at a remote location but connected through software such as Skype so that all of the group members can see one another. Alternatively, all group members can be connected through some form of computer-mediated communication.

Although technology offers many opportunities for people to connect when they cannot meet in the same place, intact groups benefit from being able to meet occasionally in a face-to-face environment. When group members agree to meet at a specific place and time, commitment is shown that helps build cohesive relationships.

Social media can also allow group members to connect so that tasks can be accomplished without regular face-to-face contact. Again, however, occasional face-to-face contact is necessary to build cohesion. In addition, research on social media use and conflict is beginning to show that people are much more likely to get angry and use abusive language when managing conflict over social media. Have you had any experience with this problem when using social media?

Group members can interact in a variety of face-to-face and computer-mediated contexts.

Small Group Conflict

All groups experience conflict. Even the most cohesive groups will encounter problems based on social relationships between members or differences of opinion on task issues. Conflict exists when there is an expressed struggle between interdependent parties who perceive incompatible goals, scarce rewards, and interference from others in obtaining their goals (Wilmot & Hocker, 2011). Although there are different ways of describing conflict in groups, let's consider the styles or communication behaviors people use when involved in conflict.

Putnam and Poole note that most work on interpersonal conflicts has centered on **conflict styles.** Conflict style refers to a person's characteristic manner or habitual way of handling a dispute. Models of conflict style vary somewhat, but most are consistent with an early model proposed by Blake and Mouton (1964) and revised by Hall (1969). The model is based on two dimensions: concern for your personal goals in the conflict, and the importance of your relationship with the other person in the conflict. Both are rated on a 1 to 9 scale (low to high). Your "style" of conflict presumably can be located by the coordinate of your ratings on these two dimensions. Although there are eighty-one possible coordinates, each coordinate falls into one of five basic style categories.

1. **The 1/1 Avoiding Style.**   This style is based on low concern for personal goals and for the relationship. The avoider refrains from arguing, withdraws from the situation, or otherwise tries to remain disconnected from the conflict.

2. **9/1 Forcing Style.**   The forcer has high concern for personal goals in the conflict, but low concern for the relationship. Consequently, the forcer is aggressive, competitive, and confrontational in an effort to get his/her way.

3. **1/9 Accommodating Style.**   When high concern for the relationship is coupled with low concern for personal goals, the result is an accommodating style. The accommodator glosses over differences or downplays disagreements in an effort to maintain the relationship.

4. **9/9 Collaborating Style.**   The collaborator has high concern for personal goals *and* for the relationship. The collaborator faces the conflict directly and works toward an integrative solution. An integrative, or "win-win," solution embraces the goals of both parties in the conflict. Hence, the collaborating style often is viewed as the ideal in conflict management. Since this approach addresses the conflict directly, it is sometimes referred to as the *confronting* style.

5. **5/5 Compromising Style.**   Given a moderate concern for personal goals in the conflict and a moderate concern for the relationship, the compromiser is willing to "split the difference" with the other party in the conflict, where each party gets something, but the end result is probably less than ideal for both. This is sometimes called the *viable solution* approach to conflict.

Even the most cohesive groups will experience conflict.

Although collaborating has often been identified as the optimal style to use in conflict, each of the five strategies identified above has strengths and weaknesses. *Collaboration* has the potential to manage conflict creatively and produce high-quality solutions. On the other hand, collaboration requires very skillful communicators and critical thinkers. If group members do not possess these skills, collaboration will not work. Also, collaboration takes time, and sometimes groups are pressured to produce quick solutions under time pressure. *Accommodating* involves "giving in" to another person; however, it can be used successfully to "right a previous wrong." For example, if one person forced an earlier decision resulting in hurt feelings, accommodation at a later point can restore cohesive group relationships. *Compromise* results in each side receiving something, and it can be done very efficiently. On the other hand, if all parties in a group know that compromise will be used, they may exaggerate their initial position to manipulate what they ultimately receive. *Forcing* may create tense relationships within the group. There are times however, when a group member is an expert and recognizes that the group is about to select a disastrous option. Forcing may prevent the group from making a bad choice. *Avoiding* does not allow a group to confront a problem they are facing. However, avoiding may be appropriate when the task facing the group is simple and all members need not participate. Also, a conflict issue may be better to avoid altogether if the group has recently managed a very difficult topic.

Because each style of conflict has strengths in particular situations, it is important to develop experience and skills in using each one. What have your experiences been in using different conflict styles in groups and in seeing the success and failures of others in using each of these five styles?

SUMMARY

Learning about communication in small groups is important because it is such an essential part of the human experience, allowing us to build the society in which we live. In this chapter we defined small group communication, and we covered communication competence in groups, small group development, establishing group culture, group cohesiveness, and groupthink. We also discussed leadership in small groups; problem-solving and decision-making; technology, social media, and group communication; and conflict in groups. The more knowledge we have about these aspects of group communication, the more likely we will become productive group members who contribute to problem-solving and decision-making and who can maintain cohesive group relationships. Building skills through group communication exercises and real-life group experience will also make us better group members.

REFERENCES

Adams, K., & Galanes, G. (2011). *Communicating in groups: Applications and skills.* New York, NY: McGraw-Hill.

Avolio, B. J. (1999). *Full leadership development: Building the vital forces in organizations.* Thousand Oaks, CA: Sage.

Baird, J. E., Jr., & Weinberg, S. B. (1981). *Group communication: The essence of synergy* (2nd ed.). Dubuque, IA: Wm. C. Brown.

Bales, R. F. (1976). *Interaction process analysis.* Chicago, IL: University of Chicago Press.

Bass, B. M. (1985). *Leadership and performance beyond expectations.* New York, NY: Free Press.

Bass, B. M. (1996). *A new paradigm of leadership: An inquiry into transformational leadership.* Alexandria, VA: U.S. Army Research Institute for the Behavioral and Social Sciences.

Bass, B. M., & Avolio, B. J. (1997). *Full range leadership development: Manual for the multi-factor leadership questionnaire.* Palo Alto, CA: Mindgarden.

Benne, K. D., & Sheats, P. (1948). Functional roles of group members. *Journal of Social Issues, 4,* 41–49.

Blake, R. R., & Mouton, J. S. (1964). *The managerial grid.* Houston, TX: Gulf Publishing.

Bormann, E. (1969). *Discussion and group methods.* New York, NY: Harper & Row.

Burns, J. M. (1978). *Leadership.* New York, NY: Harper & Row.

Cragan, J. F., & Wright, D. W. (1999). *Communication in small groups: Theory, process, skills* (5th ed.). Belmont, CA: Wadsworth.

Fisher, B. A. (1970). Decision emergence: Phases in group decision-making. *Speech Monographs, 37,* 53–66.

Gudykunst, W. B., Yoon, Y., & Nishida, T. (1987). The influence of individualism-collectivism on perceptions of communication in in-group and out-group relationships. *Communication Monographs, 54,* 295–306.

Hall, J. (1969). *Conflict management survey: A survey of one's characteristic reaction to and handling of conflicts between himself and others.* Monroe, TX: Telemetrics International.

Herring, H. B. (2006, June 18). Endless meetings: The black holes of the workday. *The New York Times.* Retrieved March 31, 2014, from http:// http://www.nytimes.com/2006/06/18/business/yourmoney/18count.html?_r=0

Hirokawa, R. Y., & Rost, K. M. (1992). Effective group decision-making in organizations: Field test of the vigilant interaction theory. *Management Communication Quarterly, 5,* 267–288.

Hofstede, G., & Bond, M. (1984). Hofstede's culture dimensions: An independent validation suing Rokeach's value survey. *Journal of Cross-Cultural Psychology, 15,* 417–433.

Infante, D. A., & Gordon, W. I. (1987). Superior and subordinate communication profiles: Implications for independent mindedness and upward effectiveness. *Central States Speech Journal, 38,* 73–80.

Janis, I. (1972). *Victims of groupthink.* Boston, MA: Houghton Mifflin.

Kelly, G. A. (1955). *The psychology of personal constructs* (Vol. 1). New York, NY: Norton.

Kirkbride, P. (2006). Developing transformation leaders: the full range leadership model in action. *Industrial and Commercial Training, 36(1),* 23–32.

Littlejohn, S. W. (1992). *Theories of human communication* (4th ed.). Belmont, CA: Wadsworth.

Myers, S. A., & Anderson, C. M. (2008). *The fundamentals of small group communication.* Thousand Oaks, CA: Sage.

Poole, M. S. (1981). Decision development in small groups I: A comparison of two models. *Communication Monographs, 48,* 1–24.

Poole, M. S. (1983a). Decision development in small groups II: A study of multiple sequences in decision-making. *Communication Monographs, 50,* 206–232.

Poole, M. S. (1983b). Decision development in small groups III: A multiple sequence model of group decision development. *Communication Monographs, 50,* 321–341.

Poole, M. S., & Roth, J. (1989). Decision development in small groups V: Test of a contingency model. *Human Communication Research, 15,* 549–589.

Rafferty, A. E., & Griffin, M. A. (2004). Dimensions of transformational leadership: conceptual and empirical extensions. *The Leadership Quarterly, 15,* 329–354.

Renz, M. A. (2006). Paving consensus: Enacting, challenging, and revising the consensus process in a cohousing community. *Journal of Applied Communication Research, 34,* 163–190.

Rothwell, J. D. (2012). *In mixed company: Communicating in small groups* (8th ed.). Boston, MA: Cengage.

Schein, E. (1969). *Process consultation: Its role in organization development.* Reading, MA: Addison-Wesley.

Schutz, W. (1958). *FIRO: A three-dimensional theory of interpersonal behavior.* New York, NY: Rinehart.

Secord, P. F., & Backman, C. W. (1964). *Social psychology.* New York, NY: McGraw-Hill.

Spitzberg, B., & Cupach, W. (1984). A component model of relational competence. *Human Communication Research, 10,* 575–599.

Tuckman, B. W. (1965). Developmental sequence in small groups. *Psychological Bulletin, 63,* 384–399.

White, R., & Lippitt, R. (1960). *Autocracy and democracy.* New York, NY: Harper & Row.

Wilmot., W. W., & Hocker, J. L. (2013). *Interpersonal conflict* (9th ed.). New York, NY: McGraw-Hill.

Wofford, J. C., Gerloff, E. A., & Cummins, R. C. (1979). Group behavior and the communication process. In R. S. Cathcart and L. A. Samovar (Eds.), *Small group communication: A reader* (3rd ed.). Dubuque, IA: Wm. C. Brown.

Yukl, G. (1999). An evaluation of conceptual weaknesses in transformational hand charismatic leadership theories. *Leadership Quarterly, 10(2),* 285–305.

COM 101
Course Supplement

COM 101 SYLLABUS

COURSE FORMAT

COM 101: Introduction to Speech Communication is a three-credit course that satisfies the University Competency Requirement for Oral English.

This course meets with the section instructor in the classroom for three hours weekly. COM 101 is designed to create an awareness of the basic principles and skills of human communication. Students will learn to understand communication processes, create dialogue, build interpersonal relationships, communicate in groups and teams, and speak to public audiences. During the course, students will learn about their personal communication strengths and weaknesses and be given opportunities to improve their communication skills.

You are expected to attend all classes. This is a participation and performance class. Regular attendance is essential for progress to occur. You are expected to participate as a speaker and as a member of the audience. Missing class on the day you are scheduled to speak may result in an "E" for the speech. Please read the COM 101 Attendance Policy very carefully. In addition, because this class involves in-class exercises which elaborate on the materials in the text, you must read assigned material prior to its due date. All assignments are due at the beginning of class on the due date. No late assignments will be accepted unless negotiated in advance of the class session in which they are due.

TEXTS

Graham, E.E. (2015). *Speaking and relating in the information age.* Southlake, TX: Fountainhead.

COURSE OBJECTIVES/GOALS

1. To provide you with a working vocabulary of the communication field.
2. To give you practical experience in communicating with others.
3. To heighten your awareness of the role of diversity in communication.
4. To make you aware of your communication strengths and weaknesses in public speaking and interpersonal relationships.
5. To make you aware of the complexities of communication and the various elements which define effective communication.
6. To provide for assessing and improving your communication skills.

COURSE EXPECTATIONS

1. Attend class as scheduled. **Daily attendance in COM 101 is mandatory.**
2. Complete any textbook reading assignments *before* they are discussed in class.
3. Participate in class activities.
4. Take the tests following the prescribed schedule.
5. Type all written assignments using double-spaced lines, one-inch margins, and standard type fonts.
6. Complete all assignments on time.
7. When in doubt, **ask questions.** Notify your instructor of problems IN ADVANCE—problem-solving can't occur after the fact.

ACADEMIC DISHONESTY

Academic dishonesty includes, but is not limited to, cheating and plagiarism. Academic dishonesty may result in course failure. The university student handbook highlights types of problems that have arisen in the past: (1) students who copy sections of printed material for speeches, (2) students who work together and hand in basically the same speech outlines or other assignments,

(3) students who "borrow" assignments completed in earlier semesters, and (4) students who use fictitious sources. **All types of academic dishonesty may result in course failure.**

In May 2001, the Central Michigan University Academic Senate approved the Policy on Academic Integrity. This policy applies to all university students. Copies are available on the CMU website at http://academicsenate.cmich.edu/noncurric.htm, and in the Academic Senate Office in room 108 of Bovee University Center. All academic work is expected to be in compliance with this policy.

STUDENTS WITH DISABILITIES

Students with disabilities are provided with reasonable accommodation to participate in educational programs, activities, or services. Students with disabilities requiring accommodation to participate in class activities or meet course requirements should contact their COM 101 instructor as early as possible.

CLASSROOM CIVILITY

Each CMU student is encouraged to help create an environment during class that promotes learning, dignity, and mutual respect for everyone. Students who speak at inappropriate times, sleep in class, display inattention, take frequent breaks, interrupt the class by arriving late, engage in loud or distracting behaviors, use cell phones or text messaging in class, use inappropriate language, are verbally abusive, display defiance or disrespect to others, or behave aggressively toward others could be asked to leave the class and subjected to disciplinary action under the Code of Student Rights, Responsibilities, and Disciplinary Procedures.

SPEECH AND HEARING SCREENING

The Department of Communication Disorders provides students in oral communication competency classes the opportunity to have a speech and hearing screening completed. All COM 101 students are encouraged to complete the speech/hearing screening during this semester. To make an appointment, contact The Carls Center for Clinical Care and Education at 989-774-3904.

CHARLES V. PARK LIBRARY

Students are encouraged to utilize CMU's library services. The Reference Desk is on the second floor of the Park Library building. Librarians are available to assist students with research questions. Reference Librarian hours are posted at http://library.cmich.edu/forms/libref.php, or they can be contacted by phone at 989-774-3470.

ORAL ENGLISH COMPETENCY

You need to earn at least a C grade—73 percent or 438 points—in COM 101 (not a C-) to receive Oral English Competency credit. Broadcasting majors need to earn a B in this course. Please keep track of your progress and any absences.

COM 101 ATTENDANCE POLICY

COM 101 students are expected to attend all classes and participate knowledgeably. Students are allowed a **limited number of absences.** Your instructor will not attempt to differentiate between *excused* and *unexcused* absences. An absence is an absence.

Students in **Monday/Wednesday/Friday** sections are allowed three absences without a penalty. Each subsequent absence will result in a five-point deduction from your attendance and participation points. An absence does not excuse a student from a speech, an assignment, or an in-class activity.

Students in **Tuesday/Thursday** or **Monday/Wednesday** sections are allowed two absences without a penalty. Each subsequent absence will result in a 7.5-point deduction from your attendance and participation points. An absence does not excuse a student from a speech, an assignment, or an in-class activity.

Students in **evening sections** are allowed to miss one evening class without a penalty. Each subsequent absence will result in a fifteen-point deduction from your attendance and participation points (five points per hour missed). An absence does not excuse a student from a speech, an assignment, or an in-class activity.

An ongoing pattern of tardiness or leaving early will also affect a student's attendance and participation points. If a student is tardy and attendance has been taken, it is the student's responsibility to talk to the instructor after class to make sure the student is marked present for that class period.

In the case of foreseeable absences, students are expected to notify the instructor in advance. In special cases, it may be difficult to immediately notify the instructor, an absence may be reported by a third party, or the absence is expected to extend more than one week. When this happens, students may seek assistance from the Office of Student Life (989-774-1345) to provide an Absence Report to their instructors. These situations still count against your given absence total.

A student who will miss class due to participation in an official CMU activity must notify the instructor well in advance of the activity. These situations still count against your given absence total. Students in university-sponsored activities are NOT allowed any additional absences. If the student's activity requires him or her to miss more than the allowed absences, it is suggested the student take COM 101 another semester.

BE CAREFUL. IF YOU TAKE YOUR ABSENCES EARLY IN THE SEMESTER, WE WILL NOT MAKE CONCESSIONS OR EXCEPTIONS REGARDING PERSONAL CRISES LATER.

It is your responsibility to keep up with class work, turn in assignments on time, and stay informed about speaking dates. Missing class will affect your ability to do this. Late assignments and missed speeches will result in an automatic 10 percent deduction on the assignment or the speech. In-class assignments will be impossible to make up.

A student who adds the class after the semester has begun must count the missed classes toward his/her allowed absences.

Students are required to attend class during the final exam period. Plan ahead to attend your final exam period. Missing the exam period will count as one absence and a loss of ten points for the final exam activity.

WHY HAVE A COM 101 ATTENDANCE POLICY?

COM 101 is a highly participatory and interactive course. A student who misses a class session has reduced not only his or her learning opportunities but also those of others in the class. Communication is a two-way, interactive process, and you need to be in class every day in your role as speaker, respondent, participant, and observer. Perhaps students can miss meetings of large lecture classes without seriously compromising their education. COM 101 is neither large nor a lecture course.

Students who miss class disrupt their instructor's preparations, imposing unnecessary burdens on them and the class. Student absences often force instructors to alter planned class activities. Also, instructors must spend additional time explaining assignments and concepts to absent students. This is an inefficient use of instructional time.

In assigning a final course grade, an instructor is claiming that the student has had certain kinds of experiences. A student who has missed several classes has missed several course experiences. Your COM 101 instructor has an obligation to register such missed opportunities to those who rely on the student's transcript. Your instructor cannot grade on the basis of *what might have been*. The COM 101 has an attendance policy that is firm but fair.

COM 101 GRADING SCALE

Evaluation Criteria	Total Points Possible	Points Earned
Examinations		——
Exam #1	100 points	
Exam #2	100 points	
Speeches and Assignments		——
Speech One	20 points	
Speech One Outline	10 points	
Speech Two	100 points	
Speech Two Outline	25 points	
Speech Three	100 points	
Speech Three Outline	30 points	
Final Exam Activity	10 points	
Instructor Discretion	45 points	
Participation/Attendance	60 points	
TOTAL	600 points	

GRADING SCALE

A	93%–100%	or	558–600 points		C	73%–76%	or	438–461 points
A-	90%–92%	or	540–557 points		C-	70%–72%	or	420–437 points
B+	87%–89%	or	522–539 points		D+	67%–69%	or	402–419 points
B	83%–86%	or	498–521 points		D	63%–66%	or	378–401 points
B-	80%–82%	or	480–497 points		D-	60%–62%	or	360–377 points
C+	77%–79%	or	462–479 points		E	59% & below	or	0–359 points

GRADING POLICIES

1. Extra credit work will not be given.

2. An "Incomplete" as a final course grade will **not** be given in COM 101.

COURSE ASSIGNMENTS

1. EXAMS

There will be two examinations in this course. The format for each exam is multiple choice, and the questions are on textbook and blackboard content. You must take the exam at the scheduled time. Missing the scheduled examination day may result in an "E" for the exam. **Attendance is mandatory.**

Please refer to the Central Michigan University Policy on Academic Integrity for a discussion of the penalties for cheating and academic misconduct.

2. SPEECH 1—INTRODUCTION SPEECH

Your first speech will be a speech of self-introduction. The main purpose of this speech is to give you an opportunity to speak in front of a group. Look to your instructor for specific requirements on this speech. For Speech 1 you should demonstrate evidence of planning and preparation, and have a clearly identifiable thesis, introduction, body, and conclusion. Specific instructions for Speech 1 are in this course supplement along with a sample outline. Please review the Speech 1 evaluation form and outline grading form. The evaluation forms explicitly describe the criteria for Speech 1.

Speech 1, unless you are otherwise instructed, is an informative speech. Missing class on the day you are scheduled to speak may result in an "E" for the speech. At a minimum, 10 percent will be deducted from your speech score.

Time Requirement:	2–4 minutes
Outline:	full content, sentence format
Point Value:	speech = 20 points
	formal sentence outline = 10 points

3. SPEECH 2—INFORMATIVE SPEECH

The purpose of the informative speech is to convey information and to do so clearly, accurately, and interestingly. This speech should be an extemporaneous speech in which you educate the audience about a particular area of interest. The goal is not to alter listeners' attitudes or behaviors but to facilitate their understanding of the subject and their ability to retain this new information. Although several classifications of informative speeches are possible, our text examines five types: (1) speeches about people; (2) speeches about objects; (3) speeches about events; (4) speeches about processes; and (5) speeches about concepts. Specific instructions for Speech 2 are in your course supplement along with a sample outline. Please review the Speech 2 evaluation form and outline grading form. The evaluation forms explicitly describe the criteria for Speech 2.

Missing class on the day you are scheduled to speak may result in an "E" for the speech. At a minimum, 10 percent will be deducted from your speech score.

Time Requirement:	5–7 minutes (**Up to 5 points will be deducted from final speech score for going over or under 1 minute and up to 10 points will be deducted for going over or under 2 minutes.**)
Outline:	full content, sentence format
Research:	evidence of research
Bibliography:	sources are to be listed according to APA VI
Source Requirement:	minimum of 5 sources cited verbally (**Each missing citation will result in a 1-point deduction from your speech score.**)
Point Value:	speech = 100 points
	formal sentence outline = 25 points

4. SPEECH 3—PERSUASIVE SPEECH

A persuasive speech attempts to influence listeners to change their beliefs, attitudes, values, and/or behaviors. The three purposes of persuasive speaking are to (1) **strengthen audience responses** by rewarding the audience for sustaining their beliefs, attitudes, values, or behaviors; (2) **change audience responses,** altering an audience's behavior toward a product, concept, or idea; and (3) **move audience members to action** by motivating them to do something or change a specific behavior. Using one of the organizational strategies described in the text, this speech should be designed for a particular audience. Specific instructions for Speech 3 are in your course supplement along with a sample outline. Please review the Speech 3 evaluation form and outline grading form. The evaluation forms explicitly describe the criteria for Speech 3.

Missing class on the day you are scheduled to speak may result in an "E" for the speech. At a minimum, 10 percent will be deducted from your speech score.

Time Requirement:	5–7 minutes (**Up to 5 points will be deducted from final speech score for going over or under 1 minute and up to 10 points will be deducted for going over or under 2 minutes.**)
Outline:	full content, sentence format
Research:	evidence of research
Bibliography:	sources are to be listed according to APA VI
Source Requirement:	minimum of 5 sources cited verbally (**Each missing citation will result in a 1-point deduction from your speech score.**)
Point Value:	speech = 100 points formal sentence outline = 30 points

5. ORAL/WRITTEN COMMUNICATION DESCRIPTIONS AND ASSESSMENTS

Each instructor will present the oral/written communication description and assessment points in his or her Personal Policy Sheet. In-class assignments will be impossible to make up.

6. ATTENDANCE AND PARTICIPATION

COM 101 students are expected to attend all classes and participate knowledgeably. Each student is encouraged to help create a classroom environment that promotes learning, dignity, and mutual respect for everyone. Students will lose attendance points for exceeding the limited number of absences as discussed in the COM 101 Attendance Policy. In addition, students may lose participation points for classroom incivility such as speaking at inappropriate times, sleeping in class, displaying inattention, taking frequent breaks, interrupting the class by arriving late or leaving early, engaging in loud or distracting behaviors, using cell phones or text messaging in class, using inappropriate language, verbally abusing others, displaying defiance or disrespect to others, or behaving aggressively toward others. If such behavior occurs, the COM 101 student will not only lose participation points, he or she may be asked to leave the class and be subjected to disciplinary action under the Code of Student Rights, Responsibilities, and Disciplinary Procedures.

COM 101
Course Resources

FORMAL OUTLINING

When you complete a formal outline, there are a few things to remember. This is a guide to formal outlining.

I. The outline should be in sentence form.

    A. That means that each section of the outline must be a complete sentence.

    B. Each part may only have one sentence in it.

II. Each Roman numeral should be a main section of the speech.

    A. Capital letters are main points of the thesis.

        1. Numbers are sub-points under the capital letters.

        2. Little letters are sub-points under the numbers.

    B. Sub-points need to correspond with the idea it is under.

        1. This means that capital letters refer to the idea in roman numerals.

        2. This means that numbers refer to the idea in capital letters.

III. All sub-points should be indented the same.

    A. This means that all of the capital letters are indented the same.

    B. All numbers are indented the same.

IV. No sub-point stands alone.

    A. Every A must have a B.

    B. Every 1 must have a 2.

    C. You don't need to have a C or a 3, but you can.

    D. There are no exceptions to this rule.

Your speech outline should look something like the one in the sample.

Your outline will also include the full sentence details of your speech, including source citations.

The number of sub-points will differ in each speech and for each main idea.

Formal Sentence Outline Format

Student's name

Instructor's name

Course reference number

Topic: Key statement that describes the topic of your speech

General purpose: To inform OR to persuade

Specific purpose: Your specific purpose identifies the information you want to communicate (in an informative speech) or the attitude or behavior you want to change (in a persuasive speech).

Thesis: The central idea of your speech (should predict, control, and obligate).

I.   Introduction

    A. **Attention-getter:** Something that grabs the attention of the audience. Examples of this: startling statistics, stories, rhetorical questions, quotations, scenarios, etc. This point should be more than one sentence long.

    B. **Reason to listen:** Why should the audience listen to your speech, make it personal to each of them.

    C. **Thesis statement:** Exact same statement as above.

    D. **Credibility statement:**

        1. What personally connects you to this topic?

        2. What type of research have you done to establish credibility?

    E. **Preview of main points:**

        1. First, I will describe…

        2. Second, I will examine…

        3. Third, I will discuss…

II.   Restate thesis, exact statement as above.

    A. Statement of the first main point; you should not use a source in this sentence.

        1. Idea of development or support for the first main point

            a. Support material (ex: statistics, quotation, etc.)

            b. Support material (ex: statistics, quotation, etc.)

        2. More development or support

            a. Support material (ex: statistics, quotation, etc.)

            b. Support material (ex: statistics, quotation, etc.)

        3. More development if needed

Transition: *(Required)* Statement of movement that looks back (internal summary) and looks forward (preview).

B. Statement of second main point. Do not use a source in this statement.
   1. Idea of development or support for the first main point
      a. Support material (ex: statistics, quotation, etc.)
      b. Support material (ex: statistics, quotation, etc.)
   2. More development or support
      a. Support material (ex: statistics, quotation, etc.)
      b. Support material (ex: statistics, quotation, etc.)
   3. More development if needed

Transition: *(Required)* Statement of movement that looks back (internal summary) and looks forward (preview).

C. Statement of third main point. Do not use a source in this statement.
   1. Idea of development or support for the first main point
      a. Support material (ex: statistics, quotation, etc.)
      b. Support material (ex: statistics, quotation, etc.)
   2. More development or support
      a. Support material (ex: statistics, quotation, etc.)
      b. Support material (ex: statistics, quotation, etc.)
   3. More development if needed

III. Conclusion
   A. **Review of main points:**
      1. Restate your first main point.
      2. Restate your second main point.
      3. Restate you third main point.
   B. **Restate thesis:** Exact same as above.
   C. **Closure:** Develop a creative closing that will give the speech a sense of ending. This point may be more than one sentence. You should refer back to your attention-getter.

References

APA VI format; all references need to be sited in APA VI format. See section in Course Pack for further details.

Be sure to make sure that the references are in alphabetical order.

Clarify with your instructor as to what types of references you may use.

Double-spaced: All references should be double-spaced and indented.

Five source minimum: You must have at least five sources cited in your outline and listed on your reference page.

Make sure to provide all necessary information in the references.

SPEECH 1 ASSIGNMENT

Speech 1, unless you are otherwise instructed, is an **artifact speech.** The objective of Speech 1 is to provide you with an initial speaking experience. It should be a learning experience! From this experience you will gain feedback and ideas to keep in mind when you prepare for Speech 2. After you give Speech 1, give yourself some feedback. What did you do well? What areas of your speech could be improved? Keep this in mind for future speeches.

As part of the assignment, you are required to turn in a formal sentence outline. An example of the formal sentence outline for Speech 1 is provided.

Your instructor will assign Speech 1 and will let you know how you will receive feedback. Please review the Speech 1 evaluation form and outline grading form. The evaluation forms explicitly describe the criteria for Speech 1. Following is a list of criteria that should be met for Speech 1:

Introduction

- The introduction should include an attention-getter, a clear thesis (purpose), and a preview of main points. In other words, grab the audience's attention in an appropriate manner, indicate the main idea of your speech, and let us know what two or more points you will be discussing to develop your speech.

Body

- The body of the speech should include clearly-stated main points and development of each main point.
- The development of each main point should include a restatement/explanation and support material. Support for each main point could be information involving statistics, testimony, or examples.

Conclusion

- Restate the main points (remind us what they were), redirect to the thesis (guide us back to your general speech purpose), and provide closure.
- Don't just run away or end things abruptly! Let the audience know that you have reached the end of your speech.

Delivery

- Deliver the speech extemporaneously—speak in a conversational manner with notes to remind and guide you as you speak. Do not read your speech to the audience.
- Maintain appropriate eye contact with your audience. Plan ahead so that you will be comfortable and prepared for your speech. That doesn't mean that your speech should be memorized—it should be extemporaneous.
- Your speech should be two to four minutes long. Your instructor may time you with a stopwatch, so be sure to practice.

Missing class on the day you are scheduled to speak may result in an "E" for the speech. At a minimum, 10 percent will be deducted from your speech score.

Example of Artifact Speech Outline

Kevin Stevens

Artifact Speech Outline

Dr. Wendy Papa

CRN: 22208024

I.   Introduction

    A.   **Attention-getter:** Sing the Victory Song for AAGPBL

        We are the members of the All-American League.

        We come from cities near and far.

        We've got Canadians, Irishmen, and Swedes,

        We're all for one, we're one for all

        We're All-Americans!

    B.   **Reason to listen:** Not many people can say a close family member was directly involved in a unique piece of our country's history. Through the use of this film artifact, I will describe how this film is a major part of my life in numerous ways.

    C.   **Thesis statement:** *A League of Their Own* symbolizes my family's history, my love for sports, and my fascination with Hollywood filmmaking.

    D.   **Preview of main points:**

        1.   First, I will share some background information on my grandmother's professional baseball career and her involvement with the film.

        2.   Second, I will describe how sports have tremendously impacted my life.

        3.   Finally, I will express my love of film.

II.   *A League of Their Own* symbolizes my family's history, my love for sports, and fascination of Hollywood filmmaking.

    A.   This film represents of piece of my family's history.

        1.   My grandmother played in the AAGPBL from 1947–1949 as a member of the Rockford Peaches and Grand Rapids Chicks.

        2.   My grandmother also appears in the movie.

Transition: Now that you know something unique about my family and my grandmother's involvement in the AAGPBL and film, I will move on to how sports have had such a positive impact in my life.

    B.   *A League of Their Own* represents my love of sports.

        1.   I believe sports teach players important lessons and values that stick with individuals for the rest of their lives, including teamwork, communication, staying positive, and being competitive while striving for the best.

    2.   My minor at Adrian College was Business Administration, however I took more classes that focused on sports marketing.

Transition: Now that you understand my love of sports—not only participating in them, but also the benefits of competitive sports in general—I will describe my fascination with Hollywood filmmaking.

    C. Quite simply, I love movies.

        1.   I find the subject of film history extremely interesting and extensive, particularly the Hollywood continuity system.

        2.   Film is a very powerful medium, and learning about the art versus business of filmmaking also interests me.

III.   Conclusion

    A. **Review of main points:**

        1.   First, I shared how this film represents of part of my family's history.

        2.   Second, I explained how this film symbolizes my love of sports.

        3.   Third, I described my fascination of films and filmmaking.

    B. **Restate thesis:** *A League of Their Own* symbolizes my family's history, my love for sports, and my fascination with Hollywood filmmaking.

    C. **Closure:** "It's supposed to be hard. If it wasn't hard, everyone would do it. The hard is what makes it great" (Tom Hanks as Jimmy Dugan, General Manager of the Rockford Peaches).

SPEECH 2 ASSIGNMENT

You will present an **informative speech** to your COM 101 class. This speech must use organization from one of the speech structures presented in your text. This should be an expository speech in which you educate the audience about a particular area of interest (people, objects, events, processes, or concepts). The speech should be delivered extemporaneously, and you should demonstrate effective speech delivery. It should be evident that you spent time planning, preparing, researching, and rehearsing the speech.

As part of the assignment, you are required to turn in a formal sentence outline. An example of the formal sentence outline for Speech 2 is provided.

Your instructor will assign Speech 2 and will let you know how you will receive feedback. Please review the Speech 2 evaluation form and outline grading form. The evaluation forms explicitly describe the criteria for Speech 2. Requirements for Speech 2 are as follows:

1. Your speech should last from five to seven minutes.

    • Your grade will be reduced if your speech is too short or too long.

    • Your instructor may stop you if you go over the time limit.

2. Deliver your speech extemporaneously.

    • Do not read or memorize your speech.

    • Talk to your audience.

3. Deliver your speech from a speaking outline rather than from your sentence outline; do not simply read your sentence outline to the audience.

4. Place your speaking outline on note cards (either 3 x 5 or 5 x 7).

5. Create a clear and obvious thesis sentence and specific purpose.

    • Make sure that these elements will be appropriate for and effective with your audience of COM 101 students.

    • By the end of your speech, your audience should be able to write down these central ideas.

6. Clearly demonstrate the use of one of the organizational patterns discussed by your instructor.

7. Support your speech with a variety of supporting materials that are relevant and believable for COM 101 students.

    • Justify these choices to your audience.

    • **Verbally cite a minimum of five sources for your support material.**

8. With the required elements included, use creativity (and appropriateness) in the introduction and conclusion steps.

9. Include references to your audience in your introduction and throughout the body of your speech; select examples and illustrations that relate to your audience.

10. Appropriately and effectively establish your credibility with your audience.

11. Select arguments that will inform your audience.

   • Use understandable facts. Don't use too many technical terms or figures.

   • Demonstrate how those arguments relate directly to your audience.

12. Establish "common ground" between you and your listeners throughout your speech.

13. Conclude in a way that is appropriate and effective for the audience and occasion.

14. The delivery of your speech should enhance the speech rather than distract from it.

   • Be animated, conversational, and direct.

   • The delivery should be appropriate and effective for your audience and the occasion.

15. The organization of the informative speech should be clear and logical and follow one of the organizational patterns described in the class and text (chronological, topical, spatial, or cause-and-effect).

16. **Missing class on the day you are scheduled to speak may result in an "E" for the speech. At a minimum, 10 percent will be deducted from your speech score.**

Example of Informative Speech Outline

Kelsi Stoltenow

Informative Speech Outline

Dr. Wendy Papa

CRN: 22130359

Topic: Wine tasting (grape juice will be used for demonstration)

General purpose: To inform

Specific purpose: To demonstrate to my audience the three steps to tasting and analyzing a glass of wine

Thesis: Wine is properly tasted and is best enjoyed in three steps: swirling, smelling, and sipping.

I. Introduction

    A. **Attention-getter:** Wine is a tremendous beverage. It's amazing because, unlike anything else we drink, wine is alive. As wine bottles sit in those tidy store-shelf rows, the sugar, yeast, and grape juice inside of them is constantly at work, forever evolving the wines. For that reason, Kevin Zraly says in his 2010 book, *Windows on the World: A Complete Wine Course,* when a bottle is brought home and opened with the pop of a cork, it will taste different than it would have on any other day of its life.

    B. **Reason to listen:** Wine is the sophisticated person's drink of choice the world over, and while most gulp it greedily, greeting each glass with curiosity and know-how will help make the most of every drop.

    C. **Thesis statement:** Wine is properly tasted and best enjoyed in three steps.

    D. **Credibility statement:**

        1. My mom has been a wine drinker for years, and she taught me all she knows.

        2. Since turning twenty-one years old, I have gone on wine excursions throughout the United States, honing my tasting skills and devouring all the literature and personal tutelage I can find.

    E. **Preview of main points:**

        1. First, I will explain how to swirl a glass of wine.

        2. Second, I will describe how to smell a glass of wine.

        3. Finally, I will discuss how to correctly taste a glass of wine.

II. Wine is properly tasted and best enjoyed in three steps: swirling, smelling, and sipping.

    A. Wine must be swirled in its glass because the action releases the wine's aroma, or *bouquet,* as it is called among experienced wine tasters.

        1. Swirling the wine allows oxygen to mix with the wine, which releases the bouquet, says Zraly, as previously cited.

        2. The type of wine you are drinking dictates how you swirl.

a. No matter the wine type, always begin with a glass that is no more than two-thirds full to prevent spilling and to provide yourself ample swirling room.

b. White wine is typically served chilled, so to avoid warming it while swirling, place one hand at the bottom of the glass and proceed to make small, quick circles on a flat surface.

c. Red wine is typically served at room temperature, so you can place one hand on any part of the glass to swirl it.

   i. Placing one hand on the body of the glass gives you the best control, allowing you to swirl red wine with small, quick circles.

   ii. Red wine, Zraly says, should be swirled for approximately fifteen to twenty seconds, while white wine needs only ten seconds (2010).

3. While swirling, you should also determine the wine's age and grape variety by tipping the glass on its side and examining the wine's color.

a. In his 1994 book, *Wines of Italy,* Burton Anderson explains that white wines begin their lives emitting a light yellow color, and as they age turn gold and eventually brown.

b. Red wines, Anderson says, start with a purple hue, turn red, and eventually adopt a maroon or brown color.

c. Popular grape varieties can be recognized by the color of wine they produce.

   i. For example, the popular white wine, Riesling, is typically a light, almost translucent yellow, while Chardonnay, the darkest white wine, is often marigold or light brown.

   ii. Pinot Noir, a middle-of-the-road red-wine grape, often dons a straightforward shade of red.

Transition: Now that I talked about how to swirl a glass of wine and release its bouquet, I will explain how to properly smell the wine.

B. Smelling a glass of wine is the most important step in the process of wine tasting, as doing so tells you what flavors to expect before placing it in your mouth.

1. According to the National Science Teachers Association article "Got Smell?" (2010), our senses of smell and sense of taste are wired to work as one, so when we do not smell, as when we have colds, we cannot taste either.

a. Additionally, as stated in his article "The Human Sense of Smell" (2004), Gordon M. Shepherd recently discovered that humans smell just as well or better than all other mammals, including dogs.

b. Zraly mentions that humans can detect only four tastes—salty, sweet, sour, and bitter—but are capable of identifying more than 2,000 smells, so smelling, not tasting, is the key step to fully enjoying a glass of wine (2010).

2. To smell wine properly and pick up on those scents, place your nose inside the wine glass directly after swirling and inhale deeply for three to five seconds.

      a. Repeat this process at least two additional times.

      b. If you are unable to detect any vivid aroma, swirl the wine again.

  3. While smelling, try to identify scents and share them with fellow tasters.

      a. Many white wines may smell like grapefruit, green apple, pineapple, nuts, butter, vanilla, or even marshmallows.

      b. Common red wine scents include oak, berry, chocolate, coffee, smoke, pepper, and cheese.

      c. In their article "Psychology of Novice and Expert Wine Talk" (1990), Gregg Eric and Arn Solomon explain that it takes practice to accurately identify the scents in a wine's bouquet, but once learned, the ability will build on itself.

         i. Eric and Solomon point out that humans retain 70 percent of the information we gather from our sense of smell, so with time wine tasters will be able to remember and distinguish among hundreds of wine aromas (1990).

        ii. Having control over one's aroma vocabulary is what separates rookie wine tasters from experts.

Transition: Now that we have learned the importance of smelling a glass of wine and how to do it properly, I will detail how a glass of wine should be tasted.

  C. Tasting, the final step of exploring a glass of wine, should be done slowly and thoughtfully.

    1. To taste a glass of wine, put the glass to your mouth and take a sizable sip.

      a. Hold the wine in your mouth for five to eight seconds before swallowing, allowing it to wash over every part of your tongue.

      b. Because smelling the wine already gave you a solid sense of what flavors the wine has, focus now on the tactile sensations you are experiencing in your mouth.

      c. Richard Gawel, author of *A Mouth-feel Wheel* (2000), says the following are the most common sensations experienced while tasting wine: soft, supple, sappy, grippy, drying, smooth, and sugary.

      d. The darker the wine, the more apparent the sensations will be.

    2. A tell-tale sign of a quality wine is how long its taste lingers after you have swallowed; the longer it lingers the better it is.

      a. Ultimately, the only person who can declare a wine good or not is the taster.

         i. If you do not like green apple, you will not like Chardonnay.

        ii. If you are not into smoky flavors, you won't like Pinot Noir.

      b. Most novice tasters favor sweet wines like Riesling and eventually acquire a taste for dry or bitter wines.

III. Conclusion

  A. **Review of main points:**

    1. Today I first discussed how to swirl a glass of wine.

2. Second, I explained how to smell a glass of wine.

3. Finally, I talked about tasting a glass of wine.

B. **Restate thesis:** Wine is properly tasted and best enjoyed in three steps: swirling, smelling, and sipping.

C. **Closure:** If you greet each glass with patience and curiosity it will tell you the story of its life, and like any good storyteller, it will entertain you until the last drop.

References

Anderson, B. (1994). *Wines of Italy.* New York, New York: Italian Institute for Foreign Trade.

Eric, G., & Solomon, A. (1990). Psychology of Novice and Expert Wine Talk. *The American Journal of Psychology, 103(4),* 495–517.

Gawel, R., Oberholster, A., & Francis L. (2000). A 'Mouth-feel Wheel': Terminology for Communicating the mouth-feel characteristics of wine. *Australian Journal of Grape & Wine Research, 6,* 203–207. doi: 10.1111/j.1755-0238.2000.tb00180.x

Got Smell? Retrieved from http://www.nsta.org/publications/article

Shepherd, G. M., (2004). The Human Sense of Smell: Are We Better Than We Think? *PLoS Biology, 2,* 572–575. doi: 10.1371/journal.pbio.0020146

Zraly, K. (2010). *Windows on the World: A Complete Wine Course.* New York, New York: Sterling Publishing.

SPEECH 3 ASSIGNMENT

Speech 3 is a **persuasive speech.** The persuasive speech should be based on a topic of social significance. You must integrate five credible and scholarly sources into your outline and speech, as well as adapt the speech to a particular audience that will be selected in consultation with your instructor. Design the speech for a particular audience, and reveal direct and obvious references and appeals to your particular audience.

The speech must be five to seven minutes long. As part of the assignment, you are required to turn in a formal sentence outline. An example of the formal sentence outline for Speech 3 is provided.

Your instructor will assign Speech 3 and will let you know how you will receive feedback. Please review the Speech 3 evaluation form and outline grading form. The evaluation forms describe explicitly the criteria for Speech 3. Refer to requirements 1–14 listed for Speech 2 on page 195, and additional requirements for Speech 3 are listed below.

Key differences between an informative speech and a persuasive speech:

1. A persuasive speech attempts to influence and change the beliefs, attitudes, values, or behavior of a listener.

    - The purposes of persuasive speaking are to create new audience responses, enhance existing audience responses, change audience responses, or motivate audiences to action.

    - This should be reflected in your purpose and thesis statements.

2. Focus on persuasive appeals based on logic, emotion, and credibility.

3. The organization of the persuasive speech should be clear and logical, and should follow one of the organizational patterns described in Chapter 10 (problem-solution, problem-cause-solution, or Monroe's Motivated Sequence).

4. **Missing class on the day you are scheduled to speak may result in an "E" for the speech. At a minimum, 10 percent will be deducted from your speech score.**

Example of Persuasive Speech Outline

Michael Gustin

Persuasive Speech

Dr. Wendy Papa

CRN: 22109018

Topic: Vaccines and autism

Audience: You are speaking to a group of military wives. There are twenty-five women present at this biweekly coffee. Most women are between twenty-three and thirty-five years old, although there are a few older women present. About three quarters of the women are married to enlisted men, while one quarter are married to officers. Most women have at least two children under the age of three. The women do not know who you are or what your topic is.

General purpose: To persuade

Specific purpose: To persuade the audience of the importance of vaccinating children

Thesis: Fear of vaccines will most definitely have severe consequences, and it is our children who will have to suffer them.

I. Introduction

   A. **Attention-getter:** Jim Carrey is giving children measles! Sound ridiculous? You might think Britney and Paris are the ones doing harm to America's children. Yet, people like Jim Carrey, Jenny McCarthy, and even Oprah are actually making them sick. Wonder how? Well it's simple really. It all has to do with vaccines.

   B. **Reason to listen:** Each of these celebrities has played a part in an ever-growing movement against today's vaccines claiming they cause autism—a claim unsubstantiated by science and dangerous to the public health.

   C. **Thesis statement:** Fear of vaccines will definitely have severe consequences, and it is our children who will have to suffer them.

   D. **Credibility statement:** As a Biomedical Science major, I have taken medical and specialty courses in Biology and Chemistry at Central Michigan University.

   E. **Preview of main points:**

      1. In order to remedy this issue and eliminate unnecessary risks to our children, we must understand the problems posed by the anti-vaccination movement.

      2. Next we will look back to understand how such misinformation has spread.

      3. Finally we will take action to eradicate this infectious myth.

II. Fear of vaccines will definitely have severe consequences, and it is our children who will have to suffer them.

    A. The largest problems posed by the anti-vaccination movement are the recent rise in preventable diseases among American children and the increasing dangers of lower vaccination rates.

        1. According to an August 22, 2008 Morbidity and Mortality Weekly Report from the Centers for Disease Control, there has been an average of sixty-three reported American cases of measles per year for the past seven years.

            a. However, within seven months of 2008, the number of reported measles cases had increased to over twice that amount.

            b. Why the jump? An August 21, 2008 article of *The New York Times* states, "public health officials [blame the increase on] growing numbers of parents who refuse to vaccinate their children" (p. 8).

        2. The necessity of high vaccination rates is paramount.

            a. In a September 2, 2008 interview with *Newsweek Magazine,* Jane Seward, an immunization expert from the CDC, said the chicken pox vaccine is only about 85 percent effective, meaning that having only *your* children vaccinated is not guaranteed to protect them.

            b. Only when large portions of a population are vaccinated does it drastically reduce the risk of disease outbreak by creating a condition known as "herd immunity," as reported in a September 1, 2008 article in *USA Today.* If vaccination rates decrease, those who don't get their children vaccinated are putting their children and everyone else's children at risk.

Transition: While the decrease in vaccination rates poses a serious threat to America's children, we must ask why so many parents are taking this risk.

    B. To understand this, we must look back to see what gave the anti-vaccination movement its start and see how it is perpetuated today.

        1. The myth began ten years ago when a study was published in *The Lancet,* a British medical journal, claiming that the combination measles, mumps, and rubella vaccine causes autism by releasing toxins from the gastrointestinal tract.

            a. Since then, the study has been refuted and discredited numerous times.

            b. As a September 9, 2008 editorial in *The New York Times* reports, a brand new study from Columbia University has failed to replicate the original study's results.

        2. Even though it was only a single false study, it has managed to create a firestorm of backlash against vaccines.

            a. Leading this battle is Jenny McCarthy, an actor and former Playboy playmate.

            b. In a June 4, 2008 interview with *Good Morning America,* McCarthy claimed current vaccines contain things like mercury, ether, and anti-freeze which she believes contributed to her son Evan's autism and the rising autism epidemic.

            c. Even the claim that autism is an epidemic is faulty.

      i.   An article in the May 2008 issue of *Developmental Child Neurology* found that 25 percent of adults who had been diagnosed with a pragmatic impairment or developmental language disorder would be diagnosed with autism under today's diagnostic criteria.

      ii. This suggests the increase in autism is not a true increase but instead an expansion of what is considered "autism" combined with an increase in awareness.

3.   Quite simply, McCarthy is completely wrong.

   a.   David Gorski, a surgical oncologist of the *Science-Based Medicine* blog posted February 18, 2008, says neither anti-freeze nor ether is present in vaccines.

   b.   Even more incorrect is the claim that vaccines contain mercury which causes autism.

      i.   A study published on September 27, 2007 in the *New England Journal of Medicine* reports no link between the mercury-containing preservative thimerosal and "neurophysiological functioning."

      ii. Even so, a September 9, 2008 article published by the American Academy of Family Physicians reports that in 2001, thimerosal was removed from all routine vaccines.

      iii. If mercury in vaccines was really the cause of autism, then we should have expected to see a decrease in autism diagnoses, yet since 2001 they have continued to increase without any change in rate.

Transition: Jenny McCarthy's misinformation has created a fear of vaccines which has already managed to cause an increase in reported measles cases. If the current trend continues, it won't be long until diseases we thought had been eradicated make a deadly resurgence. However, the trend does not have to continue.

C.   By encouraging government vigilance, media integrity, and individual responsibility, we can stop the spread of vaccine misinformation.

1.   Fixing the problem starts with the CDC.

   a.   Although their statement as of February 8, 2008 on thimerosal is, "there is no convincing scientific evidence of harm caused by the low doses of thimerosal in vaccines," in 2001, the CDC removed all thimerosal from vaccines as a preventative measure.

   b.   Clearly, the anti-vaccinationists have more influence then we imagined.

   c.   It is obvious that our medical experts need to focus on medicine and not the whim of the masses.

      i.   Contact the CDC through their website, cdc.gov, and tell them the evidence of science should be the only basis for their health recommendations.

      ii. *Live Science* of September 5, 2008 warns, "This issue shows why public health policy must be guided by science instead of celebrity."

2.   The media is the next problem to be fixed.

   a.   The *North County Journal* of September 9, 2008 asserts unwarranted media frenzy has made childhood immunizations "controversial."

   b.   The media sensationalizes rumors for the sake of making profits.

      i.   "Vaccines cause autism!" There's a headline you can sell.

     ii.   "Very little has changed in the scientific opinion of vaccines." Not so exciting.

  c.   We have to demand a higher quality of news reporting.

      i.   Write to your local and national news stations and tell them you won't continue to watch their programming without more credible scientific reporting.

     ii.   Once networks see an effect on their bottom lines, you can be sure they'll fix the problem.

  3.   Finally, we must turn our sights inward.

    a.   The most important thing you can do is get your child vaccinated, but just as importantly, we must encourage other parents to do the same.

    b.   A statistic reported by the *Chicago Tribune* on August 26, 2008 stresses the importance of vaccines: In a 1989 measles outbreak, 123 deaths were reported, almost all of which occurred in unimmunized preschoolers—123 deaths that could have easily been prevented.

    c.   Get involved with your local skeptical and scientific organizations and spread the word.

    d.   Jenny McCarthy might have celebrity influence, but truth trumps the appeal of a Playboy centerfold.

III. Conclusion

  A. **Review of main points:**

    1.   Today I have discussed the health problems posed by the anti-vaccination movement.

    2.   Secondly, I have addressed the causes behind its prevalence and influence.

    3.   Finally, I have reviewed the solutions to help combat it.

  B. **Restate thesis:** Fear of vaccines will most definitely have severe consequences, and it is our children who will suffer them.

  C. **Closure:** Vaccines are too vital to public health to let celebrity influence diminish their effect. It's time for us stand up and give this viral idea a shot of truth. It's time for us to defend science and protect our children.

References

Bishop, D., Whitehouse, A., Watt, H., Line, E. (2008) Autism and diagnosticsubstitution: evidence from a study of adults with a history of developmental language disorder. *Developmental Child Neurology 50(5)*. Retrieved from www.ncbi.nlm.nih.gov/pubmed

Brady, J., Dahle, S. (2008, Jun. 4). Celeb couple to lead 'green vaccine' rally. *ABCNews*. Retrieved from http://abcnews.go.com/GMA/OnCall/story?id=4987758

Common vaccine beliefs. (2008, Aug. 26). *Chicago Tribune*. Retrieved from www.chicagotribune.com/features/lifestyle/health

Debunking an autism theory. (2008, Sep. 9). *The New York Times.* Retrieved from www.nytimes.com/ 2008/09

Gorski, D. (2008, Jan. 7). Mercury in vaccines as a cause of autism and autism spectrumdisorders (ASDs): A failed hypothesis. *The Science Based Medicine Blog.* Retrieved from www.sciencebasedmedicine.org

Harris, G. (2008, Aug. 21). Measles cases grow in number, and officials blameparents' fear of autism. *The New York Times.* Retrieved from www.nytimes.com/2008/08

Kranbuhl, H. (2008, Sep. 9). House Call: Vaccines don't pose danger to kids, but skipping them does. *North County Journal.* Retrieved from http://northcountyjournal.stltoday.com/articles/2008/09

Mercury and vaccines (thimerosal). (2008, Feb. 8). *CDC.* Retrieved from www.cdc.gov/vaccinesafety/ concerns/thimerosal.htm

Novella, S. (2007). Vaccines and autism: myths and misconceptions. Retrieved from www.csicop.org/ si/2007-06/novella.html

Radford, B. (2008, Sep. 5). Autism and vaccines: Why bad logic trumps science. *LiveScience.* Retrieved from www.livescience.com/health

Sabo, L. (2008, Sep. 1). Chicken pox vaccine does a number on the number of cases. *USA Today.* Retrieved from www.usatoday.com/news/health

Shoof, A. (2008, Sep. 3). Fears of Autism Not Affecting Immunization Rates. *American Academy of Family Physicians.* Retrieved from www.aafp.org/online/

Springen, K. (2008, Sep. 2). A CDC expert on the success of the chickenpox vaccine and why every child should get a booster shot to prevent new outbreaks of the potentially serious disease. *Newsweek.* Retrieved from www.newsweek.com/id/156654

Stobbe, M. (2008, Aug. 21). Measles cases highest since '97. *Time.* Retrieved from www.time.com/time/ printout/0,8816,1834693,00.html

Thompson, W. W., Price, C., Goodson, B., Shay, D. K., Benson, P., Hinrichsen, V. L., et al. (2007). Early Thimerosal Exposure and Neuropsychological Outcomes at 7 to 10 Years. *New England Journal of Medicine, 357(13),* 1281–1292. doi: 10.1056/NEJMoa071434.

Update: Measles. (2008). *Morbidity and Mortality Weekly Report, 57(33).* Retrieved from www.cdc.gov/ mmwr/preview/mmwrhtml/mm5733a1.htm

LIBRARY ASSIGNMENT

Objective: Students will become familiar with the facilities and electronic resources of Park Library and obtain information for their selected speech topics. As students acquire more information, they will be better able to support the arguments in their speeches.

Procedure: Once students have selected a speech topic, they must go to the library, find the following items, and answer the questions listed below. **Important note:** A topic can be too broad or too narrow. The topic "pollution" is too broad, but it could be narrowed to "water pollution in the Great Lakes." The topic "Taylor Swift" could be too narrow for an entire book. One way to broaden it would be "women in popular music" and then see if matching books have information on Taylor Swift.

1. **Find a book** related to your topic. (Hint: Search the library catalog Centra. It can be searched at the library and online at http://catalog.lib.cmich.edu/. For help finding a book, go to the library's online tutorial. Go to www.lib.cmich.edu and click on Library Tutorials, Park Library Online Tutorial, and Finding Books.)

    a. Identify the library call number.

    b. Where is the book located in the library?

    c. Cite the book according to APA VI format. (For examples, go to www.lib.cmich.edu and click on Virtual Reference and then Style Guides.)

    d. Provide one direct quotation from the book.

2. **Find a journal article** on your topic. (Hint: Visit the Find an Article page at www.lib.cmich.edu/databases/. Choose General/Multidisciplinary, then WilsonSelect. For help finding an article, go to www.lib.cmich.edu and select Library Tutorials, Park Library Online Tutorial, and Finding Articles.)

    a. Either give the library call number for the journal or give the name of the database in which you found an online version of the article.

    b. If the journal is physically located in the library, on what floor is it shelved?

    c. Cite the article according to APA VI format.

    d. Write a one-paragraph abstract of the article (in your own words).

3. **Find another article** on your topic. The article may be from a popular magazine or journal. (Hint: See the Find an Article tutorial for the differences between magazines and journals. Visit the Find an Article page at www.lib.cmich.edu/databases/ and choose a database that fits your topic.)

    a. Either give the library call number for the magazine or give the name of the database in which you found an online version of the article.

    b. If the magazine is physically located in the library, on what floor is it shelved?

    c. Cite the article according to APA VI format.

    d. Write a one-paragraph abstract of the article (in your own words).

4. Using a journal article you found in steps 2 or 3, give the name of an expert in the area of your topic. (Hint: The authors of journal articles are considered experts.)

   a. Identify this person's credentials. (Hint: Journal articles usually provide information about the author's background and where he/she teaches.)

   b. If you could interview this person, list at least three questions you would ask during the interview.

5. Where else could you get information on this topic?

Note on format: Park Library receives material in a variety of formats including print, microfilm, microfiche, and electronic. For example, some journals can be found in both paper and digital media through one of the library databases. Both of these formats provide the text of the journal and can be used for this assignment.

For help with this assignment, please visit the Reference Desk on the second floor of the Park Library.

Source: Adapted from Bridges, T. M., Crowell, T. L., & Scholl, J. C. (1999). *Instructor's resource manual to accompany public speaking: Challenges and choices.* Boston, MA: Bedford/St. Martin's. Revised by Park Library Reference Department 10/2003.

COM 101
Evaluation Forms

EVALUATION FORM FOR SPEECH 3

Monroe's Motivated Sequence

Speaker _____ Topic _____ Time _____

4 = excellent   3 = competent   2 = needs improvement   1 = insufficient   0 = did not do

Introduction

4 3 2 1 0 Captures attention and interest
4 3 2 1 0 Provides a reason to listen
4 3 2 1 0 Introduces a clear thesis and specific purpose
4 3 2 1 0 Credibility is established
4 3 2 1 0 Preview of main points

Body

4 3 2 1 0 Speech is adapted to the audience's interests, knowledge, and attitudes
4 3 2 1 0 Establishment of need
4 3 2 1 0 Explains how the solution satisfies need
4 3 2 1 0 Visualization
4 3 2 1 0 Main points are clearly identified
4 3 2 1 0 Transitions with internal summaries are evident and effective
4 3 2 1 0 Evidence of research and support material
4 3 2 1 0 Used acceptable logic, reasoning, and emotional appeals

Delivery

4 3 2 1 0 Poised and confident
4 3 2 1 0 Professional appearance and appropriate attire
4 3 2 1 0 Delivery is extemporaneous (conversational, did not read)
4 3 2 1 0 Effective use of voice (not monotone, too soft, too fast, etc.)
4 3 2 1 0 Language and grammar are appropriate
4 3 2 1 0 Maintained eye contact with audience
4 3 2 1 0 Effective nonverbal communication (gestures, visual aid, etc.)
4 3 2 1 0 Freedom from distractions (pacing, swaying, fidgeting, "um," "ok")

Conclusion

4 3 2 1 0 Signals the end of speech
4 3 2 1 0 Reaffirms main points
4 3 2 1 0 Statement of desired action
4 3 2 1 0 Vivid and memorable closure

Topic Choice and Time Guidelines

4 3 2 1 0 Topic meets assignment
4 3 2 1 0 Communicated enthusiasm for topic

_____ / 100 points

_____ Sources cited ☐ ☐ ☐ ☐ ☐

_____ Observes 5–7 minute time limit

PEER EVALUATION

Speaker's name: _____

+ great
✓ ok
– needs work

_____ Introduction	_____ Conversational
_____ Organization	_____ Voice
_____ Main ideas	_____ Eye contact
_____ Support material	_____ Gestures
_____ Transitions	_____ Visual aid
_____ Cited sources	_____ Topic choice
_____ Conclusion	_____ Time

Identify two speaker strengths:

_____

_____

Identify two areas in which the speaker could improve:

_____

_____

Other comments that might help the speaker do a better job:

_____

_____

PEER EVALUATION

Speaker's name: _____

+ great
✓ ok
– needs work

_____ Introduction	_____ Conversational
_____ Organization	_____ Voice
_____ Main ideas	_____ Eye contact
_____ Support material	_____ Gestures
_____ Transitions	_____ Visual aid
_____ Cited sources	_____ Topic choice
_____ Conclusion	_____ Time

Identify two speaker strengths:

_____

_____

Identify two areas in which the speaker could improve:

_____

_____

Other comments that might help the speaker do a better job:

_____

_____

PEER EVALUATION

Speaker's name: _____

+ great
✓ ok
– needs work

_____ Introduction	_____ Conversational
_____ Organization	_____ Voice
_____ Main ideas	_____ Eye contact
_____ Support material	_____ Gestures
_____ Transitions	_____ Visual aid
_____ Cited sources	_____ Topic choice
_____ Conclusion	_____ Time

Identify two speaker strengths:

_____

_____

Identify two areas in which the speaker could improve:

_____

_____

Other comments that might help the speaker do a better job:

_____

_____

PEER EVALUATION

Speaker's name: _____

+ great
✓ ok
– needs work

____ Introduction		____ Conversational
____ Organization		____ Voice
____ Main ideas		____ Eye contact
____ Support material		____ Gestures
____ Transitions		____ Visual aid
____ Cited sources		____ Topic choice
____ Conclusion		____ Time

Identify two speaker strengths:

_____

_____

Identify two areas in which the speaker could improve:

_____

_____

Other comments that might help the speaker do a better job:

_____

_____

PEER EVALUATION

Speaker's name: _____

+ great
✓ ok
– needs work

____ Introduction		____ Conversational
____ Organization		____ Voice
____ Main ideas		____ Eye contact
____ Support material		____ Gestures
____ Transitions		____ Visual aid
____ Cited sources		____ Topic choice
____ Conclusion		____ Time

Identify two speaker strengths:

_____

_____

Identify two areas in which the speaker could improve:

_____

_____

Other comments that might help the speaker do a better job:

_____

_____

PEER EVALUATION

Speaker's name: _____

+ great
✓ ok
– needs work

____ Introduction		____ Conversational
____ Organization		____ Voice
____ Main ideas		____ Eye contact
____ Support material		____ Gestures
____ Transitions		____ Visual aid
____ Cited sources		____ Topic choice
____ Conclusion		____ Time

Identify two speaker strengths:

_____

_____

Identify two areas in which the speaker could improve:

_____

_____

Other comments that might help the speaker do a better job:

_____

_____

PEER EVALUATION

Speaker's name: _____

+ great
✓ ok
− needs work

___ Introduction	___ Conversational
___ Organization	___ Voice
___ Main ideas	___ Eye contact
___ Support material	___ Gestures
___ Transitions	___ Visual aid
___ Cited sources	___ Topic choice
___ Conclusion	___ Time

Identify two speaker strengths:

_____
_____

Identify two areas in which the speaker could improve:

_____
_____

Other comments that might help the speaker do a better job:

_____
_____

PEER EVALUATION

Speaker's name: _____

+ great
✓ ok
− needs work

___ Introduction	___ Conversational
___ Organization	___ Voice
___ Main ideas	___ Eye contact
___ Support material	___ Gestures
___ Transitions	___ Visual aid
___ Cited sources	___ Topic choice
___ Conclusion	___ Time

Identify two speaker strengths:

_____
_____

Identify two areas in which the speaker could improve:

_____
_____

Other comments that might help the speaker do a better job:

_____
_____

PEER EVALUATION

Speaker's name: _____

+ great
✓ ok
− needs work

___ Introduction	___ Conversational
___ Organization	___ Voice
___ Main ideas	___ Eye contact
___ Support material	___ Gestures
___ Transitions	___ Visual aid
___ Cited sources	___ Topic choice
___ Conclusion	___ Time

Identify two speaker strengths:

_____
_____

Identify two areas in which the speaker could improve:

_____
_____

Other comments that might help the speaker do a better job:

_____
_____

PEER EVALUATION

Speaker's name: _____

+ great
✓ ok
– needs work

___ Introduction	___ Conversational
___ Organization	___ Voice
___ Main ideas	___ Eye contact
___ Support material	___ Gestures
___ Transitions	___ Visual aid
___ Cited sources	___ Topic choice
___ Conclusion	___ Time

Identify two speaker strengths:

_____

_____

Identify two areas in which the speaker could improve:

_____

_____

Other comments that might help the speaker do a better job:

_____

_____

_____

PEER EVALUATION

Speaker's name: _____

+ great
✓ ok
– needs work

___ Introduction	___ Conversational
___ Organization	___ Voice
___ Main ideas	___ Eye contact
___ Support material	___ Gestures
___ Transitions	___ Visual aid
___ Cited sources	___ Topic choice
___ Conclusion	___ Time

Identify two speaker strengths:

_____

_____

Identify two areas in which the speaker could improve:

_____

_____

Other comments that might help the speaker do a better job:

_____

_____

_____

PEER EVALUATION

Speaker's name: _____

+ great
✓ ok
– needs work

___ Introduction	___ Conversational
___ Organization	___ Voice
___ Main ideas	___ Eye contact
___ Support material	___ Gestures
___ Transitions	___ Visual aid
___ Cited sources	___ Topic choice
___ Conclusion	___ Time

Identify two speaker strengths:

_____

_____

Identify two areas in which the speaker could improve:

_____

_____

Other comments that might help the speaker do a better job:

_____

_____

_____

COM 101
Chapter Activities

Communication Is Irreversible

Think about a time when you said something, face-to-face or computer-mediated, that could not be taken back. Describe the experience in detail.

Think about a time when someone said something, face-to-face or computer-mediated, that you wish had not been said. Describe the experience in detail.

We use social networking to build and maintain relationships. Is it easier to share information through technology than face-to-face? Why?

What I Value

Below is a list of personal values common to all of us. Consider what values are most important to you, and rank the top five (with 1 being the most important). Although many of the values listed below will be important to you, choose the five you feel are most important as to how you live your life.

_____	Family	_____	Knowledge (education)
_____	Patriotism	_____	Friendship
_____	Wealth	_____	Being ethical
_____	Status	_____	Social responsibility
_____	Health	_____	Forgiveness
_____	Cleanliness	_____	Humility
_____	Individuality	_____	Patience
_____	Attractiveness	_____	Tradition
_____	Generosity	_____	Obeying the law
_____	Loyalty	_____	Hard work
_____	Religion (spirituality)	_____	Getting along with others
_____	Love	_____	Saving face

INTERPRETATION

Once you have completed this challenging task, compare your answers with those of your classmates. How do your own priorities overlap or differ with those of your classmates based on gender, family, religious background, ethnicity, or age? Why do you think so? How might your parents' or grandparents' rankings be different or similar to your own?

see reverse

Did you rank "being ethical" on your list? How frequently does the value of *being ethical* appear on your classmates' lists? How prominent a value is *being ethical* to you? How important is this value to you when it comes to your perception of the following people?

President of the United States

Parents

Significant other

Close friends

Academic advisor

Instructor in this class

Notice how this list of values is common across all people. That is, each characteristic on the list is something we all value; yet each of us ranks the values on the list somewhat differently. How might our different rankings influence how we communicate with or perceive one another?

Sense of Self

Read each of the following scenarios. Put yourself in each situation and answer the following questions.

Situation: A friend and classmate ask if you want a copy of a stolen answer key s/he has obtained for the upcoming COM 101 exam. How do you answer?

Situation: Someone you are really attracted to invites you out to a party; however, you had already agreed to do something with a friend that evening. How do you answer?

What role did your self-concept play in your responses?

What role did others' possible impressions of your behavior play in your responses?

Make a list of three characteristics of yourself:

1. _____
2. _____
3. _____

Now determine how you got those characteristics (family, friends, media, culture...):

1. _____
2. _____
3. _____

What are three characteristics you think others perceive about you?

1. _____
2. _____
3. _____

Do the characteristics you have for yourself match those that you think others have for you? Why?

How much of your sense of self is shaped by those around you and the culture you live in?

Guessing

Each student should pick a partner that they do not know and fill out this questionnaire about them. You must *guess*—you cannot ask your partner for the answers to any of these questions.

Fill out this page about your partner by guessing the correct answers.

Hometown:

Major:

Size of family: a. only child   b. 1–3 siblings   c. 4–7 siblings   d. 8 or more siblings

Favorite beverage:

      a. orange juice   b. Coke/Pepsi   c. 7-UP   d. beer

      e. milk   f. coffee   g. champagne   h. other _____

Would prefer spending his/her money on which of the following?

      a. clothes   b. traveling   c. things around the house

      d. books   e. entertainment   f. savings account

Person's favorite color:

Person's favorite musician/singer:

This person probably handles conflict by:

      a. avoiding it   b. trying to solve it peacefully   c. meeting it head-on

      d. starting a fist fight   e. reporting the other person to the authorities

What one thing would you and this person disagree on?

If this person could be given his/her favorite food it would be:

Describe this person in one word (an adjective):

Assume it is twenty-five years from now, and this person has just made the headlines. What would the headline say?

Language Ambiguity Worksheet

Answer the following questions to the best of your ability.

1. Ken is **independently wealthy.** What is his total personal worth? _____

2. Lucy is **very old.** How old is she? _____

3. Luke is a **big** smoker. How many cigarettes does he smoke everyday? _____

4. Casey watches **quite a bit** of television. How many hours a day does she watch? _____

5. Joe has been playing the violin for a **long time.** How long has he been playing? _____

6. The price of fruit at that store is **insane!** How much is the fruit? _____

7. Mr. Gravish has a **large** farm. How many acres does he have? _____

8. Bob the mechanic is **paid well** for his services. What is his hourly wage? _____

9. Torch Lake is **far away** from here. How many miles away is it? _____

10. She is a **veteran** golfer. How many years has she been playing? _____

11. A trip to Africa is **expensive.** How much would it cost for a week? _____

12. Yesterday was **very hot.** What was the temperature? _____

13. Professor Huntley let us out of our 12:00 class **quite early** today. We usually get out at 1:00. What time did we get out? _____

14. The building is **so tall.** How many stories is the building? _____

15. My grandpa quit school at a **young age.** How many years did he go? _____

16. Jody comes from a **rural** town. What is the town's population? _____

Can you think of any other ambiguous terms that are often used today? Write them below, along with an improved, more descriptive way to state the same idea.

1.

IMPROVED:

2.

IMPROVED:

The Nature of Language

1. List the three DIRTIEST words you can think of.

   _____

   _____

   _____

2. List the three COLDEST words you can think of.

   _____

   _____

   _____

3. List the three KINDEST words you can think of.

   _____

   _____

   _____

4. List the three SCARIEST words you can think of.

   _____

   _____

   _____

5. List the three MOST TACKY words you can think of.

   _____

   _____

   _____

6. List the three MOST IRRITATING words you can think of.

   _____

   _____

   _____

7. List your three MOST FAVORITE words.

   _____

   _____

   _____

8. List your three LEAST FAVORITE words.

   _____

   _____

   _____

Nonverbal Ethnography Report

You are communication researchers working to uncover the many subcultures that exist within the CMU campus. In order to uncover the culture, you will observe the daily activities of people in a particular section of campus. What constitutes a *culture?* It is the daily interactions between people, the messages they send and receive, and how meanings are attached to these messages that become commonplace over time.

As an individual, in pairs, or in groups of three, observe people in a particular area of campus. Identify the specific nonverbal messages they send and how these messages are received from others. What meanings do you derive from the interactions? Please review the following types of nonverbal messages to assist you with your observations.

Body movements
Body appearance

Facial communication
Eye communication

Proxemics distances
Territoriality

Color communication
Clothing and body adornment
Space decoration
Smell communication

Touch communication
The meanings of touch
Touch avoidance

Paralanguage
Silence

Time communication

What nonverbal messages did you observe, and how do you derive meaning from these nonverbal messages? Through your observations, determine the goals and activities of the people you are observing. What do you know about the people you are observing: types of relationships, power, conflict, leadership, emotions, decision-making, etc.?

On the back of this page, you will produce a written ethnographic report to be turned in and discussed in class. Your report will identify specific nonverbal messages being sent and the meanings you derive from those messages.

see reverse

NONVERBAL ETHNOGRAPHY REPORT   Date: _____

Students' names: _____

Location of observation: _____

Source: Nathan Hodges, original activity.

Meaning between Words

Your instructor will ask for volunteers. Two students will read the following dialogue as written, after receiving special instructions from the instructor. After the dialogue has been read, the class will try to identify the relationship between the two characters.

A: Hello.

B: Hello.

A: So, uh, how are you?

B: About the same. You?

A: Nothing new to report.

B: I thought maybe you might have something to tell me.

A: Has anything changed?

B: Not that I know of. Do you know of a change?

A: No.

B: So what do you think we should do now?

A: I suppose we could go ahead and . . .

B: Yeah, seems like it's a good plan.

A: Are you sure?

B: As sure as we ever can be in situations like this.

A: Want to reconsider? A lot is at stake.

B: No, I'm ready. Let's do it.

Handshake Report Card

The handshake is part of the first impression you make. A poor handshake speaks volumes about your confidence level and your personality. Your task is to shake hands with three different people in your class. Rate them based on the five characteristics.

PERSON #1

Firmness	Poor	Fair	Average	Good	Excellent
Eye contact	Poor	Fair	Average	Good	Excellent
Movement	Poor	Fair	Average	Good	Excellent
Length	Poor	Fair	Average	Good	Excellent
Appropriate	Poor	Fair	Average	Good	Excellent

PERSON #2

Firmness	Poor	Fair	Average	Good	Excellent
Eye contact	Poor	Fair	Average	Good	Excellent
Movement	Poor	Fair	Average	Good	Excellent
Length	Poor	Fair	Average	Good	Excellent
Appropriate	Poor	Fair	Average	Good	Excellent

PERSON #3

Firmness	Poor	Fair	Average	Good	Excellent
Eye contact	Poor	Fair	Average	Good	Excellent
Movement	Poor	Fair	Average	Good	Excellent
Length	Poor	Fair	Average	Good	Excellent
Appropriate	Poor	Fair	Average	Good	Excellent

Listening Ability: A Self-Assessment Scale

The chapter on listening identifies common errors associated with listening. Take this opportunity to evaluate your own listening behavior according to those errors.

1. **I assume that all listening is passive and easy to do.**

   not at all like me   *just like me*

              1   2   3   4   5   6   7

2. **I jump to conclusions.**

   not at all like me   *just like me*

              1   2   3   4   5   6   7

3. **I have unproductive use of thinking time.**

   not at all like me   *just like me*

              1   2   3   4   5   6   7

4. **I give in to status differences.**

   not at all like me   *just like me*

              1   2   3   4   5   6   7

5. **I allow attitudes and beliefs to interfere.**

   not at all like me   *just like me*

              1   2   3   4   5   6   7

6. **I am preoccupied with myself.**

   not at all like me   *just like me*

              1   2   3   4   5   6   7

7. **I sometimes lack perspective; failing to reflect on the importance of the information.**

   not at all like me   *just like me*

              1   2   3   4   5   6   7

8. **I criticize the delivery of a speaker.**

   not at all like me   *just like me*

              1   2   3   4   5   6   7

9. **I sometimes call the subject dull.**

   not at all like me   *just like me*

              1   2   3   4   5   6   7

10. **I sometimes fake attention.**

    not at all like me   *just like me*

               1   2   3   4   5   6   7

11. **I can overreact to an idea or emotionally laden word or phrase.**

    not at all like me   *just like me*

               1   2   3   4   5   6   7

12. **I listen just for facts.**

    not at all like me   *just like me*

               1   2   3   4   5   6   7

see reverse

Now, total your score. Use the following guidelines to interpret your score.

30 and below: Excellent

31 to 50:   Not bad

Over 50:   You need to work on your skills

Listening Skill Exercise

Form listening triads. In each group, one person will be the referee (observer) and the other two will have a discussion, alternating between being the listener and the speaker. The listener and the speaker must each identify his/her position on the topic. The referee will review the speaker and listener positions and select a topic on which they disagree. The speaker will hold a pencil while communicating his/her viewpoint on that topic and then hand the pencil to the listener who must paraphrase what the speaker has said. Then the listener communicates his/her own viewpoint on the topic. The only person who may speak is the person holding the pencil. After five minutes, the participants switch roles and continue the process. The following are suggested topics that may be discussed, or the referee may select a different topic.

5 = Strongly agree   4 = Agree   3 = Neutral   2 = Disagree   1 = Strongly disagree

_____ Same sex marriage

_____ Capital punishment

_____ Legalization of marijuana

_____ Keeping abortion legal

_____ Affirmative action

_____ Animal rights

_____ Immunizations (required)

_____ Genetic engineering

_____ Prayer in public schools

_____ Welfare system is fair

_____ Child beauty pageants

_____ Law enforcement cameras—an invasion of privacy?

_____ Cheating in college (penalties should be stricter)

_____ Torture (is acceptable in certain circumstances)

_____ Driving under the influence

_____ Gun control

_____ Military recruitment at high schools

_____ Employers using Facebook to make hiring decisions

_____ Immigration reform

_____ Health care coverage provided for all United States citizens

_____ Birth control for teenagers (without parental consent)

_____ Homeless shelters in residential areas

_____ Juvenile offenders prosecuted as adults

_____ Voting process in the United States is fair

_____ Racial profiling

_____ Global warming exists

_____ Steroids (or performance enhancing drugs) used by athletes

_____ Taxes are fair for all United States citizens

Other: _____

Conversation Starter

Review each of the situations below and write two open-ended questions that would start a conversation. Break into dyads, and ask your partner the questions you have written. Take turns role-playing and responding.

SITUATION 1

You met a person online. You are on your first face-to-face date. You meet at a nice restaurant that overlooks a lake and the sun is beginning to set. You are looking at the menus.

1.

2.

SITUATION 2

You went to college but your best friend from high school decided to get married and start a family. You are visiting your friend's home for the first time since high school graduation. Your friend's two young children are playing in the next room.

1.

2.

SITUATION 3

It is the first meeting of your COM 101 class. You sit down next to a person you have seen on campus and have been attracted to for some time but have never approached.

1.

2.

SITUATION 4

You have dated someone in college for one semester. You are meeting his/her parents for the first time. You are alone with the parents in their living room.

1.

2.

The Ocean Liner Worksheet

An explosion destroyed an ocean liner traveling to San Francisco. A lifeboat was thrown clear of the explosion and ten people plus yourself have made it to safety. After a few moments, everyone realizes the boat has a puncture in it and is sinking fast. There is a small rubber raft aboard the boat that will be able to take you and four passengers to safety. Everyone else will die. You choose the four people who will go on the raft with you and survive. Below is a list of the ten passengers currently on the boat with you. Which four fellow survivors will you choose?

1. Dr. John Keller

   Age 67, he specializes in rare diseases and has given his life to the service of medicine and selflessly helping others.

2. Rev. Michael Maller

   Age 35, he is an African-American who has a military style. He is a political and spiritual leader to troubled youth.

3. Lucy Taylor

   Age 30, she is a successor to Naomi Wolf and a spokesperson for the Women's Rights Movement.

4. Bliff Smith

   Age 42, he is a wealthy banker, has done a large amount of community service, and is the father of triplets.

5. Laura Smith

   Age 22, she is pregnant and Bliff's wife. She is a prominent member at the country club and is in her ninth month of pregnancy.

6. Thomas Sowell

   Age 21, he is a student at the local university and a leader of a group dedicated to cleansing the campus of liberals. He is also the sole supporter of his mother and younger sister.

7. Jimmy Lorenzo

   Age 50, he is a reformed criminal and is on his way to testify against the largest organized crime ring in history.

8. Joseph Brooks

   Age 40, he is a former member of the Navy Seals and is dying of cancer.

9. Erin Mueller

   Age 47, she is a nurse, gets regular panic attacks, and can't swim.

10. Bob Pratt

    Age 29, he has an Olympic gold medal and is the father of six.

What's Your Leadership IQ?

Instructions: The following quiz will help you determine if you have what it takes to be an effective leader. In the space provided after each question, indicate if the statement is true (T) or false (F).

1. True leaders are born, not made. _____

2. If I take on a leadership role, I'll improve my popularity. _____

3. The very best leaders know the value of keeping a low profile. _____

4. If you usually get along well with those in charge, you will probably be a good leader. _____

5. The best leaders always know what to do. _____

6. An effective leader must try to maintain a forceful personality. _____

7. My physical appearance has little or nothing to do with my becoming a leader. _____

8. I prefer reading fiction to nonfiction. _____

9. I usually stick to my decision even when it is unpopular with my group. _____

10. Being a quick decision-maker is an important trait in a good leader. _____

SCORING THE LEADERSHIP IQ QUIZ

To tally your score, give yourself 1 point for each response that matches yours.
1. False 2. False 3. False 4. True 5. False 6. False 7. False 8. False 9. False 10. False

A score of 8–10 points:
You would be or are an effective leader. You are sensitive to the needs of those you would direct, and if you are not already in some type of supervisory role, you are probably not developing to your fullest potential.

A score of 4–7 points:
You have an average ability to lead a group. Like most others in this broad category, you probably can improve your capacity to take charge if you receive some extra training.

A score of 0–3 points:
You are a solid follower and not a leader of others. This does not mean you will fail in those endeavors you choose, but only that you will probably not achieve your goals if they have to be reached through others. People with low scores often work better on their own or as a team member rather than as a leader.

Patterns of Conflict Behavior

Reflect on your conflict history and identify two conflicts you have had recently. These should be conflicts that occurred with people who are important to you or in the relationships that matter most. Answer the following questions:

CONFLICT SITUATION #1

The conflict: Describe whom the conflict was with and what the conflict was about.

How I managed it: What did you say? How did you behave? How did others respond? How did you react?

The results: How did you feel about the final outcome of the conflict? How did the others involved feel about the outcome? Are you happy with the results?

CONFLICT SITUATION #2

The conflict: Describe whom the conflict was with and what the conflict was about.

How I managed it: What did you say? How did you behave? How did others respond? How did you react?

The results: How did you feel about the final outcome of the conflict? How did the others involved feel about the outcome? Are you happy with the results?

see reverse

In pairs or groups of three, discuss your conflict situations. Based on your conflict history, answer the following questions:

1. Are you satisfied with the way you have handled your conflict situations?

2. Did you come away from the conflicts feeling better or worse about yourself?

3. Are your relationships with the people involved in the conflict stronger or weaker?

4. Do you recognize any patterns in your conflict style? Which style or series of styles do you tend to use: avoiding, dominating, compromising, obliging, or integrating.

5. Do you use defensive or supportive communication during a conflict episode?

6. Review both conflict situations. Do you recognize any patterns in your conflict management style? For example, do you hold in your feelings? Do you say hurtful things? Do you single out one or two factors for blaming the other person? Do you store up grievances and then "unload" them on others? Are you sarcastic? Do you have a temper? Are you verbally or physically aggressive?

7. If you could, would you like to change the way you handle your conflicts? What ideas do you have for change?

Self-Disclosure Assessment Form

Label each topic below using one of the following codes.

L   low risk—could be disclosed to many people

M   moderate risk—might be disclosed to friends and family

H   high risk—would be disclosed only to people we trust such as our closest friends and family

P   private information—would not be disclosed to anyone no matter how close the relationship

_____   1.   Your dreams for the future

_____   2.   The classes you are taking this semester

_____   3.   How you feel about each of your parents

_____   4.   The happiest moments in your life

_____   5.   Your religious views

_____   6.   Your sexual fantasies

_____   7.   The things that you feel guilty about having done

_____   8.   Your definition of the perfect spouse or lover

_____   9.   The aspects of your physical appearance that you like least

_____   10. Your political views

_____   11. Your worries about the future

_____   12. People you know who frustrate you or make you angry

_____   13. Your financial status such as income, debts, investments, etc.

_____   14. People you have had intimate relationships with in the past

_____   15. Your successes in life

_____   16. Things that you fear

_____   17. Your unhappiest experiences from your childhood

_____   18. Your favorite pastimes

_____   19. Things that have made you cry

_____   20. Things that you like best about yourself

see reverse

SCORING THE SELF-DISCLOSURE ASSESSMENT FORM

Give yourself:

> 3 points for each L
>
> 2 points for each M
>
> 1 point for each H
>
> 0 points for each P

Total your score and interpret it using the following descriptions:

0–20 POINTS   PRIVATE PERSON

You tend to reveal only small amounts of information in your relationships with others. You might want to make sure that you're not missing out on relationship opportunities because of your reluctance to talk about personal topics.

21–40 POINTS   AVERAGE DISCLOSER

You share information about a fairly wide range of topics.

41–60 POINTS   HIGH DISCLOSER

You are comfortable conversing about a wide range of personal topics. Be sure that you are pacing your self-disclosure to match the disclosure of your partner(s). Some people take advantage of people like you by using this private information to hurt you later.

Design a Speech Topic Purpose

Below are twenty-one topics. Select any three, and for each of the three compose a specific purpose statement and thesis statement for an informative speech. Next, evaluate the suitability of the topics for your audience.

Residence hall food	Cholesterol management	Homelessness
Health care crisis	Child abuse/neglect	Preparing for a wedding
Fraternity/sorority life	Campus security	Student stress
Offshore drilling	Special Olympics	Affirmative action
Presidential elections	Recycling	Financial aid for students
Privacy and Facebook	Solar energy	Insanity plea in court
Legalization of marijuana	Toxic waste	Underage drinking

Topic #1: _____

Specific Purpose:

Thesis:

Topic #2: _____

Specific Purpose:

Thesis:

Topic #3: _____

Specific Purpose:

Thesis:

Audience Analysis Exercise

Form small groups (3–5 members) with your classmates. Interview each other and fill out the form below in preparation for your public speaking assignment. Move from group to group until you have spoken with most of the people in your class. Use the concepts from the text to help you complete this form.

1. What is your general topic?

2. What is your specific purpose?

3. Identify the composition of your audience.

   Total size: Males   Females

   Age range:

   Variety of majors:

   Variety of career goals:

   Individual differences:

4. Explain what you and your audience have in common? How are you and your audience members different?

5. What is your audience's knowledge of your topic?

6. What aspects of your topic would your audience like to learn more about?

7. How can your topic benefit your listeners? How can they use the information you present? How will this information make their lives better?

8. Identify your audience's interest level or attitude toward your topic?

9. What are the ideas or examples from your speech with which your audience might identify?

10. How will you adapt your speech to the audience's knowledge, interest, and attitude toward your topic? Identify the strategies you will use.

Research Activity

> Science is constantly changing. It's never dull. To me, it's all absorbing,
> like a wonderful hobby that allows you to do what you really like to do.
> *Marshall Nirenberg, Ph.D. (Nobel Prize in Medicine/Physiology – '68)*

This is a fun activity to help you become more familiar with the CMU library. In pairs, or a small group of three, choose one of the diseases or disorders listed below. Each pair or group must select a separate disease. If you would like to learn more about a disease or disorder that is not listed, please feel free to research a disease of your choice.

AIDS	cancer	heart disease
diabetes	multiple sclerosis	sickle cell anemia
arthritis	Lyme disease	scoliosis
epilepsy	cerebral palsy	Parkinson's disease
retinitis pigmentosa	Asperger syndrome	spina bifida
lupus	dyslexia	Marfan's syndrome
SIDS	SARS	bipolar disorder
ADHD or ADD	pectus excavatum	cystic fibrosis
progeria	Williams-Beuren syndrome	

Now that you have selected a disease or disorder to research, go to the CMU library, investigate the disease or disorder and describe the following points:

- A description of the disease

- How widespread the disease is

- The cause of the disease, if known, and how it was discovered

- Key researchers involved

- The status of current knowledge of the disease

- Organizations sponsoring research of the disease

see reverse

In researching your topic, you must identify the following sources. Make sure to cite all of your sources in APA format.

1. Find a journal article on your topic.

   a. Cite the article according to APA format.

   b. Identify the library call number or online citation.

   c. Where is the journal located in the library?

2. Find a book on your topic (or a book that contains information about your topic).

   a. Cite the book according to APA format.

   b. Identify the library call number.

   c. Where is the book located in the library?

3. Find a magazine or newspaper article on your topic.

   a. Cite the magazine or newspaper according to APA format.

   b. Identify the library call number or online citation.

   c. Where is the magazine located in the library?

4. Provide a web citation on your topic.

   a. Cite the exact web citation.

   b. Explain the process or steps involved in finding this web citation.

Ethical Speaking Checklist

This checklist is a practical guide to assist you in making ethical choices when preparing your speeches. Please review this checklist before presenting each speech.

_____ My motives in presenting this speech topic are ethically sound.

_____ Audience members cannot use the information I present in a harmful way.

_____ I have thoroughly researched my topic on my own.

_____ I have examined my sources for reliability and accuracy.

_____ I have written my own speech using my own mind and words.

_____ The sources for all quotations and paraphrases are cited.

_____ My speech is free of deception and false statements.

_____ All support material is accurate: statistics, facts, testimony, etc.

_____ I used logical and valid reasoning for all of my arguments.

_____ My emotional appeals are genuine and appropriate.

_____ I am careful to avoid abusive or offensive language.

_____ My visual aids represent honest and reliable information.

_____ I know my responsibility to be fully prepared for this speech.

Adapted from Lucas, S. E. (2011). *Instructor's Manual to Accompany The Art of Public Speaking*, 11th ed. New York, NY: McGraw-Hill, Inc.

You Are a Speech Writer

You must create an introduction and conclusion for each of the following speakers and the situation for which s/he will be speaking. Consider all of the aspects of an introduction and conclusion.

Barack Obama is speaking at a commemoration ceremony for Iraq and Afghanistan veterans.

Introduction:

Conclusion:

Miguel Cabrera is speaking to those attending a fundraising dinner for Special Olympics.

Introduction:

Conclusion:

see reverse

Bruno Mars is speaking at a seminar for the American Federation of Musicians.

Introduction:

Conclusion:

Angelina Jolie is speaking at a luncheon for the Future Mothers of America, Inc.

Introduction:

Conclusion:

Dr. Oz is speaking to those attending a meeting of Overeaters Anonymous.

Introduction:

Conclusion:

Outline Worksheet

Begin to create a tentative outline for your speech. Include ideas for a specific purpose, thesis, attention-getter, reason to listen, credibility, main points, support material, visual aids, and a clincher in the conclusion.

Topic:

Purpose:

Thesis:

I.   Introduction

   A.   Attention-getter:

   B.   Reason to listen:

   C.   Thesis statement:

   D.   Credbility statement:

      1.

      2.

   E.   Preview of main points:

      1.

      2.

      3.

Ideas for support material

Ideas for visual aids

Ideas for closure

Personal Report of Communication Apprehension

Please indicate the degree to which each of the following statements apply to you by writing the number showing whether you:

1	2	3	4	5
agree strongly	agree	are undecided	disagree	strongly disagree

_____ 1. I dislike participating in group discussions.

_____ 2. Generally, I am comfortable while participating in group discussions.

_____ 3. I am tense and nervous while participating in group discussions.

_____ 4. I like to get involved in group discussions.

_____ 5. Engaging in group discussion with new people makes me tense and nervous.

_____ 6. I am calm and relaxed while participating in group discussions.

_____ 7. Generally, I am nervous when I have to participate in a meeting.

_____ 8. Usually I am calm and relaxed while participating in meetings.

_____ 9. I am calm and relaxed when called upon to express opinions in meetings.

_____ 10. I am afraid to express myself at meetings.

_____ 11. Communicating at meetings usually makes me uncomfortable.

_____ 12. I am very relaxed when answering questions at a meeting.

_____ 13. While in a conversation with a new acquaintance, I feel very nervous.

_____ 14. I have no fear of speaking up in conversations.

_____ 15. Ordinarily I am very tense and nervous in conversations.

_____ 16. Ordinarily I am very calm and relaxed in conversations.

_____ 17. While conversing with a new acquaintance, I feel very relaxed.

_____ 18. I'm afraid to speak up in conversations.

_____ 19. I have no fear of giving a speech.

_____ 20. Certain parts of my body feel very tense and rigid while giving a speech.

_____ 21. I feel relaxed while giving a speech.

_____ 22. My thoughts become confused and jumbled when I am giving a speech.

_____ 23. I face the prospect of giving a speech with confidence.

_____ 24. While giving a speech, I get so nervous I forget facts I really know.

see reverse

SCORING THE PERSONAL REPORT OF COMMUNICATION APPREHENSION FORM

To calculate your score for each of the four communication contexts measured by this instrument, add or subtract your scores for each item as described below. Begin your adding or subtracting with 18 points in each case.

Group Discussion	18 points + scores for items 2, 4, and 6
	– scores for items 1, 3, and 5
Meetings	18 points + scores for items 8, 9, and 12
	– scores for items 7, 10, and 11
Interpersonal Communication	18 points + scores for items 14, 16, and 17
	– scores for items 13, 15, and 18
Public Speaking	18 points + scores for items 19, 21, and 23
	– scores for items 20, 22, and 24

To determine your overall score on the PRCA, add the points you earned on all four of the contexts together.

NORMS FOR PRCA-24

Range of Scores:	24–120
Average Score:	65 (plus or minus 15)
High Level of CA:	above 80
Low Level of CA:	below 50

Source: McCroskey, J. C. (1982). *An introduction to rhetorical communication* (4th ed.). Englewood Cliffs, NJ: Prentice-Hall.

Choosing a Method for Delivery

Consider each of the following speaking situations. Decide what method of delivery would be best suited for each situation. Be able to discuss your reasons for why you chose each method of delivery.

1 = manuscript

2 = memorized

3 = impromptu

4 = extemporaneous

5 = mediated

_____ You are asked by the chairperson of your department to prepare and deliver a speech to introduce the winner of the Outstanding Alumni Award at the annual student/alumni banquet.

_____ As human resources director, you have to deliver a speech explaining the new procedures for filing health care benefits, travel reimbursement, and sick leave request forms online. You record your speech so it may be accessed on your company website.

_____ You are assigned to give campus tours during New Student Orientation and point out information about the history of CMU's campus and the significance of various locations on campus. You have to present the same speech, twice a week, for the next eight weeks.

_____ You have to answer a question asked by an audience member at the end of your speech in your COM 101 class.

_____ You are running for Student Government Association President. You and your campaign team write a speech that you will deliver with the aid of a teleprompter at Plachta Auditorium in Warriner Hall.

Adapted from Nelson, P. & Pearson, J. (2004). *Confidence in Public Speaking* (8th ed.). Dubuque, IA: Brown & Benchmark Publishers.

see reverse

Develop an Informative Speech Topic

Divide yourselves into pairs or groups of three people. Select four of the topics and formulate a specific purpose statement and thesis statement for an informative speech. The four specific purpose and thesis statements must include one topic for a speech of *demonstration,* one topic for the speech of *explanation,* one topic for a speech of *definition,* and one topic for a speech of *exploration.* In addition, identify the main points and support material you would select in presenting your topic to your audience. If you do not like any of the suggestions below, feel free to choose your own.

Apple iPad	domestic violence	Detroit Tigers
tornadoes	cloning and genetics	voting
vegetarianism	pilates	kleptomania
Bill Gates	Prince William	hanging wallpaper
alternative fuel	capital punishment	safe sex
Grand Canyon	identity theft	other: _____

Be prepared to present your topics along with specific purpose, thesis statements, main points, and support material to the class.

Speech of Demonstration

Topic:

Specific purpose:

Thesis and main points:

Support material: Examples, illustrations, narratives, testimony, statistics, definitions, and presentational aids

see reverse

Speech of Explanation

Topic:

Specific purpose:

Thesis and main points:

Support material: Examples, illustrations, narratives, testimony, statistics, definitions, and presentational aids

Speech of Description

Topic:

Specific purpose:

Thesis and main points:

Support material: Examples, illustrations, narratives, testimony, statistics, definitions, and presentational aids

Speech of Exploration

Topic:

Specific purpose:

Thesis and main points:

Support material: Examples, illustrations, narratives, testimony, statistics, definitions, and presentational aids

Using Visual Aids to Enhance Delivery

For each of the following speech topics, describe in complete detail the type of visual aids you would use to enhance the delivery of the speech. Be creative when thinking of ways to utilize visual aids in the following topics.

- How to perform the Heimlich maneuver to help a choking victim

- The location of the five best restaurants in Mount Pleasant, Michigan

- The proportion of the electorate that votes in major national elections in the United States, France, Germany, England, and Japan, respectively

- Where to research for information about student scholarships

- The wing patterns of various species of butterflies

- The increase in the amount of money spent by Americans on health care since 2006

- How to change a bicycle tire

- The basic equipment and techniques of rock climbing

Monroe's Motivated Sequence: The Benefits of Buying Walking Shoes

Group Names: _____

Audience: _____

Attention:

Need:

Satisfaction:

Visualization:

Action:

Goals of Persuasion

How would you use persuasion in the following situations? What arguments would be most effective? Why? Are you trying to strengthen (or weaken) attitudes, beliefs, or values? Are you trying to change attitudes, beliefs, or values? Or are you trying to motivate to action?

1. You have been pulled over by a police officer for driving five miles over the speed limit. You want to convince the officer not to issue you a ticket.

2. You have volunteered for your favorite nonprofit organization, the American Cancer Society. You want to solicit donations from the people in your community.

3. You purchased a product and you are extremely dissatisfied. You return the product to the store and you are seeking a full refund.

4. You are attracted to a person in one of your classes and you would like to take the relationship further. You want to ask this special someone out for a date.

5. You have received your final grade in one of your classes and the grade is lower than you expected. You want to request a grade change from your instructor.